"Every business leader can bring out their inner Elon Musk, inspired by the driving techniques mentioned in Michaël Valentin's work."
Emmanuelle Ducrost, *L'Opinion*

"Here comes Teslism – the 21th century's new industrial model. This theory is tempting. The Fourth Industrial Revolution was left behind from a show-case system; we'd imagined that after the American and Japanese models, the next ones would be Chinese, even European – German (Indutry 4.0 is full of extraordinary sites) or even French, with, for example, Michelin. But Tesla is so disruptive!"
Christine Kerdellant, Publishing Director, *L'Usine Nouvelle*

"This book offers readers ways in which to break through historical brands and create a new production model, Teslism, which (according to Valentin) should become the industry's fourth-age Toyotism."
Emmanuel Botta, *L'Express*

"I really encourage you to read this book to understand the changes and issues of our industrial world. It is a clear, structured and pedagogical book, which alternates theoretical analysis, concrete example, fields trips and testimonies from industrials leaders."
Fatie Toko, AI Business Transformation Director at La Poste and blogger at *L'ère digitale en résumés*

The Tesla Way

*The disruptive strategies
and models of Teslism*

Michaël Valentin

KoganPage

Publisher's note

Every possible effort has been made to ensure that the information contained in this book is accurate at the time of going to press, and the publishers and authors cannot accept responsibility for any errors or omissions, however caused. No responsibility for loss or damage occasioned to any person acting, or refraining from action, as a result of the material in this publication can be accepted by the publisher or the author.

First published in French as *Le modèle Tesla* by Dunod in 2018

First published in Great Britain and the United States in 2019 by Kogan Page Limited

2nd Floor, 45 Gee Street
London
EC1V 3RS
United Kingdom

122 W 27th St, 10th Floor
New York, NY 10001
USA

4737/23 Ansari Road
Daryaganj
New Delhi 110002
India

www.koganpage.com

© Michaël Valentin 2019

The right of Michaël Valentin to be identified as the author of this work has been asserted by her in accordance with the Copyright, Designs and Patents Act 1988.

ISBNs

Hardback   9781789660135
Paperback   9780749497033
Ebook   9780749497040

British Library Cataloguing-in-Publication Data

A CIP record for this book is available from the British Library.

Library of Congress Cataloging-in-Publication Data

A CIP record for this book is available from the Library of Congress.

Typeset by Integra
Print production managed by Jellyfish
Printed and bound by CPI Group (UK) Ltd, Croydon CR0 4YY

CONTENTS

FIGURES

ABOUT THE AUTHOR

Michaël Valentin is Associate Director at OPEO, a consultancy specialized in industrial transformations. Having accumulated significant experience both as an operational manager in the automotive sector and as a McKinsey & Company consultant, Valentin now helps small to medium enterprises (SMEs) and large groups become industries of the future. Widely recognized as a global expert in this field, he is also an author of books such as *The Smart Way*, which talks about how the industry of the future can be used to transform today's factories into nuggets of gold.

ACKNOWLEDGEMENTS

This book is a collective adventure that has only been possible by the kind collaboration of a very large number of people, colleagues, industrial leaders, Tesla employees and partners. I would particularly like to thank all those who helped me start and finish the project, from the early reflective stage through the fieldwork analysis and manuscript editing phases.

My first thanks are to Charles Bouygues for his help and energy in organizing interviews in Silicon Valley. A special thanks goes to Renan Devillières for his special insights into the ins and outs of software hybridization; to David Machenaud for his general support; and to Raphaël Haddad for helping to structure the book.

Thanks as well to all the persons and companies who agreed to speak here, teaching me an enormous amount about the technical and human aspects of this topic.

Thanks to all my associates who participated indirectly in this book, starting with Frédéric Sandei, Philippe Grandjacques and Grégory Richa.

Thanks as well to Odile Ricour and to Adélaïde Lechat for their assistance; and to Bidane Beitia, Laurène Laffargue, Soizic Audouin, Abir Bruneau, Denis Masse, Antoine Toupin, Robin Cellard, David Fernandez, Clément Niessen, Quentin Lallement, Hadi Mahihenni, Anass Khamlichi, Romain Pigé, Jean Baptiste Sieber and Sébastien Desbois for their very concrete help in helping me contact Tesla and more generally the lighthouses of the industry of the future.

Thanks to Julie El Mokrani Tomassone, Esther Willer and Chloé Sebagh for their help and enthusiasm in copy-editing this book; for improving it and for keeping communications going.

Finally, my heartfelt thanks go out to Marie-Laure Cahier, whose support was indispensable to the book's final form; to Alan Sitkin and Susan Geraghty, for their help with its English language version; to Ro'isin Singh, for her detailed work improving upon earlier drafts; and to my editor Julia Swales, for her faith in me.

PREFACE

My latest observations about the state of industry in most developed countries, their organizational systems and technological progress these past 10 years, as well as recent socio-economic changes, all encouraged me to write this book. In the face of increased digitalization and a decaying industry, I believe Teslism's business model, operational and management system can be the remedy. However, understanding my personal context, I believe, will give you a good understanding of how and why I came to write *The Tesla Way*.

After some good results at my school-leaving exams in 1995, I wasn't really sure of what to study next. Back then, my family insisted I study to become a doctor, a notary public or even a politician: actually, anything except manufacturing. In rural-town France, social success and factory work were considered mutually exclusive. I didn't start my path on the roads of the industrial sector until I met a friend (her name was Véronique) in the hallways of the high school I had freshly graduated from. With such grades, she said, I couldn't possibly go into medicine: in her eyes, engineering seemed like a more adequate option. She was right; I had received good marks at a whole series of science exams, and yet, due to cultural bias, I still didn't have any real understanding of the academic possibilities that this might create. After a few nights out with classmates, I started to look for an internship. Civil engineering immediately attracted me: it looked like a concrete job to me – no wonder, since it actually involved concrete.

Later, after my experience as a foreman, another friend, from the renowned Ponts et Chaussées engineering school, gave me a call. He was strongly into the field of manufacturing, and his dream was to manage a factory one day. I followed him, and a month later I found myself working at a Michelin factory in Ballymena, Ireland. That is when I caught the industrial fever. Each and every day, more than 1,000 tyres roll out of firing kilns that stand at more than 3 metres high. It was a truly impressive sight for the young graduate I was. After tyres, I wanted to see how cars were manufactured. They left me truly astonished: how does a metal sheet comes out of a rolling mill, only to get transformed in just a few hours into one of the most complex systems that humans have ever invented, a product that has more than 140,000 units manufactured worldwide every day of the week?

This fascination is what led me down the road of industry. As I went on, and was then promoted to lead a team of maintenance technicians, I started to see the strength of this rewarding sector. Many like to stereotype the industrial as stiff and bland, but they often ignore the fact that it is mostly about the people. In fact, with my team, we quickly became experts in rapid intervention, and did everything in our power to keep the lines from shutting down. Our solutions always started with teamwork and the challenges that come with it: listening to them attentively, while being able to make the tough decisions. It was sometimes based on a consensus but always involved some degree of difficulty. Why? Because manufacturing is a complex business that requires a lot of courage. Tentacular supply chains are complex. Products made out of tens of thousands of components – and just as many variants – are complex. Organizational operations, in the era of happy globalization, are complex. Even simple manufacturing is complex. Yet again, what is key in manufacturing or material transformation activities are the people – even if some will always try to save face by pretending they have everything under control.

Of course, alongside all this complexity there is the simple beauty of an environment in which frontline operatives work hand in hand, day in day out, with technicians, engineers and researchers. It's an incredible adventure, with everyone coming from different social backgrounds, working together to improve the system. It is challenging but, oh so exciting. A truly unique human adventure.

As I started making my way into consulting, this enthusiasm stayed the same, soon beating the scepticism I had over the world of consultants. I had the chance to visit hundreds of factories, to meet several work teams, get stuck into hundreds of complex and exciting issues, all in a myriad of sectors: heavy industry, mechanics, chemistry, pharmaceuticals, bio-production, machine tools, consumer goods, and even artistic businesses that the luxury sector has kept alive despite all the new technologies flooding the market. I learnt that there is no such thing as 'the industry', but there are, in fact, many faces to it.

Having said that, the year was 2008. Manufacturing had bad press. For 30 years, France's factories had been pursuing a 'fabless' strategy, with many viewing manufacturing as an activity whose time had come and gone. The trending idea was that services would dominate everything in the years to come. The elites saw this clearly and oriented public policy towards what they saw as the sectors of the future. Back then, France had a very good card to play. In the 1980s, the French and German automotive sectors were competing head to head, before German machinemakers achieved their hegemonic position, and before Japan or even China made much of a mark worldwide. By 2008, the die was cast, and things were very different. My old classmates were all working as financial analysts, traders or as internet specialists. Not many were taking manufacturing seriously. There were constant reports on TV about the factories shutting down. During elections, politicians would mention their 'rescue plans' to save manufacturing. Everyone agreed that the industrial sector was seriously ill and probably on its way out.

The crisis that followed in 2008 was a wake-up call for several countries. After spending almost 30 years trying to offshore its production, France was left wondering what kind of society it wanted to build. Did it make any sense for the devices that French people used, for their children's toys, for the clothes they wore, to be shipped halfway around the world before these items landed in their carts?

Gradually, another phenomenon was taking root. Digitalization was taking several sectors by storm, and all the talk started being about big data, machine learning and artificial intelligence. Companies that didn't even exist 15 years previously now had a market value equal to 50 per cent of French GDP. In 2018, the 10 most highly valued companies in the world were in tech, eight in the United States and two in China. Of course, at the same time Europe only accounted for 25 of the global top 100, with Siemens, the German giant and Europe's biggest industrial company, struggling to maintain its 62nd place on the list.

Digitalization had more economic and political repercussions than we could imagine. Trump, Brexit, Salvini, the yellow vests movement: these phenomena are the expression of a popular will for more sovereignty. But behind it there is a much more structural phenomenon that very few mention by its name: the deindustrialization of developed countries' more marginalized regions. Their inhabitants feel like runaway globalization has robbed them of their freedom. The big urban centres, which for a long time had partnered their peri-urban and rural counterparts, were now striking out on their own. Globalization meant that small provincial towns are having to compete with low-cost countries, thus provoking the closing of factories, poor results among retailers, and a rise in unemployment. In 1970, the Vosges district, where I was born, was France's leading industrial centre. By 2017, the tables had turned. In the Ile-de-France region around Paris, 57 per cent of all active workers were employed in white-collar jobs, while in the Vosges that figure was only 15 per cent. The Moselle Valley region has been devastated, like so many similar areas in France or other countries that once had a proud industrial tradition. How can France, and other similar developed countries, preserve their economic model, when at the same time a large part of the population feels excluded?

This is where *The Tesla Way* comes in. This book aims to participate in the industry revitalizing efforts by showing how Elon Musk's Tesla can be a model to rejuvenate our industrial sector – and the principles of this needed change. The Tesla Way stands as a unique opportunity, part of what different people have called the industry of the future, or industry 4.0, or even smart manufacturing.

What is the upshot of all this? It's quite simple. You take two threats – rising digitalization and declining industry – and you turn them into a fantastic opportunity.

Tech is exploding and it is incumbent upon us to take full advantage of it. In most developed countries, irrespective of whether or not they have been behaving like 'start-up nations', there is everything needed to succeed. By hybridizing industry with tech – software, artificial intelligence, etc – but also by counting on the skills of business managers and stellar engineers, I remain certain that France, and other countries, can move their industry to the next phase, which is industrial platformization. The needs are huge, however. In France, a recent PwC survey found that 75 per cent of all industry executives consider industry 4.0 as the current main issue; but 80 per cent are still unsure what to do about it. They lack the skills, the expertise and sometimes the vision. In France, manufacturing remains a more or less virgin territory for tech. Yet it is the sector that has historically benefited the most from science, being responsible for 80 per cent of all research and development.

The skills, the good practices, the vision – it can be found by looking closely at the practices and the ideas borrowed from the tech sector that Tesla, and many other companies that I describe in this book, successfully applied in their organizational systems.

I believe that the Tesla Way can help industry to leave this rut. But it can also do much more. By reinvigorating industry in the numerous countries where it is collapsing, we will of course give our economies and our GDPs the boost they need – but we will also help with environmental concerns by nearshoring and shortening distances. Not to mention the added benefit assuaging social tensions by reconnecting big urban centres with heretofore marginalized zones. We can go back to a renewed socio-economic system, where we will re-create a relationship of trust between the elites and the people.

Through my work as a consultant I have visited a vast number of factories and have met many senior managers. With my help, they come up with ideas capable of accelerating their company's further expansion. Sometimes these ideas are part of their core business, but sometimes they spill over into other sectors of activity. In both cases, executives rarely have the time or methodology to follow up on them. I hope that *The Tesla Way* will help to fill the information and process gaps encountered by these executives, as well as to give every reader an insight into the industry of tomorrow.

Online resources for this book are available at koganpage.com/Tesla

Introduction

For several years now, a powerful wave of change has submerged the world of factories. Industrial and digital activities have gradually hybridized to give birth to a new paradigm where services and products combine and intertwine in response to the new characteristics of demand in the 21st century. Influenced by smartphones and other new neural appendages, modern consumers have transformed into hyper-connected users whose demand is increasingly geared towards the immaterial world in a search for greater instantaneousness, user friendliness, customization, collaboration, sharing and responsibility.

These aspirations, imported from the digital sphere, seriously challenge the industrial (and more broadly, the economic) world. It started with accelerated technological progress, increasing the level of competence that all industrial sectors would require. Then came a phenomenon known as disruption, with new players accumulating substantial market share by pursuing business models that were very different from what came before. In turn, this led to a hyper-concentration of value, talent and resources, translating into greater opportunities for some parties but also – and conversely – into a need for more vigilance than ever before against the risks associated with rising social, geographic and environmental tensions. The changes were monumental in technological, economic and societal terms, causing some observers to posit the existence of a 4th Industrial Revolution. The question, however, is why so much attention has been paid to one kind of activity – industrial – that accounts today for a mere 16 per cent of global GDP, a number that has been steadily declining in most Global North countries. The answer is that the 16 per cent in question have had a disproportionate effect on the rest of the economy, with industry generating 70 per cent of all exports and 77 per cent of all R&D in the world (Figure 0.1).

FIGURE 0.1   Manufacturing contribution to export, innovation, productivity and employment

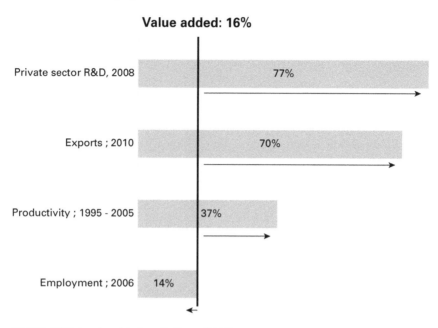

Value added: 16%

Private sector R&D, 2008 — 77%

Exports ; 2010 — 70%

Productivity ; 1995 - 2005 — 37%

Employment ; 2006 — 14%

SOURCE   OPEO, based on data from McKinsey (2012)

Aware of these new challenges, the world's leading industrial economies have progressively launched national strategies centring on investment, innovation, training and the structuring of strategic branches of activity. Germany kickstarted the process with its 2011 'Industrie 4.0' plan, which had an explosive effect everywhere and convinced other leading nations that it was time to do the same.

The stakes have been high for Germany, Europe's leading industrial nation, and it has embraced digital transition as a way of maintaining its position in a sector where competition can be extremely fierce. The new policies unveiled at the 2011 Hanover Fair were widely lauded for being forward looking. The strategy had three goals: developing an offer of production-related digital equipment and services; continuing the industrial sector's digitalization; and extending this to include smart services (La Fabrique de l'industrie, 2017). The strategy's particularity lay in its transversality in the sense that it sought to create a technology branch capable of interlinking a variety of different production systems.

Next up was the United States with its 2013 'National Network for Manufacturing Innovation', followed by Japan's 'Connected Industries', South

FIGURE 0.2 Main 'industry of the future' policy themes

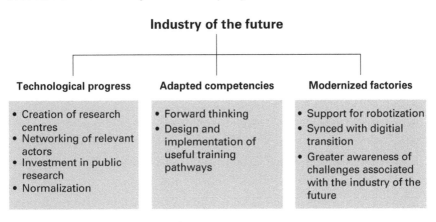

Industry of the future

Technological progress	Adapted competencies	Modernized factories
• Creation of research centres • Networking of relevant actors • Investment in public research • Normalization	• Forward thinking • Design and implementation of useful training pathways	• Support for robotization • Synced with digitial transition • Greater awareness of challenges associated with the industry of the future

SOURCE La Fabrique de l'industrie (2016)

Korea's 'Manufacturing Industry Innovation 3.0 Strategy', China's 'Made in China 2025', France's 'L'Industrie du futur' and, finally, Italy's 'Calenda' plan in late 2016. Interestingly enough, many countries' 'Industry of the Future' programmes have featured the same levers, with most if not all seeking to: 1) develop their own technological offer; 2) adapt or develop employee competencies; and 3) modernize industry while encouraging upgrading (Figure 0.2).

Looking more closely now at national specificities, Japan offers a good example to start with. In March 2017, the country launched a new industrial strategy called 'Connected Industries'. The primary aim was the further digitalization of Japanese industry. Starting with the premise that the sector was facing a serious risk of contraction, the initiative promoted a widespread use of data to boost national productivity. Japan subsequently settled on a number of ambitious objectives, including the creation of 50 small factories by the year 2020, entities whose operations mainly revolve around connected objects.

In China it was Prime Minister Li Keqiang who launched a very similar dynamic with a 10-year plan entitled 'Made in China 2025'. The country, long viewed as the factory of the world due to its huge product output, has started planning to improve its industry's image, relying towards this end on R&D, new technology and a new organization of its manufacturing sector. It is a perfect example of a policy aimed at modernizing industry, specifically with a view towards ensuring its upgrading.

It is the same idea that drove the South Korean government to launch the 'Manufacturing Industry Innovation 3.0 Strategy' initiative in July 2014. Like Japan, South Korea's goal is to build more smart factories. This mainly involves developing and investing in hi-tech industry to bring previously unknown products into the country, including the medicine of the future and smart clothing.

In the United States and the UK, the impetus has been slightly different. Here the general idea is not to increase public investment in existing companies but to create research centres dedicated to specific technologies such as 3D printing. The proliferation of partnerships between factories and universities is actually one of the markers attesting to this strategic choice. It is also the goal specified in the US's 'National Network for Manufacturing Innovation' initiative, namely the creation of a public–private partnership network involving industry, universities and government, ensuring the convergence of thinking in this area. Today the network counts 14 members and has made a real contribution towards the development of new industrial technology in the country. The most telling example is the Digital Manufacturing and Design Innovation Institute (DMDII) that Barack Obama created in 2015. Thanks to the strong support the entity receives from the Department of Defense, it is the most fully developed of all bodies within its field, having invested nearly $90 million in total in more than 60 industrial digitalization research projects.

France has been no exception to the trend, given its industrial sector's re-energization in recent years. Evidence for this includes Prime Minister Edouard Philippe's new plan, presented to the National Industry Council on 22 November 2018 and entitled 'Territoires d'industrie'. The initiative identified 124 areas with strong industrial potential, all of which are meant to benefit from a specific commitment and personalized support from the French State. Spending of €1.36 billion will prioritize these locations, with public policy having identified four main needs: recruiting new talent; attracting further investment; further innovation; and simplified administrative procedures. The actions implemented pursuant to these four priorities should offer a response to the challenges that are part of this new environment. With the new approach, French industry policy will be driven by a whole new dynamic. It is a new stage in the country's move towards greater decentralization, with policy being directed by regional authorities operating in greater proximity to frontline actors.

These repeated examples of public policy favouring the development of the industry of the future demonstrate that what we are witnessing today is a real increase in global awareness of the transition towards a 4th Industrial Revolution. All four corners of the world have experienced greater digitalization, with a 2016 PwC study estimating that within the next five years there should be a further increase of 42 per cent in the Americas, 34 per cent in Asia and 41 per cent in Africa (PwC, 2016).

Notwithstanding all these initiatives, an enormous gap remains between the level of energy deployed by the public- or private-sector actors operating in the industrial world and the measurable results of their efforts. According to a recent study entitled 'Industry 4.0: Global Digital Operation Survey 2018', only 10 per cent of all companies in the world can be considered cutting edge in industry 4.0 terms, with two-thirds yet to start their digital transition. Asia-Pacific countries lead with respect to their percentage of digital champions, followed by the Americas (11 per cent) then Europe, Middle East and Africa, where only 5 per cent of all companies can be categorized thus (PwC, 2018).

From a macro-economic perspective, recovery has been minimal in industrial GDP and employment terms. From a micro-economic perspective, there are doubts as to whether companies have changed quickly enough, given how fast everything else happens nowadays. The 2018 PwC survey of 1,293 chief executive officers (CEOs) in 87 countries undertaken on behalf of the World Economic Forum revealed that 76 per cent of all respondents were extremely concerned by the speed of technological change and the potential problems they faced in accessing the competencies they needed to cope – with 32 per cent convinced that their own sector would end up being disrupted. This has changed the terms of the debate, with the new question being how to obviate the trend's negative side-effects even as the overall movement continues to accelerate. There are least three explanations for the perceived gap between the speed of progress and the speed at which companies have adapted to it.

First, it is not at all natural for human beings to think exponentially. Most of the natural laws governing our daily existence are linear in nature, with our brains being accustomed to certain ways of thinking for thousands of years already. As difficult as it is for any one individual to apprehend the phenomenon of exponential technological progress, the challenge is far greater when an entire company is involved.

Second, until now very few companies have been able to define a transformation methodology enabling them to transition from the Old World to the New World. Yet most of the changes taking place have been so substantial that it would be impossible to improvise a response. Simply investing in a technology is not enough to ensure that a company will capitalize upon it. This was the dilemma underlying *The Smart Way* (Valentin, 2017), telling the story of an entrepreneur seeking to transform his company into an industry of the future.

The final explanation involves the absence of a target model, creating uncertainty about which strategy should be adopted – hence which operational or management system (and ultimately which organization) is advisable. Note that all these questions play out against a background of three other debates, namely how to find growth drivers in a constantly changing world where the very concept of the sector no longer makes sense; how to avoid being disrupted; and how to attract and retain talented people.

To ensure their industries' transformation, companies will need new competencies. Only 27 per cent feel that staff have been sufficiently trained to handle all these changes – making talent a key aspect of the digital transformation. This explains the global emergence of new training programmes adapted to the new needs. In the United States, for instance, there is Harvard University's 'Digital Initiative', a digital transformation-oriented programme including inter alia studies of the industries of the future. In Saclay near Paris, the Boston Consulting Group has created an 'Operational Innovation Centre' that is basically a 4.0 version factory where students come face to face with frontline realities, familiarizing themselves with concrete applications and cases involving operations in digitalized factories. This type of centre is destined to spread across France over the next few years and will underpin the new Industrial Revolution. Indeed, the country's top engineering schools, such as Arts et Métiers, Paris Tech or Centrale Paris, all offer industry of the future training programmes today.

The big picture is that nations worldwide are all seeking to create a framework that will support companies by implementing structures enabling innovation to thrive. By so doing, it is an entire ecosystem that they have started to galvanize.

Each of economic history's three previous industrial revolutions had three drivers: disruptive technological progress; new societal needs; and an organizational model adapted to the new context to ensure that technological progress would lead to measurable economic development. This can be exemplified by Fordism, which became an obvious reference in the 2nd Industrial Revolution, if only because of the massive productivity gains it generated. The leading model for the 3rd Industrial Revolution was Toyotism, which unleashed impressive gains in responsiveness. For the moment, however, the 4th Industrial Revolution has no 'lighthouse' system that it can showcase. It is true that the pure digital player sector is full of natural leaders like the GAFA (Google, Apple, Facebook and Amazon) quartet, who might then be used as target models. But, in the industrial and manufacturing sectors, there is a sense that no one actor has been sufficiently recognized by its peers for its system to be deemed a universal change driver. The question then becomes which model will assume in the 4th Age of Industry the role that Toyota played previously.

This book shares the belief that the 4th Industrial Revolution is well and truly under way and that there exists one emerging system that is primed to take full advantage of it. This system, which will drive industry's shift from the 3rd Age of Industry into a hybrid digital and industrial sector, is the brainchild of Elon Musk, the charismatic and controversial leader of Tesla, San Francisco's famous (and widely hyped) industrial icon. Tesla carries within itself the genes that can spawn this New World. It was born in a digital cradle and culture, replete with the kind of capitalist structure that has become de rigueur for technology start-ups. The company has achieved the exploit of already being competitive with Ford, Renault and GM in terms of market capitalization, while steadily becoming a leading manufacturer in the highly emblematic automotive sector – in a country where the industry had seen little that is new since the early 20th century. Nor is it any surprise that the model attached to the 4th Age of Industry could come from a new actor embedded in both the digital and industrial culture.

Above and beyond this macro-level observation, however, what the present book details is the Teslism model – construed here as the successor to Toyotism. The aim is to understand how it responds to the challenges of the 4th Industrial Age. Seven fundamental principles can be scrutinized towards this end.

Like any system, the one that Elon Musk has devised is far from perfect and can be criticized in several ways. Not to mention the fact that it would be reductionist to limit Teslism to Tesla itself. Indeed, this is what Musk himself has said about the role that his company plays in society, noting that even if Tesla is not that significant in and of itself, it has been powerful enough to incentivize all of the world's other carmakers to invest massively in electric cars (Fabernovel, 2018).

That being the case, the purpose of the present book is not to promote the brand itself but instead to get readers to take a step back and think about the main principles associated with the Tesla model, since these might well be capable of orientating the organizations of the future by ensuring their adaptation to future situations. Hence the choice of consolidating each of the principles described in this book with what other cutting-edge industrial companies say about them – without forgetting a list of reflections that readers may wish to meditate upon individually when adapting the Tesla model to their own contexts.

01

The 3rd Industrial Age is over: So far so good

SUMMARY

Successive industrial revolutions have been marked by an exponential acceleration in technological progress. As illustrated by the legend of Balhait, the human mind struggles to apprehend exponential progress, explaining why current changes can be so disconcerting.

The period following the Second World War was characterized by a globalization phase marked by supply chains' global dispersion, the offshoring of manufacturing and a belief in corporate gigantism – all in a context defined by financial market liberalization.

The end of the 3rd Age of Industry witnessed the emergence of Toyotism, a response adapted to consumers, shareholders and employees' changing needs. Today this model is showing its limits. New imperatives like adaptability, responsiveness, customization and meaningful work have arrived, driven by the rise of digital technologies capable of transforming business models, the competitive landscape, consumer habits and employee expectations. The world of physical objects is having to adapt to a universe populated with information and data flows.

Not so long ago, companies used to talk about 'happy globalization'. With the explosion in transportation options and volumes, and with the rise of globalized supply chains and productive facilities (driven by territorial arbitrages, themselves dictated by labour costs), companies have been incentivized to expand in order to achieve economies of scale, in a context defined by the liberalization of trade and financial markets. Toyotism, which would later be known as lean manufacturing, seemed like an organizational model that was particularly adapted to this era since it enabled improvements in quality, shorter production times and reduced stock – all of which helped companies' working capital positions. Unbeknown to many, however, the Digital Era was already starting to destabilize this model, with established industrial companies' operational modes being challenged by a host of factors, including the growing demand for immediacy, transparency and meaning; the exponential acceleration in technology (overturning long-standing competence platforms); and the arrival of new competitors from the digital universe.

Innovation and industrial revolution, the inevitable acceleration

Homo erectus first appeared a million years ago. Human beings stood up and progressively learnt to use their arms and differentiate themselves from other animals. Homo sapiens arrived 900,000 years later, bringing the first transformations of materials, culminating in the first use of tools; 90,000 years later, mankind began raising animals and growing crops; 9,000 years later, it was the printing press that would forever change communications between people (and indeed, build bridges between generations); 700 years later, James Watt invented the steam machine in what would soon be known as the 1st Industrial Revolution, but which actually marked the beginning of a kind of accelerated progress that people could actually perceive.

From this date onwards, major scientific breakthroughs occurred so frequently that the world that subsequent generations experienced would be characterized by constant renewal resulting from technological progress, with everyone living very differently than their parents had (or indeed, than their children or grandchildren would). The term 'disruption' is appropriate for qualifying the three major eras that followed, all marked by a movement that transcended simple technological change to generate new ways of working and a systematic response to certain very new economic and social needs arising in society. With the 1st Industrial Revolution, this occurred in the late 18th century, when the priority was to satisfy the demand for infrastructure, hence to build buildings and expand the transportation of people and goods. The steam machine would enable a mechanization of tasks leading in turn to new ways of working. Humans would learn to work with machines, with all the social consequences that came with this.

The next stop on this fresco of industrial progress was the 2nd Industrial Revolution about 100 years later. From a scientific perspective, the discovery of electricity was the trigger. But, once again, the consequences far transcended the actual invention. Electricity made it possible to organize factories differently by replacing a configuration based on one huge central steam engine with many small autonomous electricity-powered machines spread across the facilities. This ultimately gave birth to the principle of assembly-line production, leading in turn to massive productivity gains that made it possible to satisfy the mass demand that exploded from the early 20th century onwards. Socially, this revolution was accompanied by a new collective imagination symbolized by Charlie Chaplin's famous film *Modern Times*. This was widely referred to as 'assembly-line work'. In reality this marked the beginning of Fordism, an organizational model rooted in principles that an engineer named Taylor developed and that would make it possible to increase the efficiency of labour by a factor of 10, thanks to the specialization of tasks.

Sixty years later, a much more discrete revolution would occur. With the re-emergence and amplification of globalization, the first computers paved the way to robotics and the automation of tasks. The problem was that this latter innovation – necessitating enormous calculational power – quickly exceeded the capacity of the human brain, wired as it is for repetitive tasks. At this level, it is worth recalling Moore's Law, named for the famous Intel engineer who invented the microprocessor and predicted that memory capacities double every 18 months. For the first time ever, people realized with this new Industrial Revolution that progress could be exponential. Even so, Moore was relatively conservative in his predictions. Fifty years later, his 'times two' law still applies, driving the ongoing rise in memory, storage and calculating capabilities. A closer look at the speed with which different human innovations have succeeded one another closely resembles an exponential law: homo erectus, 1 million years ago; homo sapiens, 100,000 years ago; agriculture, 10,000 years ago; printing, 600 years ago; steam engines, 300 years ago; electricity, 100 years ago; computing, 40 years ago… and today, the smartphone! (Figure 1.1)

FIGURE 1.1 Mankind and technological progress

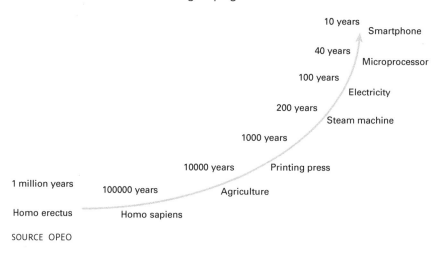

SOURCE OPEO

The human brain and exponential law

People are used to living linearly. This is how our lives unfold and how our brains learn, bit by bit, each and every day. One useful way of representing mankind's difficulty in conceptualizing the exponential law is the ancient Indian legend of King Balhait.

One day, when he was bored, Balhait decided to organize a competition offering a fabulous reward to anyone who could come up with a good distraction. A wise man named Sissa accepted the challenge with malice aforethought, inventing for this purpose (according to legend) the game of chess and presenting it to the king, who was totally enchanted and offered Sissa anything his heart desired in return for this extraordinary gift. Sissa's response was to request that his sovereign reward him by placing one grain of rice on the chessboard's first square, two on the second, four on the third and so on, doubling the amount of rice on each square until the whole board was full. When the king's advisers tried to pay the debt, they soon realized that there was not enough rice in the kingdom to fill even half the chessboard. The king then understood that Sissa had played him and sentenced the man to death – meaning that Sissa ended his days as one of the first collateral victims of the exponential law that we still find difficult to understand.

This legend suggests the difficulties that the human brain has in conceptualizing a law that has yet to reach its ultimate form. Yet the modern era, which some pundits insist on still calling the '3rd Industrial Age', is already governed by a principle of exponential progress. Indeed, this might explain the widespread sense of flux today – and the collective malaise regarding accelerated progress. Modern civilization has got close to the point where the slope of the curve accelerates, with progress becoming visible not only from one generation to the next but also within a single lifetime. All of which explains why it is worth detailing – before any discussions about the existence of a new Industrial Revolution (the 4th in history) – the characteristics of the 3rd Age of Industry, an economic, technological and organizational model that had unprecedented strengths and advantages but also clear limits.

The happy globalization paradigm

The West rebuilt after the Second World War to progressively evolve from mainly agricultural economies to ones specializing in industrial (and subsequently service-oriented) uses. Doped by increasingly abundant oil resources and looser barriers to trade, by the 1960s global trade had intensified again. From year to year, personal (and then merchandise) transportation began to democratize and expand, notably after the Berlin Wall fell in 1989. According to International Civil Aviation Organization (ICAO), air traffic reflected this general trend, rising from 10 million passengers in 1950 to 500 million in 1970 and 3 billion in 2010. This cut transportation costs and made it easier to manufacture goods far from their place of consumption.

Anecdotally, from the 1980s onwards, delocalization would become a huge phenomenon in the world's industrial countries, particularly favouring the emergence of new Asian giants, starting with China. Together with the arrival of industrial IT systems, supply chain fragmentation would mean a global manufacturing of increasingly sophisticated products using highly complex production and transportation chains working on an end-to-end basis (ie covering anything from simple components to final products). Even without final assembly operations necessarily being delocalized, this would create a situation where today more than 50 per cent of all value added is 'exported' elsewhere than the market where a good is consumed, even where hi-tech products are involved. Commercial trade would skyrocket at the same time as supply chains atomized – increasing transportation distances for basic industrial components and product modules alike.

Financial market liberalization further extended the movement as the free circulation of capital helped create polymorphic groups that would link and delink depending on trends that could be completely disconnected from the real economy. The end result was the disappearance of entire swathes of traditional manufacturing from the West. Textiles, for instance, would go entirely offshore, followed by other basic consumer goods such as toys and simple electronic products. The factory-free Fabless approach made famous by Serge Tchuruk when he ran Alcatel became very fashionable in Europe, raising questions as to why any company should ever produce low-margin goods locally in a sector subject to constant renewal. The value of a company would increasingly be deconnected from the value of its manufacturing assets, whose location depended more on Global North versus Global South labour cost differentials.

The dominant strategic model – reflecting both the race for growth (to cover overheads) and supply chains' fragmentation (to take advantage of global labour cost differentials) – would enable both economies of scale and value creation through the optimization of global operations. This type of growth could occur either organically or via acquisitions, involving in both cases a race for size materializing in an asset aggregation strategy. Little by little, actors in the different chains would become more interdependent, with the interest of each being to protect their margins by achieving excellence in their core businesses.

Toyotism, a providential model

Consumers, shareholders and employees became increasingly demanding. Consumers wanted greater customization, responsiveness and timeliness in the products they bought, putting greater pressure on supply chain logistics and factory responsiveness alike. Shareholder structures also evolved, notably following the emergence of huge pension funds. Short-term return imperatives tightened at the same time as people became more risk averse, squeezing companies whose response was to operate with less working capital. Lastly (and reflecting other changes in society), employees in this 3rd Age of Industry were increasingly demanding that their ideas be listened to, and that they have opportunities for professional development.

The net effect of these three phenomena was to induce most industrial companies to question their own models. The early years of automation and robotization helped reduce the number of arduous and repetitive tasks that companies performed while partially satisfying their short-term profitability imperatives. A number of companies also began to implement enterprise resource planning (ERP) systems enabling different functions to share data sourced either externally from the marketplace or internally from their global manufacturing processes, all with a view towards making their supply chain more robust.

Despite all this, the 3rd Age of Industry lacked an organizational model capable of facilitating the management of large companies and complex supply chains without this costing too much in working capital or end-user service quality terms. This explains the emergence of a system whose operational principles broke with the Taylorism that had guided the preceding era. The new system, first known as Toyotism – later referred to as lean manufacturing – responded to the three aforementioned challenges by promoting a value-added concept that put the end user at the heart of all internal practices. It was a concept based on three underlying principles. The first was 'lean flows' piloting, responding to the need to decrease working capital by reducing inventories. The second was the quality monitoring system, based on the idea that things be 'right first time' to guarantee excellent quality service at the lowest possible cost. Third, participative management systems made it possible to fully leverage the intellectual firepower at a company's disposal, including its operatives and not just executives or engineers.

In the 1980s and 1990s the world began to discover a Toyota model that for a period of 40 years penetrated all parts of the economy and enabled considerable progress in cost, production time and product quality terms. In most sectors today the model has remained more or less operative since, and the challenges associated during the 3rd Age of Industry – with consumer, shareholder and employee demands – still apply. The question then becomes why things should change.

Limitations of the model

Like any transition between two worlds, change cannot be enacted from one day to the next in the way that a light switch is turned on. For a certain time at least, benchmarks from both worlds will overlap. Thus, even as benchmarks associated with the 3rd Age of Industry largely continued to apply, several major changes began taking shape, including an awareness that grew more or less rapidly depending on the sector of activity and each industrial actor's trajectory.

Among all these changes, the most striking is undoubtedly the rise of social networks enabling instantaneous access to product, brand and service information as well as a viral propagation of information. One consequence is customers' new habit of demanding end-to-end transparency from all parties involved in an industrial chain. This was a problem for the model associated with the 3rd Age of Industry, more focused on optimizing production costs globally by choosing industrial locations based on two factors alone (transportation versus local labour costs). A tension has arisen between pure profitability objectives and other aims relating to a company's image, comprised inter alia of its working conditions, the traceability of the raw materials it used, its environmental performance and its fiscal citizenship in the countries where it ran manufacturing operations.

In addition to industrial actors' straightforward adherence to minimum ethical thresholds, there is also the arrival on the labour market of so-called generations Y and Z, who demanded far more meaning from work than their predecessors had done. The end result has generally been greater public criticism of where companies locate their industrial units, development centres or support functions, a scrutiny further complicated by the recent return (at both the national and the regional level) to old-fashioned chauvinism. One notable example is the growing dichotomy between large globalized metropolises and the 'peripheries' where citizens increasingly felt ignored by politicians (Guilluy, 2014). The 3rd Age of Industry had caused these peripheral areas to compete with one another where they used to simply supply raw materials or transformed foodstuffs to metropolises that would then perform requisite redistributive and administrative functions. Small towns in US farming states such as Iowa used to be able to rely on the nearest big city, 'subcontracting' more manual and industrial activities to the metropolis in exchange for its administering the educational system and redistributing tax receipts levied on the consumption of these very same products. This had generally been a win-win situation for all involved. Now these same small towns were having to compete with mid-sized cities in Mexico, Eastern Europe or Asia. This is because the 3rd Industrial Revolution had concretized in a form of offshore subcontracting totally disconnected from any sort of proximity-based relationship involving political trust. All of this explains the lesser tolerance today (exemplified in certain recent Global North election results) for a model that had aggravated inter-regional imbalances and exacerbated all kinds of tensions.

The growing demand for business ethics also had shareholder behaviour in its crossfire. Financial market liberalization was followed by a grand era of capital dilutions involving complex financial arrangements. This was clearly hobbled by the 2008 financial crisis when the entire world became aware that the system could go out of control irrespective of what this meant for the real economy. The disruption sparked a twofold reaction. On one hand, there was renewed consideration for physical and concrete value – with the idea growing that the industrial sector could become flag bearer for this approach. On the other hand, there is greater mistrust of shareholders, accused of being overly focused on financial returns hence having too short-term a view and being disconnected from companies and their employees. Manufacturing history is full of examples of factories purchased several times by funds who may have had a few long-term development ambitions but were ultimately forced (often because of leveraged buyouts) to cut into the 'meat' of an industrial apparatus by neglecting its basic need for mainte-nance and modernization investments. With the acceleration of technology, this kind of strategy – which might work for one or two years without any notable consequences – became more apparent than ever before. Greedy investment funds no longer had very good press and contributed to a number of people rejecting the system as a whole.

Another major shift was that the digital economy began to export its model to other sectors. This especially applied to one attribute that is specific to immaterial exchanges, namely the demand for transactional immediacy. In the world of industry, information always ends up transformed into a physical good. Despite the very fast acceleration in production times, indus-try during this 3rd Age would be turned totally upside down by a new demand that seemed impossible to satisfy given materials' transformation and shipment delays. The paradigmatic idea that big groups benefited using their size to realize economies of scale also lost currency. The new idea taking shape was that size is no longer necessarily an advantage but can be a big obstacle to rapid adaptation and instantaneous responsiveness.

The technologies of this 3rd Age of Industry were also progressively reach-ing their limits in terms of being able to satisfy the new demand for responsiveness and adaptability. It is hard to respond to a kind of demand that increasingly requires single batches yet where no one product looks like another. At the time, machines and processes were being sized according to a series logic. Robots were enclosed in cages and could only be accessed using specialist technicians, with ERP being implemented to process all manage-ment data and ensure that industrial planning was re-set once a year. Of course, systems designed in this fashion might also take several years to set up. Insufficiently adapted to market volatility and to the demand for customization, it increasingly became clear that they needed to be reinvigorated – and that a good way of doing this might involve agile solutions such as collaborative robots capable of learning, as well as specialist applications that could be installed very quickly and operated on a Software as a Service (SaaS) basis.

It remains that new technologies would have another effect that was even more pernicious in terms of the traditional ways that 3rd Age industrial companies had operated. Exponential change required increasingly cutting-edge competencies that had to be renewed more and more quickly. It also required intensified cooperation between experts. Yet developing all these cutting-edge competencies internally was almost impossible. The very principle of innovative activities and industrial secrets' facing significant barriers to entry no longer applied. Quite the contrary, innovation would require greater access to external competencies and engagement in partnerships sometimes including one's competitors. The problem here was reconciling the growing need to innovate in order to remain competitive in the marketplace while differentiating oneself from the competition and remaining open to the discovery of useful competencies. The greatest dilemma in this technological change was that mistrust no longer only applied to a company's traditional competitors but also to actors in other sectors coming either from the same value chain (upstream or downstream) or from a totally different world (like the GAFA world of pure digital players whose digital platforms were threatening entire industries).

With its demands for ethics, immediacy, customization and disruptive innovation, the world created by the 3rd Age of Industry still had some miles left in it – but clearly the big changes that it was going through raised serious questions about its seminal principles. The question here was whether these changes should be met with indifference while waiting for the situation to stabilize (like a pain that someone ignores until it gets really bad) or whether the time was ripe for another disruptive change. Up until then everything had gone well – so far so good – but it was unclear whether this could last. What had yet to be ascertained was whether all these upcoming disruptions were going to be so earth-shattering as to deserve being called a new Industrial Revolution, the fourth in human history.

02

The 4th Age of Industry: Real disruption or false revolution?

SUMMARY

- Four new challenges face the industrial world: everyone's hyper-connectivity with everyone else; the exponential nature of progress; winner-take-all hyper-concentration; and the use economy. The four challenges have combined to force the industrial world to change. Even so, many business leaders continue to question the shift.

- Doubters have three main arguments. In their opinion, there has been no disruption (only an acceleration in the standard speed of industrial change); the changes that have occurred are contradictory and do not lend themselves to any clear characterization; it is impossible to replicate in the world of physical objects the kinds of logic that apply to intangible flows.

- The main thing that industrialists are missing, in the wake of Fordism and Toyotism, is a benchmark organization model adapted to this new industrial age. The model would have to be agile, connected, capable of disruptive innovation and attractive to tomorrow's talents, ie able to cope with the challenges of the 4th Age of Industry.

- The Tesla Way – inspired by the system that Tesla established – could become the matrix of a new model of productive organization. This might be structured into three concentric circles and seven principles: story-making, cross-integration, tentacular traction, start-up leadership, software hybridization, hypermanufacturing, and men and machine learning.

Many observers remained sceptical that a real industrial revolution was taking place. Instead of welcoming a disruption approach, they preferred inaction or at most simple incremental reforms. It is true that the absence of a target organizational model made things harder for anyone seeking real transformation. After Taylorism, Fordism and Toyotism, the question now was which organizational model was most likely to emerge and allow companies to take full advantage of all the technological changes taking place while satisfying customers' new demands.

Four new challenges for industry

Before talking about the 4th Industrial Revolution, it is worth revisiting the main challenges mentioned above, as well as their primary effects (Figure 2.1).

The first challenge was the new hyper-connectivity between machines, humans, products and individuals' professional and private lives. Everyone would be connected in the New World, enjoying access to information no longer limited to just a few persons and teams who sought greater meaning and autonomy in their work. Modern consumers would also want things to happen in real time, with responsiveness being a key value for them. This meant that companies would have to leverage increasingly massive connectivity even as customers were demanding greater responsiveness.

FIGURE 2.1 The four challenges 4th Age of Industry

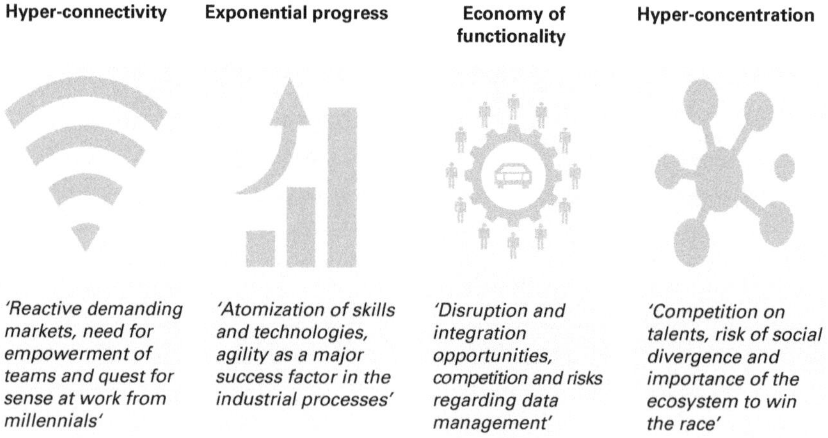

Hyper-connectivity	Exponential progress	Economy of functionality	Hyper-concentration

| 'Reactive demanding markets, need for empowerment of teams and quest for sense at work from millennials' | 'Atomization of skills and technologies, agility as a major success factor in the industrial processes' | 'Disruption and integration opportunities, competition and risks regarding data management' | 'Competition on talents, risk of social divergence and importance of the ecosystem to win the race' |

SOURCE OPEO

The second challenge was the exponential nature of progress. Moore's law shows that calculational power doubles every 18 months, with most technologies following this exponential trend. The end result was a proliferation of technologies that were increasingly atomized but also becoming more specific and cutting-edge. This was accompanied by the atomization of the associated competencies in an environment characterized by liquid progress. Agility (based on permanent adaptation) would become the key value, with the question being how best to benefit from the constant change in industrial robotics, 3D printing, the internet of things, artificial intelligence and digital tools.

The third challenge was hyper-concentration or the possibility that the biggest players in the digital sphere would become dominant, both in market value terms and geographically. Most global R&D is concentrated on a few small sites (with 10 clusters accounting for three-quarters of total global R&D). Concentration to this extent has created a social imbalance with people starting to worry about job security and the possible disappearance of the middle class. On top of this, inter-regional disequilibrium also worsened. Ambient business models were no longer good enough and wider support systems became necessary. The key value system was the ecosystem, with questions at this level being how to create a safety net ensuring that the digital world (with its endemic winner-takes-all principle) did not lead inevitably to social or environmental devastation. Similarly, responses would also have to be found to the new generations' need for meaning both at work and in their consumption behaviour.

The fourth and final challenge related to changing perceptions of value. From a society rooted in the consumption of goods there would be a steady shift towards a world where the use of goods became paramount. Successful people would be the ones who founded new business models and used data to create innovative services – like digital platforms – before anyone else. Everyone was trying to figure out how to create more customized services and products to satisfy the demands of 21st-century consumers more interested in how goods could be used than in the status afforded by their ownership.

The issues raised by these challenges were both essential and structuring, implying very strongly that the model created in response would have to be disruptive in nature. Reality is more complex than that, however, since any adaptation to challenges of this kind would need to be substantial, occasionally contradictory, and, in any event, hard to conceptualize. Hence the scepticism that many leaders felt, with others remaining perplexed as to the best way of taking advantage of the new movement.

Doubters' wrong right reasons

The first reason not to change anything was the most obvious. As noted above, the 4th Industrial Revolution had to some extent been a continuation of the 3rd but featuring an accelerated speed of technological progress. It would have been unclear under these conditions why any change should occur. Robots were already well known, as were information systems (with ERP having long been on the scene); as were digital approaches, seen as little more than the logical successor to PCs' workspace deployment. As for Toyotism and lean manufacturing, they had also been in place for many years. Hence the idea of intensifying efforts in all these areas, hoping blindly that something good might come out of this. Notwithstanding the depth of the challenge required to simply stay in business, this is what many companies were saying at the time – and indeed, still are today.

A second reason not to stick with the status quo was the internal contradictions between some of the concepts associated with the 4th Age of Industry. Some analysts felt stymied by a situation where success required agility and an adaptive start-up mindset even as the world was becoming increasingly complex, calling for highly sophisticated and robust operational processes that were seemingly at odds with the happy improvisation usually associated with a start-up activity. It was a contradiction also exemplified by the pervasive idea at the time that investment returns would be undermined if the new paradigm called for major investments in new system architecture, focusing on long-term interests but not expecting any short-term bottom-line benefits. This seemed totally at odds with the financial and operational agility that the markets were demanding. Note that a similar phenomenon had also been witnessed in each of the previous industrial revolutions, materializing in the lengthy delays between when new technologies became available and the materialization of their concrete economic effects. The enthusiasm phase had mainly occurred when combinations of innovations started to generate greater value than the sum of the values they produced individually. In the early 20th century, for instance, the invention of electricity took more than 20 years to translate into major change – notably when factories started to adopt an assembly-line approach and apply Taylor's principles based on the electrification of smaller, more flexible machines. The problem is that the modern world's increasingly financialized perspective made it harder to adopt a long-term shareholder view.

The final reason for refusing change was the infamous conceit that 'we do things differently'. Clearly industrial activities were not like services – but that also made it unclear how a model based on purely intangible flows might be replicated in the world of physical flows.

On top of all this, the industrial sector was mainly comprised of companies that function on a business-to-business (B2B) basis. At the same time, the immense majority of known unicorns ran according to business-to-consumer (B2C) models, despite the fact that selling products to private parties was clearly very different from selling to fellow professionals. The specific conundrum at this level became how to respond to consumers' growing demand for authentic manufactured products. Traditional or artistic professions – even recently automated ones (like watchmaking or luxury leather goods) – already benefited from a certain value-creating aura. As such, their digitization did not necessarily make much sense.

Continuity despite acceleration, contradictory conditionalities, widespread denial about the need for change – all of these seemingly well-founded arguments would raise doubts as to the existence of a 4th Industrial Revolution. But in the absence of an organizational model adapted to the characteristics of this new era, it was also possible that there was yet another reason for the ambient scepticism.

The 4th Age of Industry orphaned by a lack of organizational disruption

Many observers tend to view industrial revolutions as events largely dominated by radical technological disruption. Yet historically, each industrial revolution has corresponded to a triple movement: revolution in markets and in society; technological revolution in response to this initial change; but also, and above all, an organizational revolution in businesses trying to connect the dots. A new organizational model is indispensable to any company seeking to fully leverage technological innovation in response to new market needs while ensuring the long-term survival of all the activities, competencies and human motivations that take shape within the new context. Hence the systematic emergence of new organizational models during earlier industrial revolutions, which they helped to intensify and consolidate.

The 1st Industrial Revolution was born out of the early 19th-century need for infrastructure to parallel the emergence of the steam engine, whose productivity far outweighed anything humans could do. In organizational terms, this was the beginning of mechanization.

The 2nd Industrial Revolution translated into rising mass consumption during the early part of the 20th century. In technological terms, the discovery of electricity transformed factories by replacing core equipment with production lines characterized by autonomous machinery. This change enabled the advent of Taylorism, followed by Fordism, and more specifically, a specialization of tasks leading to substantial productivity gains.

The 3rd Industrial Revolution started in the early days of the globalization wave that broke out during the 1960s. In technological terms, this was the beginning of robotization and industrial IT. Companies adapted their organizations by creating global supply chains and progressively implementing new principles like just-in-time or lean manufacturing, with a view towards satisfying consumers' demand for greater responsiveness in a globalized market. The keynote organizational model born during this era was Toyotism.

Compared to the past when the scientific organization of work, Fordism, Toyotism and lean manufacturing had all adapted to the dominant economic and technological paradigms of their times, the 4th Industrial Revolution seems orphaned, lacking a disruptive organizational model helping it to respond to the four aforementioned mega-challenges. Whatever model coincides with this new revolution will have to be connected, agile and capable of innovating disruptively; attract talented people; and ensure that competencies develop at a pace matching accelerated technological progress. The question then becomes how to conceptualize a model responding simultaneously to all these challenges, ie one that is sufficiently disruptive to transform doubt, scepticism and perplexity into opportunity – in other words, that can play the same role as Toyotism did during the 3rd Age of Industry.

Such a model exists but unlike previous industrial revolutions it merges different business attributes. As befits the 4th Industrial Revolution, anyone applying traditional reasoning is bound to be confused by the new model, being a synthesis of everything that is best in all industrial sectors, at a strategic level and in organizational, technological and human terms.

Having said that, there is one company that – due to its leader's audacity and extraordinary capacity for innovation – has shown the ability to epitomize a new organizational model adapted to the 4th Age of Industry. This company is Tesla, the California start-up that for the first time since Ford, General Motors and Chrysler appeared in the early 20th century has added a new name to the list of major US carmakers. Its model is called 'Teslism' (Figure 2.2).

The remainder of the book will analyse the new model's DNA to better understand its foundations. It will do this by drilling down into Tesla's

FIGURE 2.2   Teslism, a potential organizational paradigm
              for the 4th Industrial Revolution

Market and society

Organization

Teslism

Toyotism

Mechanization   Taylorism

Technology

1st Industrial Revolution	2nd Industrial Revolution	3rd Industrial Revolution	4th Industrial Revolution
1800	1900	1970	2020

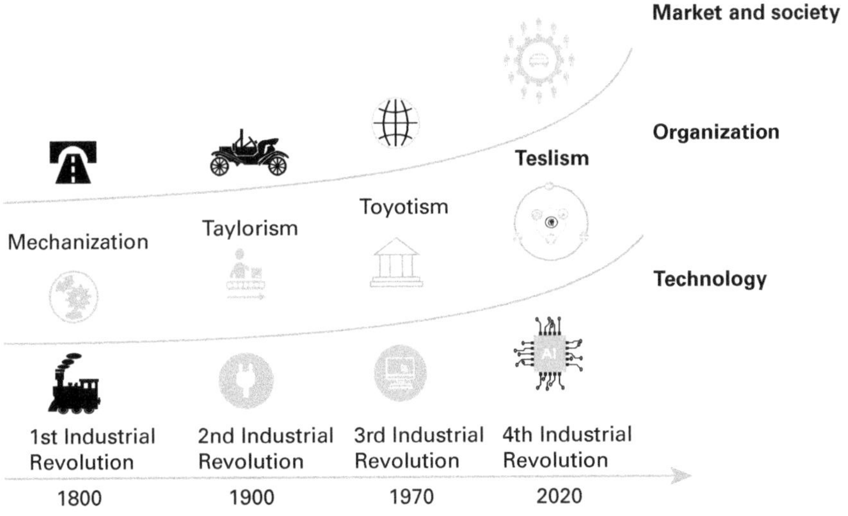

SOURCE OPEO

operational levels and by using targeted illustrations of leading global references for each of the dimensions it discusses.

Teslism as a potential organizational model for the 4th Age of Industry

The author's analysis and observations of the Tesla model (and of other potential 'lighthouses' of Industry 4.0) have revealed 'Teslism' deserves to be called a 'system' and that it revolves around three concentric circles.

One is outside facing. Another is inside facing. The third is the core system, focused on humans' but also machines' ability to learn quickly. The system features seven principles: story-making; cross-integration; tentacular traction; start-up leadership; software hybridization; hypermanufacturing; and human and machine learning (Figure 2.3).

Before delving into these seven principles, it is worth spending a little time trying to understand how Teslism might become a credible response to the strategic and technological challenges of the 4th Age of Industry.

FIGURE 2.3 The seven principles of Teslism

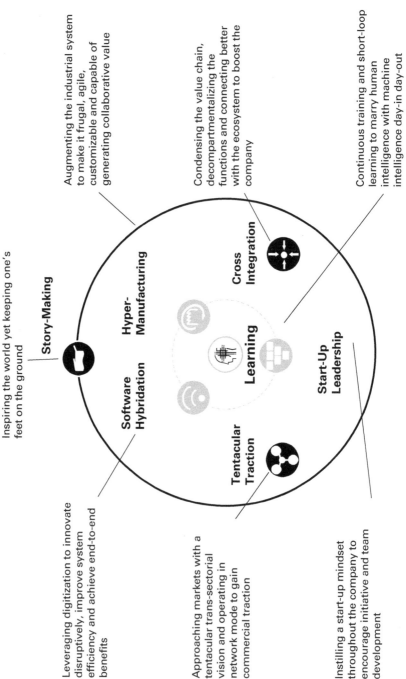

Inspiring the world yet keeping one's feet on the ground

Story-Making

Augmenting the industrial system to make it frugal, agile, customizable and capable of generating collaborative value

Hyper-Manufacturing

Condensing the value chain, decompartmentalizing the functions and connecting better with the ecosystem to boost the company

Cross Integration

Continuous training and short-loop learning to marry human intelligence with machine intelligence day-in day-out

Software Hybridation

Leveraging digitization to innovate disruptively, improve system efficiency and achieve end-to-end benefits

Learning

Start-Up Leadership

Tentacular Traction

Approaching markets with a tentacular trans-sectorial vision and operating in network mode to gain commercial traction

Instilling a start-up mindset throughout the company to encourage initiative and team development

SOURCE OPEO

FIGURE 2.4 Teslism's four objectives

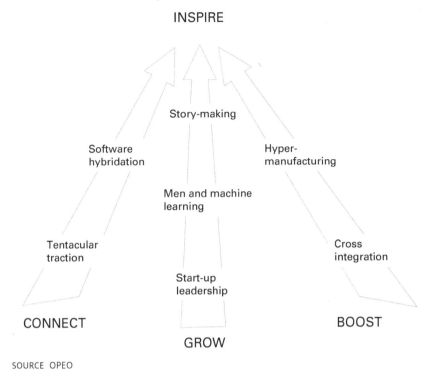

SOURCE OPEO

The book will then analyse how the seven principles respond to four main objectives: inspiring the world with a project transcending the company where it was born; boosting this company's operational systems and interfaces; digitally interlinking its businesses, ecosystem and customers; and helping its people to grow every day to get the organization as a whole to grow as well (Figure 2.4). These four objectives resonate perfectly with the four challenges associated with the 4th Age of Industry. Inspiring the world makes it possible to respond to the demand for ethics and regulation caused by the hyper-concentration of value and talents. Boosting and connecting a system both internally and externally responds to the growing need for product functionality, hence to the challenges of a use-based economy, while benefiting from hyper-connectivity between people, machines and products. Lastly, helping people to grow makes it possible to develop individual and collective competencies so that exponential progress is viewed as an opportunity and not as a race against time.

INSPIRING, CONNECTING, BOOSTING AND EXPANDING: JPB SYSTEMS, AN SME THAT UNBEKNOWN TO ITSELF HAS BEEN FOLLOWING THE TESLA WAY

The incredibly inspiring story of someone who has dug deep to further a loved one's life's work

Despite having run his own SME for more than a decade, Damien Marc has never realized that he is himself a kind of Elon Musk. This 36-year-old entrepreneur neither needed Tesla nor Industry 4.0 to develop a vision that was diametrically opposed to what everyone had been saying in his sector. Making a virtue out of necessity, Damien has always been driven by a sense that 'growing our company is the best way of keeping Dad alive'. Despite his father having passed away a long time ago, Damien is still visibly moved whenever the topic arises. It is often said that emotions can move mountains. JPB's story is all about the transmission of emotion and passion from one generation to the next. Jean-Pierre, Damien's father, was born in 1958 and had himself had an atypical profile. He was an artistic photographer, which displeased his own father who told Jean-Pierre very early on that he needed to get a real profession. Whereupon his mother signed him up for a mechanics training programme at Caen's Lemonnier Institute, following which he began a career in precision mechanics. This new direction didn't make him any less creative, however, quite the contrary. After a few years working for a man named Bernard, Jean-Pierre dared to question an aberration that the aeronautics sector had tolerated until that point, relating to the way clamp nuts were being combined with lock-wire to minimize the risk of torque loss. It was a compromise that cost a great deal in terms of time and money without ensuring complete reliability. Jean Pierre began tinkering with his own system at the workshop, but as often happens with trailblazers, few people believed in him at first. 'If changing the system is something that could be done, the industry would have done it long ago' seemed to be the doomsayers' attitude. Despite this, Bernard agreed to start a new company together with Jean-Pierre, alongside his own mechanical engineering firm.

This was back in 1995. Finalizing an operative product took Jean-Pierre more than six years, during which time Damien completed his studies. He was a more or less average student, having been far more interested in tangible topics than in academia, although he did do well on his school-leaving exams. Faced with the choice of continuing in higher education, Damien decided to pursue a technical training programme, preferring this to a more theoretical pathway. With his love of electronics, Damien found his new studies fascinating and ended up towards the top of his class. This then inspired him to enrol in an engineering school to further his education. Unlike his classmates, however, he still followed an unusual trajectory, which saw him first do an internship in Africa before gaining some initial job experience working as a foreperson. His early career went swimmingly – he loved what he was doing.

Damien and Jean-Pierre devoted little time to discussing their professional lives at this point in time. Indeed, Damien didn't have a clue about his father's business. But a sudden chain of events conspired to bring them together. Jean-Pierre's already fragile health took a sudden turn for the worse when a major heart attack put him into a coma. This was an enormous shock for Damien. Not only had he never wanted to take over his father's company but, even worse, he knew nothing about it, meaning he had to start from scratch. A few months later – and very unexpectedly – Jean-Pierre woke up from the coma. Damien didn't waste the chance, taking full advantage of what was to be a miraculous interlude (lasting 18 months) to attend to some critical business. Jean-Pierre's company had been profitable but relied on a single large customer, with three people working all day long to get everything done. Damien had to expend a great deal of energy negotiating the legalities of his assuming control of Jean-Pierre's business, which the other shareholders felt was at an imminent threat of going under. This period of endless conflict, with Damien being forced to take enormous risks, left its mark on him. In the end he gained control of the operation but there was a price, namely the fact that his mother – who supported him all throughout his legal ordeal – had to put up all her savings.

Within 10 years, however, JPB Systems would turn into an incredible success story. The company counts four of the global aeronautics sector's biggest engine manufacturers among its customers, together with their main partners. Annual turnover now exceeds €18 million. Yet its corporate culture is still influenced by the hardships it faced during these early years. Hard work and a willingness to face challenges remain fundamental values for its teams.

A single-minded focus from the very outset: growing the business
and increasing competitiveness by thinking differently

People entering a sector as demanding as aeronautics must figure things out even more quickly than players who are already up and running. By definition, a company starts as a start-up, meaning everything has yet to be done. Damien was very focused on the idea that 'excellence was our only option'. He has been very successful with that attitude and his business outperforms almost all of its rivals.

JPB Systems has been hitting a service rate of 100 per cent for several years now. Having won a number of awards, today it is universally recognized as a lighthouse for the aeronautics sector. Taking the beaten path would not have led to these fantastic outcomes, however. The main pitfalls that Damien had to avoid after taking over the company were complacency and smugness. Instead, he decided to 'always look far ahead... drive things forward, fight on all fronts'. In short, success depends on being audacious and energetic – although in and of itself, this isn't enough.

Talking with Damien about the underlying factors driving his company's dynamic, the first thing that springs to mind is the boss himself, a visionary who knows how to remain humble and results-focused regardless of the situation. 'I didn't have a choice at first and had to position myself as someone who was simply observing the system. Coming from the world of electronics, I knew nothing about mechanics.' In other words, Damien's first move was to adapt to a new situation. He was a quick learner and the fact that he did not start out as a mechanic possibly explains why he felt empowered to take certain risks that others eschewed. An example of this was his decision, once the company was on an upwards trajectory, to create an entirely automated production line starting from zero. His goal was noble in the sense that he did not want to have to offshore operations to Poland. Everyone considered this a crazy risk. Yet it turned out to be a great success. Of course, there were problems at first and it took a while to overcome certain reliability issues. But Damien's tenacity meant he was able to hold the line even when the going got tough. This was a good example for his teams, the idea being 'not to give in to doubt but keep faith with what we're doing'.

Above and beyond these slightly crazy risks, JPB's dynamic was also rooted in its ability to accelerate continuously. The company has never stopped expanding hence questioning its modus operandi. One of the clearest manifestations of this capacity for executing at speed is its systems' ability to make decisions quickly, largely based on the faith that management has in the teams and the autonomy they have been given. 'Once something has been explained to me, I never dither and usually make a decision immediately – or at the very latest by the end of the day.'

A start-up attitude is the only way small companies can survive in a world dominated by giants

It's not easy for SME bosses to become a new Elon Musk. This is especially challenging for companies with a single line of business and few staff members – if only because of how very difficult it is to acquire and develop the necessary competencies. During its early years, JPB had been mainly focused on engineering studies. The product that Jean Pierre developed was a completely disruptive innovation. Not to mention that the company was tiny at the time and highly reliant on suppliers making its parts (and on its one and only customer). The key to its further development was therefore more vertical integration and much closer connections to the rest of its ecosystem.

Towards that end, Damien adopted a typical start-up strategy, which meant understanding customer needs in sufficient detail to avoid having to work through any intermediaries (and indeed, with any big rivals). He quickly starting dealing directly with his products' end users, to wit, with process engineers. Their main goal during a design phase is to be able to show prototypes to their internal decision-makers as quickly as possible. Damien and his teams came up with a miraculous solution, investing in alpha stage equipment (metalwork machine, kiln, test bed) that could be used to develop and test new parts in less than a week. This was a revolution in the aeronautics sector and led to JPB soon winning a number of tenders.

But it also caused new headaches relating to the company's being too small, hence coming under the size threshold that potential buyers required from their suppliers. Whereupon Damien turned to peers in the local area, combining with them to reach a scale that large English or US customers might consider sufficient.

On top of these purely psychological issues, there was the basic imperative of performing well. Small companies surrounded by big competitors can struggle to survive. Damien quickly realized that he would have to integrate the different facets of his manufacturing function to have any chance of meeting the aeronautics supply chain's usual delivery deadlines. This was particularly important given his own desire for excellence, which precluded JPB's working to a more mediocre service standard. The end result was a strategic decision to gradually bring production back in-house, with Damien notably opting to automate as many processes as possible in order to continue being able to invest in France. This affected the company's in-house design flows but also – reflecting his willingness to engage in disruptive innovation – the bespoke information system that JPB's teams devised. Damien also began monitoring the ERP market but was not particularly satisfied by any of the products on offer there, finding them too old-fashioned and insufficiently responsive or user friendly. He again rose to the challenge by building his own manufacturing execution system (MES) 'with input from two recent school graduates' – adhering in this way to JPB's seminal philosophy that if things are progressing too slowly they can always be accelerated by bringing work back in-house and giving the company's highly motivated teams a crack at it.

The company is much bigger nowadays but Damien still refuses to sit on his laurels. He continues to link into wider networks but uses other channels today. These include close relationships with schools, contributing to the BPI France incubator and working with the press to get it to both publicize the company more widely and make it attractive to potential new talents. Connections of this sort remain a key success factor, especially for small ventures competing with super-sized rivals.

Growing the team: prioritizing individuals over competencies

'The most difficult thing throughout this whole adventure has undoubtedly been human resource management.' When Damien looks at all the problems he has had to overcome, the tone can get very serious. 'HRM is clearly a key success factor for us.' This is not something he had understood at the outset, especially not how complex this whole field would become – above all when there is bad news to be shared. 'I've always found that saying goodbye is the hardest thing. But it's important to have the courage to do that when necessary. Indeed, it's usually much better for both sides.' Admitting the possibility of making mistakes is part of JPB's culture – yet another trait that the company shares with the digital world.

In a similar vein, there is Damien's recognition that, 'It doesn't always work when technical staff members are asked to assume management roles.' Having said that, what counts more than anything else is the trust that exists between senior management and frontline staff. Everyone has their place in the organization as long as they are driven by a desire to do well. One funny story that Damien tells is about how some of the recruits were hired by JPB before anyone even knew what jobs they were supposed to do. He would interview people and offer them work simply because he liked them, the understanding being 'we'll figure out your position later on'. This is diametrically opposed to the kinds of rigid processes characterizing recruitment in many if not most large firms. Recently, for instance, Damien hired an acquaintance who had previously worked as CEO at an SME. The individual in question had a transition period juggling both jobs, following which he chose to run JPB's sales department. 'Our teams are driven by a passion for the business and the pride they feel when helping to grow the company.' Damien is also proud about the speed with which some managers have risen up the corporate ladder despite having little more than a vocational certificate. 'I work on a basis of trust.

Everyone has a space where they can thrive. All I can say is that the more motivated you are, the faster you will move up.'

So trust is crucial, as is the freedom to be entrepreneurial. Damien always finds it amusing, for instance, that the company runs so well – and sometimes even better – when he is away. 'I love it when a staff member shows me their latest prototype as soon as it comes out of the lab. They clearly feel a great deal of pride in their work but you know what? So do I.'

Of course, it was not as easy at first to attract new talent, with some recruits facing a pay cut when they came to JPB. Over time, however, many would be highly enthused by this very unusual adventure, with the first cohort of recruits ultimately playing a key role as trailblazers. Damien had shown the way with his inspired vision but, even so, the environment at the company has always been stringent. 'Sometimes I'll even ask machine suppliers to repaint parts even if they are barely visible. I'm very tough but it's because of my belief that a factory must be as clean and aesthetically pleasing as a lab.' In short, Damien is extremely demanding regarding everything that JPB does. He questioned things from the very outset through his decision to combine atoms (mechanical engineering) with bytes (electronics), a fusion that would soon become the company's core competency. This willingness to revolutionize the corporate culture can also be felt in the way he conducts business; his approach to potential development and production issues; and last but not least, how he recruits and develops all of JPB's human resources.

All in all, JPB Systems is an excellent example of digitization being hybridized with traditional industry. More broadly, however – and without even realizing it – there are scores of entrepreneurs who, like Damien, have driven Tesla-type transformations in their own companies. The remainder of the book will offer further insights into how the Tesla Way can best be described using the seven dimensions that have been evoked previously.

'START BY GIVING 110% – AND THEN ACCELERATE':
SODISTRA, DISTILLING THE TESLA WAY
Turning constraints into opportunities: an inspirational boss
who chooses to be confident

Operating out of France's Mayenne district in the midst of three dynamic sectorial clusters, Château-Gontier is an atypical place, a beautiful and historic little town with an abnormally high concentration of entrepreneurs. It was here that Erwan Coatanea invested five years ago when he acquired a company manufacturing innovative air treatment systems.

Erwan came with me to visit the site, just outside of the town centre, that he had acquired in September 2013. At first it is very hard to see the factory, hidden in the middle of a cluster of relatively modern buildings. The reason is that industrial parks are built here to not disfigure the surrounding natural landscape, with companies visibly working hard to ensure that the area looks clean and attractive. Erwan got very serious talking about the early days. 'I had just bought Sodistra, maybe four months before. My wife and I were already taking a big risk when we suddenly got whacked by the work inspectorate telling us that nothing on-site was up to standard.' Erwan had already had some experience with this kind of thing. When he first began in the automotive industry, his potential was quickly recognized, culminating in his being put in charge of a team with more than 1,000 people. But he didn't really enjoy working in large companies, which he found too restrictive. Hence his decision to resign from the position and take over an SME in the aluminium business. After these two useful experiences, he felt he was ready for bigger things – explaining why his new operation's negative audit just a few months after his takeover was such a shock. Compliance would require an enormous investment of several million euros.

Erwan shook off the bad news and overcame his problems. A born optimist, he viewed the new constraint as an opportunity. After cogitating deeply about the matter, he simply decided to build a new building. This was a significant risk, costing €8 million, including the machines. The bill was so high that at first no one thought he would succeed. Yet a mere five years later, Sodistra's turnover had almost doubled (going from €5 million in 2013 to €9 million in 2018). The best explanation is that Erwan did not only invest in his company but actually revolutionized it by launching his own transformation programme, one he called 'Mastering yesterday, today and tomorrow'.

Behind this catchphrase lay a whole slew of technological and managerial changes, starting with a significant improvement in working conditions. This translated Erwan's idea that humans are always found at the heart of any system, a modus operandi that starts with senior managers and frontline staff respecting one another.

Speed of execution, a crucial priority for SMEs

After driving me around a little, Erwan finally dropped me off in his new facility's car park. It was a magical sort of hi-tech atmosphere, replete with an ultra-modern building, a neatly tailored lawn and a lobby entirely surrounded by glass. What I felt inside, however, was a huge culture shock, being catapulted from a quiet French countryside to something akin to a California start-up. The main open space hosts young engineers working happily alongside more experienced colleagues. The high energy levels are palpable, because everything feels more like a beehive than an office plonked in the middle of an industrial park. After speaking with a number of team members, what I understood is that all this dynamism is the doing of one man, namely the boss. As someone whispered to me jokingly, 'He can really tire us out with his 40 new ideas a day.' But jokes asides, speed of execution was a key success factor at Sodistra from the very outset. What is clear when you enter the production floor is that everything has been designed to accelerate flows: massive upstream investment to transition as quickly as possible from a 3D plan to a physical system, widespread automation, software integrated to optimize slab cutting and minimize dormant inter-operational inventory, a visual piloting of projects, etc. This is because lag times are always crucial to gaining market share and competitiveness. Erwan repeatedly highlighted as his absolute priority the idea that the customer is crucial to everything the company does. But above and beyond these purely technical aspects, he was also very focused on people's mindsets and how they could become change drivers. This applied first of all to himself. 'I spend an enormous amount of time on the frontline, trying to explain my decisions in full, which doesn't mean that I let others make decisions in my place but simply that everyone needs to understand why a particular decision has been taken.' The aim is always to germinate a new way of managing the company. Organizations must evolve continuously if they want to become faster and more agile. This especially applies to middle management. According to Erwan, 'It's totally anachronistic to want to filter the flows between frontline operatives and senior management... You need to make simple choices and explain them clearly to your people out in the field. Otherwise you can't expect them to align with your choices.' Recruitment has also been an important lever in propelling the new dynamic, with a balance having to be found between younger workers full of energy and older colleagues benefiting from long professional experience. The key for veteran staff has been to evolve ('go with the flow' in Erwan's words) instead of running around like headless chickens.

Listening, openness and honesty – three basic values for a last connectivity that benefits everyone

Local entrepreneurs club, French Fab, BpiFrance incubator, customers, suppliers, local authorities – Erwan is highly connected. But this is very different from saying that he disperses his focus. 'Networks start with observing and listening to everything going on around you. It's natural to seek connections but you need to accept that they won't necessarily produce immediate results. The most important thing is to open up to others and cultivate relationships – each in its own time.'

When it comes down to translating intentions into acts, however, caution remains advisable, along with a few general rules. The first is only to pursue avenues that everyone fully understands. It is essential that the teams remain rooted in reality, ie that their story be written more than it is narrated. Second, customers' centrality must never be forgotten, and the same applies to work colleagues interfacing between the company and its markets. Lastly, different power bases must always be balanced, with respect shown to all stakeholders, customers and suppliers, the goal being for everyone to come out a winner. Erwan's way of summarizing this vision is to use mathematical terminology. 'I like it when relationships are bijective, even injective, but never surjective.'

Sitting in Sodistra's staff rooms, Erwan told an anecdote that was a good way of representing this spirit. Alongside the table football game that he bought when the factory started, a couple of 3D printing machines can be found, stacked in boxes below the table, along with around 20 blue plastic roosters. Curious about 3D technology and how it works, Erwan bought the equipment in 2015. No one saw any use for it, however, meaning that the machines remained untouched for months. Then one day he hired a young recruit who got very excited about the machine and began blank testing it to train himself up. Erwan then asked BpiFrance to make a plastic blue rooster as a physical materialization of the logo that had been chosen for the French Fab (Made in France) campaign. The test was successful and since then the machines have never really stopped operating, producing almost all of the small plastic blue roosters that can be seen everywhere in the events organized by this one public investment bank. It has nothing to do with Sodistra's core business but constitutes a great adventure full of opportunities linking to the networking effect – while also allowing the company to acquire certain 3D competencies that it can then leverage in any future systems that it develops.

Turning enjoyment and desire into growth drivers

The question then became how to recruit teams and help them develop in a context where the company is both growing rapidly and undergoing a real transformation. From the outset, Sodistra's response has been to focus on people's desires and motivations, even before working on their know-how. Erwan always felt that, 'The most important thing is to find people who want to learn and enjoy reaching targets.' In other words, the best way to learn is to focus on how things can be achieved rather than the obstacles encountered along the way. It's all about a person's state of mind, first and foremost being action-oriented. As a concept, experience has therefore been essential to the people looking to rise within the company. The more often learning opportunities would arise, the sooner people could capitalize upon them, which didn't mean that occasional training was not needed to acquire formal new competencies – it is just that both approaches have always been considered important. Hence the role that the boss has had to assume to ensure that the entire process remain as fluid as possible, from recruitment to continuous learning. The teams need access to all the tools that could maximize their chances of success.

In sum, Sodistra's rise has been first and foremost a collective adventure, a change clearly driven by Erwan, based on the vision he proposed, his help in accelerating the process and the way he has connected the company to its ecosystem. But what is particularly noteworthy is how the entire team has experienced this growth and performance. Erwan has excellent colleagues, people who want to be the best they can, day in day out, even and maybe especially when they encounter resistance. Lastly, Sodistra has the enthusiasm of a whole family, with Erwan often repeating that his 'inspiration' was drawn from his wife Anne, who has been there since the start. All in all, more than a business, this has been a human adventure.

In the end, Erwan has a pithy expression that is the best way of describing how Sodistra pursues the Tesla Way: 'Start by giving 110 per cent and then accelerate.'

03

The seven principles of Teslism

Principle 1: hypermanufacturing

Principle 2: cross-integration

Principle 3: software hybridization

Principle 4: tentacular traction

Principle 5: story-making

Principle 6: start-up leadership

Principle 7: human and machine learning

Principle 1

Hypermanufacturing

Augmenting the industrial system to make it frugal, agile, customizable and capable of generating collaborative value

SUMMARY

- Hypermanufacturing is an 'upgrading' of lean manufacturing and derives from the three pillars of Toyotism: customer focus; just-in-time production; and 'right first time' to minimize waste.

- But three new dimensions have been added: frugality; agility; and collaborative value.

- Tesla teaches that it is possible to combine within a single plant everything that is best about the digital world with cutting-edge industries' organizational practices.

INTRODUCTION TO HYPERMANUFACTURING

What should a factory look like in 2019? As Elon Musk himself says, it no longer has to be the kind of ugly, tedious place that Charlie Chaplin portrayed in *Modern Times*. At Musk's Gigafactory inauguration speech, he said: 'A factory is not that boring place that people believe. It is the machine building the machine, you need to design it like an integrated system' (YouTube, 2016).

Of course, the 10 million factories in service in today's global manufacturing industry still account for 20 per cent of all CO_2 emissions (Figure 3.1).

But industry today also means almost 3 million industrial robots (Figure 3.2, International Federation of Robotics, 2017), €964 billion of dedicated investment in the internet of things (Gartner, 2017) and a sector developing and manufacturing products that are becoming increasingly 'tailor-made' even as manufacturers are constantly forced to shorten their time-to-market. This can be exemplified by Germany's three leading carmakers who over the past 10 years have increased the volume of the options on offer from 47 to 113 per cent, even as products' lifespan has fallen from 10 to 19 per cent over the same period. Today's factories generate 19 cents of service for every euro they produce, with something between 30 and 55 per cent of all jobs in these factories featuring a service component (McKinsey Global Institute, 2012).

Manufacturing today is generally very 'hyper' – hyper-frugal in response to resource rarity by leveraging the latest technologies; hyper-agile and customizable in response to demand volatility and diversification; hyper-connected and open to the world in the generation of collaborative value.

FIGURE 3.1 CO_2 emissions attributable to manufacturing industries and construction (per cent of total fuel combustion)

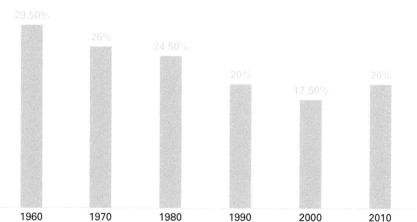

| 1960 | 1970 | 1980 | 1990 | 2000 | 2010 |

29.50%   26%   24.50%   20%   17.50%   20%

SOURCE OPEO, adapted from OECD and IEA International Energy Agency electronic file

FIGURE 3.2 Estimated worldwide operational stock of industrial robots 2016–17 and forecast for 2019–21 (in 1,000s of robots)

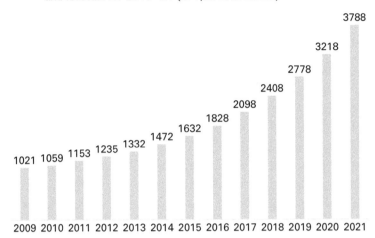

SOURCE OPEO, based on data from International Federation of Robotics, Executive Summary World Robotics 2017 Industrial Robots

But like lean manufacturing, hypermanufacturing is first and foremost a state of mind. 'Hyper' thinking is suitably summarized in Elon Musk's favourite first principle of always approaching problem-solving from a physics perspective – something he regularly says to explain his outlook, with a nod to Newton's first law of thermodynamics. This has largely materialized in a disruptive vision that challenges preconceived ideas to find innovative solutions for each of his company's key processes, notably relating to product development and technological innovation.

Applied to the world of factories, this has been partially translated in the focus on extreme rationalization to maximize the productivity of rare resources such as available space, machine capability, human competence, energy and raw materials. Note that it has also translated into an obsession with manufacturing process speed and agility, and with operations being 'open' to the rest of the world.

Hypermanufacturing has been more than frontal disruption, however. Indeed, the most accurate way of apprehending it is as an 'upgrading' of lean manufacturing. To understand its foundations, and before detailing its principles, it is therefore worth revisiting the essence of the 3rd Age of Industry.

LEAN, JUST-IN-TIME AND VALUE ADDED

By the dawn of the 3rd Industrial Revolution, commercial trade had already started to skyrocket, with supply chains gradually atomizing in a world where, as a corollary, a whole range of industrial components and sub-assemblies were starting to travel further and further. Due to economic financialization, the growing need for responsiveness, the risk of logistical deficiencies and greater working capital pressures, however, most companies steadily began to improve their operational efficiency in the hope that this might reduce the cost of this new unbridled globalization. Within this paradigm, the Toyota Production System stood out in particular. One historical coincidence is that the world discovered this system thanks to MIT (Massachusetts Institute of Technology) researchers (Womack, Jones and Roos, 1990) who studied a NUMMI (New United Motor Manufacturing, Inc) factory in Fremont (California). Anecdotally, this was the plant that Toyota had bought from General Motors in 1984 – and which, very symbolically, Tesla would acquire in 2010.

The Toyota system's efficiency was based on two pillars and three foundations, all centred on the basic principle of waste minimization. For this reason, everyone would end up calling it 'lean manufacturing' (Figure 3.3; Figure 3.4).

The first pillar of Toyotism was just-in-time, a system where each link in the chain would produce at exactly the right moment for their immediate client. This meant both the generation of very little inventory and an agile operational system capable of responding to customers' changing demands.

FIGURE 3.3 The Toyota Temple

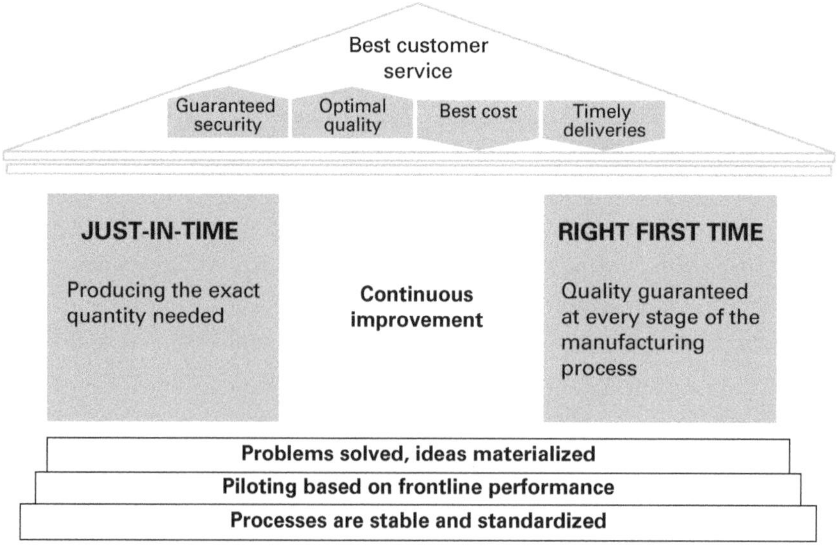

SOURCE OPEO, inspired by Womack and Jones (1990)

FIGURE 3.4 Toyotism's eight sources of waste

SOURCE OPEO, inspired by Womack and Jones (1990)

The principle seemed simple and straightforward but its implementation was very complex, requiring rigorous oversight to detect any problems and solve them as quickly as possible to avoid any supply chain blockages. Just-in-time was based on the application of five ingredients: continuity of flows; one-piece flows; production being timed to sync with end-users' needs; lean flows; and piloting processes covering the whole of the logistics chain. One of the main objectives was to avoid 'batch sizes' that might have raised machines' micro-level effectiveness by manufacturing parts in series but would also slow down overall flow speeds. Despite all this, few companies succeeded in getting their just-in-time system to meet this ultimate objective, with standard batch sizes often varying from a minimum of 10 parts to as many as several thousand, depending on the sector, with the average being around a standard 100 parts.

The second pillar of Toyotism was jidoka or 'right first time'. This was the just-in-time concept's quality dimension, with each link in the chain only continuing to produce if it was certain that the items being sent to the next link in the chain were of good quality. Otherwise, the whole system was supposed to shut down. Quality risks could be reduced by preventing defective sub-assemblies, a real risk given series manufacturing's potential for amplifying any quality problems.

These two pillars responded to Toyotism's intangible aims of focusing on end users and spending as much time as possible adding value. Just-in-time production meant avoiding over-production, ie not using company resources to create products that were not going to be sold and that were therefore completely wasted. Similarly, producing things 'right first time' meant avoiding non-quality flows and creating a product that customers might not buy.

NEW CODES FOR THE 4TH AGE OF INDUSTRY

Industrial software databases have continued to evolve at the dawn of the 4th Age of Industry, reflecting a growing need for frugality and agility as well as a new demand for collaborative value creation. The hypermanufacturing philosophy resulting from this new orientation had leveraged the 'disruptive' mindset that Elon Musk advocates in his first principle, seeking to overcome any obstacles that might prevent the creation of collaborative value.

FRUGALITY

With most global warming scientists announcing and confirming the rarefication of fossil fuels, 21st-century collective consciousness has evolved in relation to energy consumption. Alongside of this, the emergence of social networks means that everyone today possesses a clear vision of the origin of the products they consume, the journey these products have made and whether they were made ethically. In turn, this has led to the concept of frugal industry, which works according to at least four main axes.

The first has involved reducing products' end-to-end carbon footprint by developing manufacturing methods and materials that minimize the consumption of rare resources and promote renewable energies from the design phase onwards. An ancillary method has been to define manufacturing paths that optimize global transport, from the early component stage to end-user delivery.

On top of this comes the idea of low consumption production. This involves defining and operating manufacturing processes that avoid raw material waste, product returns and any unnecessary consumption of energy, while minimizing waste and helping to recycle waste residuals to comply with all solid, liquid and gaseous pollutant emission regulations.

Greater local cooperation has also been necessary to promote this circular economy, by getting local authorities and industrial partners to engage in the different locations where a company's subsidiaries operate. Methods at this level include recycling unconsumed energy or materials, minimizing noise and other kinds of local pollution, timing energy consumption in a way that regulates local production capacities – while promoting lifelong learning and raising all ecosystem participants' level of competence.

Fourth and finally, an end-to-end product ethos means that suppliers' behaviour is now being verified from the very beginning of the chain. This is achieved by means of an 'extended', robust and shared corporate social responsibility policy.

The strong demand for this kind of ethos has not, however, prevented consumers from increasingly demanding customized functionalities and speedy product delivery. Demand has therefore continued to push for extreme diversification. The industrial translation of this change has been an accrued need for agility and 'mass customization' – all combining to shape a new paradigm, one characterized by single batch sizes and same-day delivery. Many just-in-time principles have remained valid but are being pushed to their extreme. They have therefore had to be adapted. Lean flows remain a seminal principle but the idea of having a 'one-piece flow' would now need to be applied in the literal sense of the term, with batch sizes that had been standardized at 100 units being applied to single units. The concept of 'takt time' – describing the average time between two items' start of production – has been subject to particular scrutiny with each individual item now expected to have its own unique production time. Lean flows have remained the guiding principle for the overall supply chain but are now being generalized into logistics zones where people no longer move around to pick out parts ('man to goods') but where the parts are being brought to people ('goods to man').

AGILITY

In terms of doing things 'right first time' – the second of Toyotism's two pillars – most principles have remained valid, being once again characterized by the need to accelerate the system's reaction time but also to adapt the level at which it shares associated information both within a company and across the whole of its logistics chain (including end users). The upstream side of the industrial chain has therefore had to bear greater responsibility for innovation. The development method that has generalized in response involves a hybrid combining traditional industrial methods – organized sequentially and with landmarks – with so-called 'agile' methods imported from the world of software. The seminal principle for this latter sphere had always been that customer specifications constantly evolve, including very late in the innovation and development process, causing a need for much shorter loops, sometimes referred to as 'sprints' between end users and designers. In the upstream stages, the idea of being 'right first time' has also had to be adapted since the new guiding principle focuses more on 'testing and learning', an approach in which rapid action is preferred to perfect action, hence where mistakes are tolerated.

The new technologies have made it possible to respond to the adaptations required by the two pillars of Toyotism (just-in-time and right first time). Thanks to progress in robotics and notably automatic guided vehicles (AGVs), people will travel less in the future and therefore focus more on their core businesses. Connected devices (the internet of things, or IoT) have enabled an end-to-end identification of individual products within their different logistics chains, intimating a dynamic rebalancing of every workstation thanks to the intelligent programming of new manufacturing execution systems 3-D printing (or additive manufacturing) having shortened certain multistage flows, notably during the upstream prototyping phases but also during those manufacturing phases where parts do not require particularly quick production speeds. It also satisfies the need for extreme diversification and agile information flows by transforming digital specifications into immediate manufacturing orders, without any new work programme (or product range or working method) having to be qualified. Quality controls can increasingly be done on a continuous flows basis thanks to non-destructive testing and advances in industrial vision. Also, the quality alert system can now be digitized hence piloted in real time using a management organization cascading principle. Otherwise, the 'Andon' principle – allowing each manufacturing site operative to raise the alarm in case of bad or defective pieces – can now be generalized to all flow processes, ranging from initial design to the final delivery. The associated information flows have spread from Tier 1 subcontractors to the prime contractor's senior management, and even to its suppliers, partners and customers, offering them responsiveness and a full sharing of information. Collaborative digital tools can be used as early as the product development phases to enhance exchanges between the different businesses within a company and also with its partners and end users. Connected devices have helped to translate these information exchanges into physical product adaptations materializing in version updates, enabling beta versions to come to market earlier, with improvements being made as things go along. All stakeholders can engage in short-loop interactions ensuring continuous product improvement in application of the agile methods principle during a product's entire lifespan, from its development through its marketing, improvement and maintenance (so-called 'product series life') phases.

COLLABORATIVE VALUE

Lastly, the concept of added value has remained valid albeit with a limited scope. The key value for customers – now 'users' – has become collaborative value enabling quick responses to any and all needs while accounting for the customer journey and respecting a product's frugal manufacturing framework. All the way up and down the chain, the eight waste categories that Toyotism identified have evolved to incorporate the new needs of final users seeking a renewed form of value.

These observations of the most advanced industrial systems make it possible to list the eight main inhibitors blocking the creation of collaborative value (Figure 3.5).

Over-consumption   This has been the worst impediment to collaborative value since it involves using energy, raw materials and tools that could be applied to producing something else in a world where all resources are, by definition, finite. The over-consumption concept also applies when space is used suboptimally, eg when factory densities are not maximized. The massification of factories has become a crucial issue in the 4th Age of Industry, much like the miniaturization of computers was for the 3rd Age.

Unexploited data   The El Dorado of the 4th Industrial Revolution is data. Not harvesting, storing or analysing available data on customers or internal business processes reduces the amount of value that can be created to benefit

FIGURE 3.5 The eight main factors inhibiting the creation of collaborative value

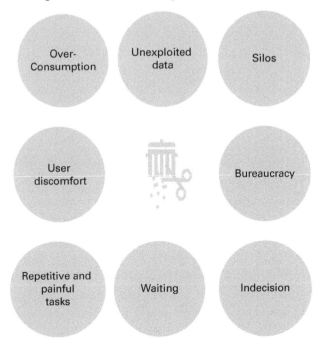

SOURCE OPEO

society, customers or employees. It can also have consequences for process efficiency and for end-to-end flow quality. One example is poor product-versioning management. Another is when problems are insufficiently leveraged into continuous improvement actions mobilizing a lifelong learning logic.

Silos   The branch of an organization that works in isolation from the rest of the structure is commonly referred to as a 'silo'. Working in silos is a significant drag on the speed at which information circulates and can also generate counterproductive decisions. It is an obstacle for responsiveness and value creation. In a digital world, all corporate departments expect to help build global value, hence to operate outside of their supposedly natural borders. The supply chain function, for instance, needs to receive commercial department sales data in very short loops if it is going to achieve maximum responsiveness. Otherwise, it might also invite itself into retail network stores to track product movements and undertake a detailed forecast of new trends. In short, the analyses that the department may require in this analysis may overlap with work done by the marketing team, which is supposed to anticipate future trends by continuously learning what customers think and do.

Bureaucracy   Some parts of an organization always apply the letter of the law or create new rules without necessarily measuring the implications. They do this to avoid taking risks or assuming responsibilities. This creates useless paperwork, sterile discussions and sometimes irritation that can destroy collaborative value. At an initial level, getting rid of bureaucracy means eliminating useless paper and unhelpful administrative process interactions between different departments or within a single one (ie like manufacturing shops). At a second level, there is also a mindset that consists of challenging system constraints in such a way as to come up with disruptive solutions. This approach is rooted in the first principle of asking which physics rules apply to a given process (and what is truly necessary to get things to work). Rules and controls used to solve past ad hoc problems often pile up. The opposite dynamic consists of taking the risk of eliminating rules to free up the system and make it more flexible. This is far from being many people's automatic reflex, however, and requires strong management impetus.

Indecision   In a world where everything moves very quickly, not taking any decisions is generally worse than taking bad decisions. Mistakes are acceptable as long as they can be quickly corrected. Conversely, doing nothing is the worst of all worlds. The idea here is therefore to have a piloting system that gets information to the right decision makers as quickly as possible, thereby associating their responsibilities as intimately possible to the things happening on the frontlines. It is also to get senior managers to spend a good proportion of their time out in the field to avoid any important decisions being delayed or poorly communicated.

Expectations   When people, machines, materials and data are inactive waiting for something to happen, it is rare resources that are not being used even though they can be vital to a company's operations and system responsiveness. In a world in perpetual movement, inaction and under-used assets destroy value. The key therefore is to invent a system that is flexible yet capable of balancing workloads and capacities and whose processes are sufficiently robust to adapt the industrial apparatus to market volatility.

Repetitive or arduous tasks   Progress in automation, robotics and artificial intelligence means that most repetitive or ergonomically difficult tasks can be replaced by machines with the company achieving a good return on investment. Not leveraging progress of this kind means exhausting the system's rarest resources – people – for tasks that do not use them to their fullest capacity. The point here is to make manual labour easier and more interesting while also helping support functions to focus on work that has value for the system, ie that creates collaborative value by resolving complex problems, defining good business and professional standards, training teams and devising innovative future-oriented solutions. Little by little, routine mechanical tasks are destined to disappear throughout business. Of course, these tasks are ones that people rarely enjoy – another good argument to lose them as soon as possible.

User friendliness   Being able to benefit from ergonomically comfortable applications and functionalities is key to customers and/or employees' creation of collaborative value since it is the kind of thing that makes everyone want to use the system and contribute to its ongoing improvement. The giants of the digital world have taught everyone that the user journey is what drives new product-technology design choices. The same applies to the teams working in the industrial world, actors who are increasingly being asked to pilot their daily activities using digital tools. Equipping teams with ergonomic interfaces adapted to their different businesses or professions has become a key factor in people's motivation and daily effectiveness.

LESSONS FROM TESLA

When Elon Musk officially opened Nevada's Gigafactory battery production site – destined to become the biggest in the world in floorspace terms – he gave a speech relaying his vision of factories being designed much like products as integrated systems whose operations can be optimized by applying the basic principles of physics. This did not mean, however, that Musk suffered delusions of grandeur. He had always had the same discourse that frugality and efficiency come before anything else. Musk's speech went on to give meaning to the idea of gigantism. For a while at least, his new plant would be the only one in the world to manufacture electric batteries, a key step in increasing automotive autonomy. The objective over time was to produce enough batteries to supply 1.5 million vehicles. Despite this ambitious objective, everything was conceptualized with a view towards site massification. In Musk's words, 'I am no expert in manufacturing but have spent the past three months on the factory's frontlines. When I think about a car factory, I always go back to my first principle. To make an analogy with physical flows, the idea is to optimize the following equation: volume x density x flow velocity' (YouTube, Elon Musk, 2016). Musk felt for two reasons that this ratio could easily be improved by a factor of 5 or 10.

First, only 2 to 3 per cent of the volume of a final automotive assembly plant is truly 'useful'. Second, the speed at which cars come out of the plant may seem high but is in fact relatively limited (at $c.$ 0.2 metres/second). In short, instead of starting with existing technologies and production modes and seeking to improve them, Musk proposed looking at the problem the other way around by working the basic equation governing the factory's flow velocity, construed here as a system. Even without finding an immediate solution, his idea was that this approach could already inspire work teams to become more ambitious. At the Gigafactory – being the first factory where this principle was applied end to end – the results were impressive. A totally digitized three-dimensional view of the factory bore a close resemblance to the inside of a computer and pursued the same volume optimization goal. This reflected Musk's belief that the manufacturing world was destined to evolve in the same way as computers had, embodied since the 1980s in the race to miniaturization. Companies would not continue to build bigger and bigger factories in response to demographic growth but instead try to miniaturize by densifying processes and accelerating velocity flows.

The first principle of hypermanufacturing consists of massifying space to avoid over-consumption. The same applies to energy consumption. The Gigafactory has been fully equipped with solar panels while also recycling a maximum amount of energy. In perfect coherence with its story-making aspect (see Principle 5), which emphasizes the goal of increasing the proportion of renewable energy, Musk would strive constantly to keep his teams motivated, his shareholders on board and his customers loyal. This would be achieved by linking his operational principles – based on a form of frugality within the industrial apparatus – with his deepest goal of reducing his transport activities' global ecological footprint. This would be achieved through better collaboration between different transport uses (with each vehicle being driven more intelligently); maximum reliance on green energy both when making and driving cars; and by connecting all vehicles to an intelligent energy network capable of smoothing out consumption peaks and troughs. Energy questions had always been present in Musk's thinking – as witnessed in his recent statement recalling that the solar energy that the whole of Planet Earth receives in one hour more than satisfies its entire annual energy consumption needs (Fabernovel, 2018).

All of which explains why Musk built a system allowing him to eliminate everything that might prevent the creation of collaborative value. His factories would be lighthouses showcasing the latest automation-related technological advance. They would also be characterized by organizational principles that broke free of silo thinking and above all facilitated quick decision making by co-locating development and production teams. Of course, team members' competencies would also be mixed, with short loops organized to incentivize decisiveness, irrespective of the topic. Musk illustrated this vision when he told biographer Ashlee Vance that acting quickly, avoiding hierarchy and getting rid of bureaucracy was a priority for him, and that rules preventing progress had to be fought (Vance, 2015). On top of this, considerable efforts would be made to maximize vehicle modularity using a catalogue of predefined functions. The ultimate goal was to give end users access to a portal where they could 'tailor' their own cars via direct flow with factories capable of producing single batches very quickly. Internal logistics flows were designed to respond to this mass customization logic, replete with an automated oversight of workstation exchanges.

The product itself would also be a great demonstration of the benefits of collaborative value. Tesla has become one of the only makers in the world to promise to increase its vehicles' values over the course of a product's lifetime thanks to permanent upgrades and by applying predictive maintenance to every car owner's vehicle – at a time when other carmakers were charging a pretty penny for their upgrades, thereby ensuring that each existing vehicle would lose value over time due to the planned obsolescence of its embedded technology.

With its daily application of Elon Musk's first principle, the Tesla model clearly seems disruptive. Visiting a Tesla plant offers a concrete translation of this principle. The walls are white, the machines red, there is maximum automation, spaces are shared (and open) between different functions, young engineers with tablets mingle with operatives and there is no visible distinction between workforce categories. Everything is structured in such a way as to remove any obstacles to collaborative value.

What is noteworthy is Musk's welcoming of disruption and how he attacks problems both pragmatically and audaciously. Thanks to the company's extraordinary energy levels, it learns very quickly, as least in comparison to Tesla's neighbouring start-ups and pure digital players in Palo Alto.

If Musk meets the challenges he set himself – marrying the best of the digital world with cutting-edge industrial organizational practices – the Tesla production system will be very hard to match. It is possible that the Fremont factory, a brownfield operation purchased from Toyota, may not turn into Tesla's dream system. Hypermanufacturing in the way that it is developing at present is likely to ascend to a higher level in the factories that Tesla has started building for the future. This includes the Gigafactory, of course, but also sites planned in Europe and Asia if growth targets are met. In just a few years, Musk has fathered a whole new global carmaker, one that resembles no one else and who could totally revolutionize the sector. As is often the case with pioneering companies, it is over the long run that the system's adaptation to its environment can be judged. Toyota did not become Toyota in a few months and also faced many crises during its long march to the top of the carmaking world.

QUESTIONS FOR LEADERS

- Have my product development choices accounted for our product's global carbon footprint and our partners' corporate social responsibility (CSR) policies?

- Does my industrial apparatus and supply chain possess indicators and continuous improvement loops allowing for a rapid reduction in waste, better waste sorting, energy savings, an increased proportion of renewable energies and a move towards energy self-sufficiency?

- Do I gather, store and sufficiently exploit the data that I have about my customers? Or about my industrial process?

- Are decisions taken quickly enough at every level of the company?

- Are there silos in my organization or externally in my dealings with partners?

- Have I launched a systematic approach automating repetitive or arduous tasks in my operational system?

- Have I encouraged my teams to minimize bureaucracy, eliminate paperwork and opt for direct exchange loops where everyone takes responsibility for their actions?

- Are there any under-exploited resources in my system and, concretely, when I visit the frontlines do I see any machines, people or decisions awaiting resolution?

- Do I myself test the solutions or products being offered to my employees or customers to make sure they are user friendly? Is this a real criterion in decisions relating to the development or improvement of our products and/ or the tools that we use?

- Is my industrial system sufficiently agile to tailor goods and adapt them to market volatility? Can I shorten my production times? Is the single batch-size principle sufficiently understood here as a goal that my teams should be striving towards?

KIMBERLY CLARK INTERVIEW
'Breaking down silos to implement hypermanufacturing'

Kimberly Clark's Toul site employs 260 persons and produces 74,000 tons of paper annually for brands such as Kleenex, Scott and Wypall. It is hard for any first-time visitor not to be impressed by the powerful paper machine that sets the pace for the whole of the factory. At the intersection between a traditional process industry and a consumer goods manufacturer, the factory was elected industrial site of the year in 2015 by the magazine *L'Usine Nouvelle*. Mathieu Gaytté, Head of Operations, arrived at the plant in 2012 at a time when a massive transformation plan was being initiated.

'No high-performance company can accept mediocre results today'

The adventure began in 2011. A new director had just become head of the Kimberly Clark business division to which the factory reports. Gaytté remembers that, 'This was a cold shower for us. Up until that point we had calibrated our improvement efforts around the staff members we had to get things done.' The new MD decided to take everyone out of their comfort zone, declaring that 'no high-performance company can accept mediocre results today'. This launched the site's long march to hypermanufacturing. 'In the past we were also but what we needed was a truly transformational approach that would make our daily behaviour much more agile.' The immediate target was for the two secondary machines and the paper machine to improve by 10 to 15 per cent within four months.

BREAKING DOWN SILOS: ONE OF THE TRANSFORMATION PROCESS'S MAIN SUCCESSES
The immediate focus was to break down the company's silos. 'We appointed a manager shared by several departments to communicate our vision of complete continuous flows inside the factory.' This was hard to change, however. Gaytté speaks about 20 years of mutual mistrust pitting the paper-manufacturing and paper-transformation teams against one another. 'Problems were always blamed on the other department.'

Alongside this, a great deal of work was done to improve teams' first-level maintenance competencies, with relations between production and maintenance staff improving markedly because people began to understand each other better. Reviewing how things had gone, Gaytté explains how attitudinal changes helped to reconnect people. 'Certain safety and quality issues were a bit more complicated than we'd thought. But it helped when we added a safety coordinator to each sector. The quality department also got better at applying its standards and started offering real support instead of just demanding things from people.' Alongside these adaptations, the management system was also restructured, cutting bureaucracy and accelerating decision making: 'The management system reconnected the frontlines with senior management, in a tentacle-like movement.'

CONSUMING LESS TO PRODUCE BETTER
One of the great sources of satisfaction in the overall plan has been improved energy consumption. 'In 2017, for instance, we cut our annual energy costs by 6 per cent, saving nearly €1 million. It's the kind of thing we've been doing for five years now.' The factory has kept certain guiding principles when defining its improvement plans. The situation must be win-win in pure performance terms but also because the ecosystem and all the teams benefit as well. One example is the way certain workstations were reorganized to increase safety, with user friendliness becoming central in the choice of projects and improvement targets.

USER FRIENDLINESS: ONE OF THE MAIN KEYS TO SUCCESS
'Whenever we attack an area to transform it, we start with a list of the irritants that the teams involved have shared with us and asked us to deal with.'
In addition, the end user of the tools being modified or created is now supposed to participate systematically in the suggested alteration. Gaytté explains the virtue of this kind of approach to competence development terms. 'Asking everyone to review their own positions or tools (whether physical or digital) has raised awareness of their own training needs and of the gap between the job now

and what it will require in the future.' The advantage of collaborative value-focused work resides in the fact that every factory stakeholder has benefited.

BETTER DATA CONTROL, WELL-CONCEIVED AUTOMATION: A MAJOR PROJECT
FOR THE FUTURE

The site still faces major future challenges. Gaytté feels that the two main issues are controlling data and using intelligent automation to reduce the number of repetitive or arduous tasks. The goal is to increase site intelligence to optimize the use of human competencies and to ensure that everyone enjoys the work. Data is a key component in process industries. In this one instance, making the paper machine more intelligent by adding algorithmic and artificial intelligence layers to it is clearly going to become a big challenge in time. But in Gaytté's words, 'This is not like some Sunday DIY work person who buys a super tool and only uses 1 per cent of its functionalities.' Instead, the plan is to raise competence across the whole of the site. As for automation, this will clearly be an important production cost factor if the site wants to remain a lighthouse and benefit from recent improvements. People at Kimberly Clark understand that they need to move on and must never stop adapting. Quite the contrary, they know that things will soon be accelerating on a daily basis. Hence senior management's recent decision to reintegrate change actors within each department to ensure that any improvements are both fluid and agile.

Principle 2

Cross-integration

Condensing the value chain, decompartmentalizing the functions and connecting better with the ecosystem to boost the company

SUMMARY

- Cross-integration satisfies a double need for responsiveness and respect for the environment, based on the integration and connections of the full range of corporate functions all the way through the final customer.

- Cross-integration plays out at four different levels (strategic, organizational, technological and peripheral).

- Integration at Tesla has enabled the in-house production of most of the components that other carmakers subcontract, even as the company remains outwardly focused by integrating all of the technological bricks that make it possible to offer customers a complete ecosystem of value.

INTRODUCTION TO 'CROSS-INTEGRATION'

Better manufacturing is a basic principle that helps to build new systems by accelerating frontline execution. The 4th Age of Industry's operational model clearly needs to boost the whole of an organization, if only because the emergence of digital solutions has abolished the concept of physical distance. Things happen more and more quickly and information circulates instantaneously all across the world. Consumers increasingly demand quick delivery and real-time service. To cope with these stresses, the industrial world has embarked upon a strong integration trajectory using digital solutions. As an example, a PwC survey of 2,000 industry leaders showed that they expected the level of vertical integration up and down their value chains to rise from 41 per cent to 72 per cent by the year 2020, with the level of horizontal integration (between different businesses within a company) rising from 34 per cent to 65 per cent (PwC, 2016).

Paradoxically, however, consumers (who are also citizens) have been demanding a return to localism. New generations want everything (including their purchasing acts) to be more meaningful. Hence the growing popularity of low-carbon products manufactured in environmentally and territorially friendly factories. The collaborative economy is also on the rise, both to make everyone's lives easier thanks to innovative services but also because it uses a sharing principle to reduce the consumption of natural resources. Teslism's second driver – cross-integration – is a response to this twofold need for responsiveness and environmental friendliness. Integration today includes corporate functions stretching all the way to the end user; all the different businesses and professions up and down the supply chain; the parties participating in various projects; and the actors comprising the company's ecosystem – all of which must be achieved while encouraging maximum connectivity and data sharing among all these actors in order to maximize both responsiveness and value creation.

GIANT DINOSAURS OVERWHELMED BY PLANNED OBSOLESCENCE

Where the 2nd Industrial Revolution tended to support highly integrated groups exemplified by the Ford factories – unwieldy giants producing every automotive part imaginable – the 3rd Industrial Revolution did the exact opposite. Opening borders, liberalizing markets, lowering transport costs and introducing market economics to the Global South, all these actions created opportunities thereby enhancing the attractiveness of an industrial model partially characterized by certain activities' delocalization to low-cost countries. The big groups have been concentrating on their core businesses and growing them until they achieve domination in a specific value-chain segment, while significantly adding to their shortlist of suppliers to save on procurement costs. In the automotive sector, for example, some very big Tier 1 players have appeared, starting with Delphi, Valéo and Faurecia. Value chains in the 3rd Industrial Age have tended to be organized into 'professions' characterized by strong leaders dominating each level in the chain. Given growing time-to-market pressures, however, each of these actors has had to progressively transform their models to accelerate both product development and manufacturing flow speed. Toyotism would respond with a streamlining strategy in which the various process stages combine under one organizational governance umbrella to increase responsiveness and offer end users a better service. This method of structuring flows and organizations around a product or family of products can generate significant responsiveness gains in each of the companies comprising a value chain, with typical response times dropping from one month to one week, or one week to one day, depending on the sector.

The best companies have started to coordinate their production lines beyond their own corporate borders. One extreme example from the automotive sector has been the rise of 'synchronous' flows enabling car seat or bumper suppliers to deliver to customer factories in less than three hours.

In most sectors, however, frictions remain at the interface between each value chain participant, translating into a loss of value for the end user. In addition, the strategy of focusing on one's core business has atomized supply chains, with hundreds or even thousands of suppliers being intertwined nowadays and as many as four or five levels working upstream from the final product manufacturer. In this way, groups have turned themselves into giant dinosaurs overwhelmed by the difficulty of managing highly complex input and output flows.

Similarly and expressed in more organizational terms, most large groups find it hard nowadays to implement a streamlining strategy that reaches all the way back to the product development stage. Upstream and downstream manufacturing functions tend to operate like silos, slowing down flows and impeding the creation of collaborative value.

Lastly, everyone has been trying to attract the best talents but thinking in this area often remains 'self-centred', with operators assuming that they can become leaders in their sector simply by acquiring the best resources. Companies open to their partners or ecosystem have constituted the exception rather than the rule. Indeed, most large groups today tend to be self-sufficient, wielding huge battalions of experts and support functions.

AN ERA OF QUADRUPLE INTEGRATION

When the digital world first emerged in the early 2000s, it seemed like an extension of the 3rd Industrial Revolution. Venture capital focused heavily on pure digital players in the hope of making big returns quickly, without necessarily investing a great deal of physical capital. Other industrial sectors were doing poorly and being offloaded onto distant emerging economies, one example being Apple's iPhone, which was designed in the United States but 80 per cent assembled in China with components that travelled around the world several times.

Things changed after the 2008 financial crisis, however – and 21st-century consumer-citizens have suddenly discovered needs that are very different from everything before. Demand for cheap mass-consumption products has been replaced by demand for high use-value products that are being developed, produced and distributed ethically, respecting both the people involved in their production and the planet in general. In addition, concepts such as 'responsiveness' and 'customer service', epitomized by Amazon's famous 'one-click delivery', have become increasingly important compared to the sales price. Indeed, 'customization' has become standard today, further accentuating a trend observed in the late 1980s when just-in-time principles were being massively deployed in most large groups, culminating in a massive decrease of manufacturing batch sizes in most sectors. Ultimately, the new paradigm looks likely to centre on single batch sizes, with the previous religion of series production starting to fade. The question now is how best to respond to the quadruple aspiration for products that are ethical, unique, characterized by high use value and can be delivered with 'one-click'.

Cross-integration is one response to this fourfold integration and connection trend, with Elon Musk having been one of the first to understand and incorporate it into a strategic and operational model. Cross-integration is characterized by four levels: strategic, organizational, technological and peripheral (Figure 3.6).

Strategic   Level 1 integration is vertical and relates to the whole of the value chain, responding to the demand for greater responsiveness emanating from all industrial chains. Thanks to new technologies and platforms, it is becoming easier to access end users, hence to disrupt existing value chains by having a company integrate to a greater extent, either internally or with its partners. This return to what used to be called vertical integration in the early 20th century has played out in three stages. The first involves the 'digital' integration of customers and suppliers within a given branch using tools like electronic

FIGURE 3.6 Cross-integration's four levels

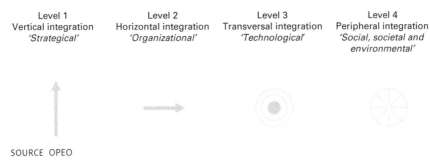

Level 1	Level 2	Level 3	Level 4
Vertical integration	Horizontal integration	Transversal integration	Peripheral integration
'Strategical'	'Organizational'	'Technological'	'Social, societal and environmental'

SOURCE OPEO

data interchange (EDI) that create a fluid connection between downstream demands and upstream counterparts' IT systems, including through the collaborative co-development of complex systems. The second stage involves disrupting a value chain's downstream segment in order to access end users. This can be exemplified by capital equipment suppliers, a greater proportion of whom now offer their end users comprehensive solutions involving services like production equipment maintenance or settings optimization. Borders between different sectors are becoming increasingly porous, notably the lines between industrial logistics and pure manufacturing. The third stage relates to industrial purchasing policies, with businesses or companies operating in upstream segments being integrated more directly into the overall chain thanks to innovative technologies such as 3D printing or simply via financial acquisitions. This is how certain businesses that disappeared from the Western world have come to be relocated and reintegrated into local production chains, increasing the responsiveness of the overall manufacturing apparatus. Polishing activities exemplify this trend in the luxury sector, which is earmarked for big changes in the years to come due to the considerable automation being undertaken currently in a bid to revive local profitability.

Organizational   Level 2 integration is horizontal and relates to industrial business functions. Digital opportunities can only be leveraged if a company decompartmentalizes. This enables rapid decision making and even more importantly allows data – the El Dorado of the 21st century – to circulate fluidly, creating extra value in this way. The consequences are twofold. On one hand, a company can now ask neighbouring businesses to harvest whatever data they possess and use it for its own benefit. One example is the growing number of consumer goods manufacturers who own their own distribution network and allow their supply chain department to harvest data from the commercial networks – including the stores themselves – because they want to obtain real-time information about the products being asked about, tried and sold. The intention here is to leverage such data to optimize inventory and planning processes.

At the other end of the spectrum, these very same supply chain management teams are also requesting access to local manufacturing or after-sales service data to find out at what stage the products being ordered can be found. This information is then used to offer end users quality information about delivery times, along with technical information about repairs. Even more than the production sphere, the new approach has affected new product development-phase activities. The agile methods that have allowed the digital world to be so quick at marketing new products or applications via 'testing and learning' can be readily transposed into the industrial world, thanks in particular to the latter sphere's high degree of digital integration. This means that an idea can start with a 3D plan before being rapidly prototyped using 3D printing, followed by short-loop exchanges with customers and finally by an almost instantaneous machine programme launch including plans, operating procedures and full product ranges. Coming at the very end of their chain, software editors such as Erméo (for maintenance applications) or Diota Soft (for augmented reality) have started to create mills that use 3-D component plans and their specifications to rapidly launch preventive maintenance manufacturing programmes or augmented reality operating modes. In the end, the lines between all of these businesses (supply chain, sales, production, industrial methods, maintenance and product development) have been increasingly blurred. This is a horizontal kind of integration where each territorial boundary comes under scrutiny in an effort to achieve end-to-end optimization.

Technological   Level 3 integration is cross-functional in nature and hybridizes traditional industrial professions both with the digital world and with change management. The transformation associated with technological change is so substantial that it cannot be achieved if people continue to work in silos. It requires architects who can wear different hats and get people from very different cultures to work together on a daily basis when they were not naturally accustomed to operating in this way. Opening a new site or transforming an industry group are tasks being increasingly allocated to people with digital backgrounds, including ex-operational or IT managers who dispose of substantial resources in industrial IT. One example was when an executive at Schmidt Group, a leading manufacturer of customized kitchens, recently said that the company had reduced its production times from 10 days to 1 day, after raising the percentage of IT engineers in the workforce to 20 per cent.

Peripheral   Lastly, Level 4 integration is also peripheral. As something that is social, societal and environmental, it enables the harmonious coexistence of a factory and its hinterland; enhances the circular economy; reduces carbon footprint, energy consumption and pollution; and facilitates local collaboration between companies within their branches but also with local authorities, schools, neighbouring residents and generally the whole of a factory's ecosystem. Lastly, and above all, it galvanizes job opportunities in places that the geographer Christophe Guilluy has referred to as 'peripheral' (Guilluy, 2014). These are areas that experienced considerable change following the Second World War, transitioning from an agricultural to an industrial economy but then generally experiencing a dramatic economic decline for the past 30 years, caused in part by an accelerated globalization of trade that led to a strong decline in industrial GDP in countries such as France. A similar example can be found in the energy business, where a number of factories in France belonging to large agribusiness groups have committed to becoming self-sufficient by the year 2030, with some having already signed electricity co-generation agreements in partnership with other local industries. Otherwise, there is also the example of a major Tier 1 automotive parts supplier founding a 'technological lab' to develop competencies that were not yet available in the marketplace, the idea being to open up the new centre to local SMEs to limit the overall investment while helping the entire region to benefit from the critical mass that it has achieved as prime contractor. Lastly, one final experimental example can be seen in recent initiatives seeking to amalgamate the different learning paths that someone has after working for various employers; or else, getting companies to engage in countercyclical activities so they can share resources and guarantee employment for people suffering today from precarious work contracts.

LESSONS FROM TESLA

Elon Musk has more or less taken cross-integration as far as it can go. Space X, for instance, manufactures 80 per cent of its rockets in the United States where its main competitor – ULA, an alliance between Boeing and Lockheed Martin – is on the record as expressing pride in its network of 1,200 worldwide subcontractors, with all the management inertia and operational slowness that this intimates. It is striking to note that Tesla's dashboards (and even its seats) are being manufactured internally, something unique in the automotive sector. From the outset, Musk has always made very clear strategic choices reflecting his prioritization of responsiveness but also the fact that his highly innovative company was never 100 per cent sure of being fully supported by traditional automotive suppliers – who were sceptical about his model and did not want to invest in a business associated with such low output rates. Not only has Musk's approach given his company an advantage in terms of production times, it has also reduced the risk of failure in one part of the value chain affecting the rest of the chain, while restoring a semblance of overall governance. According to M Mueller, chief engineer at Space X, 'We got everything covered, we have our own test site and have cut working times in half' (Vance, 2015). Musk acquired industrial automation expert Grohmann through Tesla to gain internal control over the relevant vehicle manufacturing technology. This integration drive has also stretched beyond Tesla's own sector, with Musk having invested both in energy supplier Solar City and in building several battery manufacturing plants (that he ultimately hopes to sell on to other parties). The overall strategic vision underpinning this orientation is that Tesla will do anything to create use value for the end users. Over time, the objective is to get Tesla customers to use its product (in this case, the car) to tie into a broader energy network connected to people's homes and to other automobiles via smart grids. Alongside this, Musk has also given thought to starting up an interpersonal rental service where people can easily sublet their autonomous vehicles to one another. Hence the numerous (and growing) service lines set up alongside the main automobile manufacturing lines – culminating in a need to have full control over the reactor core so that these 'ancillary' ideas might be nurtured.

For Level 2 (organizational integration), it is worth noting the surprise that Ashlee Vance felt upon discovering the way in which Space X and Tesla teams are co-located and work in a truly decompartmentalized fashion, with geeks and 'blue collars' coexisting on the shop floors day in day out, with no distinction between functional levels (Vance, 2015). What is considered virtuous behaviour here is when complex problems are resolved in 'scrum' mode, as most start-ups do worldwide. A visit to Tesla generates the strong feeling that each employee and function are on the same level. All offices are open plan, even on the production floor, with so-called support functions being totally intertwined with core functions – to such an extent that it is impossible to distinguish them at first glance. Even more fundamentally at the supply chain level, Musk has been testing entirely internalized intra-site logistics, with some analysts stating the chief goal of the recently divulged 'electric truck' project being to implement this as a new strategy. The idea here is to create a fleet of trucks that follow one another, with a driver in the first vehicle and the others self-driving. This could be very useful for inter-site logistics, for instance, when hauling batteries away from the Gigafactory. Other improvements include cheaper energy consumption and lower labour costs. The project would also be a perfect response to the need for greater autonomy in order to improve inter-site responsiveness. Moreover, if Tesla owns its own trucks, it can load them at non-peak times hence pay lower electricity rates.

Musk himself has insisted on the importance of Level 3 (technological) integration, arguing that anyone who codes must also be familiar with mechanics (Fabernovel, 2018). More than anyone, he understands that the marriage between atoms and bits will be a key factor of success in a New World where connectivity and responsiveness are expected from the outset and where digital competence per se is not enough to enact the kind of global systemic transformation that the original vision had theorized. This explains why Musk's teams are comprised of Palo Alto's best data scientists, often talents coming from Apple or Google who have gone to Tesla more for the project than the money. The factory has been broadly digitized and it is noteworthy that most employees walking around the production floor carry a tablet with them, with the open spaces being full of IT materials. Tesla's industrializing teams have explained that bringing together different businesses and professions is something quite unique in that it accelerates development despite the handicap of an organization that is often less robust and rigorous.

Lastly, and in terms of Level 4 (peripheral) integration, Musk seems to front-run his Silicon Valley counterparts, most of whom are still developing innovative solutions in the United States but manufacturing them elsewhere. Musk has spoken publicly about how, when the United States stopped making TV screens and basic general consumer electronic devices, it also lost its ability to build the flat screens and batteries that are essential for mobile phones and indeed for the whole of the 21st-century economy (Fabernovel, 2018). His speeches never forget to mention things like pride and sense of community. This partially explains his acquisition of the highly symbolic NUMMI plant that Toyota had bought from GM in the early 1980s and that introduced the principles of lean manufacturing to the United States. By so doing, Musk was allowing thousands of employees to again manufacture, locally, a very high proportion of his vehicle's total value, including basic electronic components that had long been subcontracted en masse abroad.

QUESTIONS FOR LEADERS

- Is it possible to connect my products and get data from final users in a way that allows me to both offer innovative services and 'disrupt' my own market?

- Are there strategic upstream value chain activities that I could execute more quickly if I did them myself?

- Have I already tried to integrate part of my value chain by testing new technologies related especially to the logistics chain to improve responsiveness and customization?

- Have I made sufficiently used digitization to generate data sharing and end-to-end collaboration between corporate functions (marketing, R&D, sales, supply chain, production, after-sales)?

- As leader have I promoted a mindset rooted in transparency, openness and mutual aid to ensure that data sharing generates collaborative value?

- Have I already tried working with a start-up in my ecosystem in order to co-develop a new product or digitize/test 'new tech' in my operational system?

- Have my IT and operational teams been sufficiently integrated into the transformation programmes that I lead?

- Do I work proactively with HR to recruit hybrid profiles or develop hybrid IT-operational backgrounds specifically to create 'Architect 4.0' positions?

- Do I participate in local clusters and in the different initiatives taking place within my branch or competitiveness cluster?

- Have I pushed initiatives with other regional industrialists or local authorities to improve my local ecological footprint and accelerate the circular economy?

SEW-USOCOME INTERVIEW
'Be the first to join the cross-integration train'

The SEW group is one of those great stories of entrepreneurial success that German industry is so good at creating. Especially renowned for engine motor and gearbox design and manufacturing, the company has evolved progressively to become a supplier of dedicated machine automation and industry logistics solutions. Jean-Claude Reverdell, Chief Executive, joined SEW in 2008 and has run its French subsidiary since 2015. In 2010, the executive team had recognized that the group's Haguenau site (its main production unit) was becoming too small to ensure revenue growth. Hence the decision to create a new site in Brumath. Applying standard investment thinking, the decision was taken to leverage the unique project into a lighthouse showcase for Industry 4.0. There were three reasons why this seemed useful: the company would become more competitive; it could now test certain advanced solutions; its reputation with customers and in its ecosystem would be improved. During the long journey that led to the creation of one of the world's most advanced automated logistics sites, a number of new businesses with specialized jobs and vocations would also be born. Yannick Blum was one of the technicians who had a chance to build a new profession through his participation in the project. He ended up running the company's AGV piloting process. The two men share their insights below.

VERTICAL INTEGRATION, SEW-USOCOME'S HISTORICAL AGILITY LEVER

Vertical integration has long been a strategic aim at SEW-USOCOME. In France, the company makes most of its own parts and provides most of the specialized jobs required for the engines, motors and gearboxes that roll off its final assembly lines, including cutting, machining, winding and smelting casting. 'Our corporate philosophy is to be highly integrated. We only subcontract a few standard components or operations relating to certain very specific businesses processes', according to J C Reverdell, who views this corporate structure as an incomparable advantage because it enables a much better and quicker industrialization of future products – as the company has all the competencies it needs internally. This has been decisive for him, seeing as: 'In our relationship with our holding company headquarters, we are constantly thinking about what products our customers will expect in the future. Today's customers demand solutions and services and no longer products alone. Without advanced integration, we wouldn't be able to predict market trends as quickly as we can now.'

HORIZONTAL INTEGRATION IMPROVES COMPETITIVENESS AND SHORTENS PRODUCTION TIMES

Building a new assembly site at Brumath has also reinforced horizontal integration, with much work having already been done here on internal logistics.[1] Internal and external suppliers have felt the effects, which include physical flows characterized by 'maximal leanness', smaller containers that accelerate flow rates, smaller batch sizes and sequencing optimization measures. In Reverdell's words, 'We have increased operational efficiency thanks to a high degree of internal integration and greater proximity to suppliers.' Order validation now triggers a perfectly orchestrated production process that starts with preparation of the parts needed for product assembly. The collection of all these items occurs in a storage space warehouse that has been fully automated using SEW-USOCOME's proprietary own picking solutions. Stacker cranes collect the different items from the storage-rack bays, with order pickers then using picking tables to place them on a tray corresponding to each of the products being manufactured. The tray is then sent transferred automatically to the assembly block line using an automotive guided vehicle (AGV); 37 AGVs travel more than 400 kilometres per day, powered by induction and entirely designed by SEW-USOCOME to be operational 24/7.

CROSS-FUNCTIONAL INTEGRATION OF INDUSTRIAL IT AND OPERATIONS,
THE CORNERSTONE OF PROJECT SUCCESS

The question then becomes how to shift from a traditional logistics world to a '4.0' world where handling activities are highly automated. J C Reverdell feels that one of the keys here is the degree of integration between 'the IT' and the 'operational' functions of the company. 'In the current industrial environment, manufacturing is impossible without IT. That's even truer here than elsewhere.' The Brumath site makes 4,500 products a day, all configured-to-order based on customer specifications. The gearboxes are comprised of 20 to 25 main elements from a total of 50,000 possible references. This means there are millions of variants – all of which can be combined in response to each customer's specific demand. To achieve the levels of flexibility and responsiveness needed to assemble products whose specifications make them quasi-unique, the company's production tools are connected to its IT systems responsible for managing orders and logistics flows. The automats piloting the different pieces of production equipment interface directly with ERP. Digital information flows and physical flows are perfectly synchronized from the time an order is recorded through all manufacturing stages until final product delivery.

TRUST AND QUALITY OF LIFE AT WORK, HIDDEN BUT CRUCIAL SOURCES OF VALUE

Industry 4.0 does not mean that people no longer count. In Reverdell's words, 'Digitizing is not the same thing as manufacturing a product. Digitizing will not manufacture the product.' The main focus now is on better working conditions and fewer arduous tasks – meaning that, despite the site's high degree of automation, Reverdell remains convinced that staff engagement is the key to success. After all, these are future users and therefore the people with the clearest view of how the new processes will be defined. 'The first thing to do is to speak truthfully with our people... and follow that up with a major training effort. In our company, something like 8 to 10 days are spent training each worker on the new assembly lines, and much more when the more automated processes are involved.' Giving teams a sense of responsibility and showing trust in them is also important. 'They get concretely involved in defining future lines using life-size digital models.' Brumath site visitors are often surprised to discover cardboard production lines inside the factory. They exist because management has trusted users to modulate their workstations as they see fit. Workers are treated as users, hence given the job of developing the assembly lines that they will be working on in the future, in conjunction with a lean manufacturing expert and someone from engineering. The levers actually ensure staff involvement go even deeper than this, however, and are not always found where they might be expected. A site visit with Reverdell always begins with the company restaurant and other 'non-production' zones such as the physical fitness centre and the rest areas, of which he is particularly proud. 'Even more than that, we organize events, including after-work activities, wellbeing workshops and Christmas tree competitions that only use recycled materials. They all add value and are essential in motivating our people and ensuring their wellbeing at work.' The focus on staff welfare and on ensuring that work meshes with the ecosystem is generally seen as one of the company's trademarks.

CREATION OF NEW SPECIALIZED JOBS, THE START OF AN EXCITING ADVENTURE
Among the great sources of satisfaction associated with building the new site, Reverdell focuses in on the advent of new professions enabling many staff members to blossom and acquire know-how that will be crucial for their future. One case is Yannick Blum, who came to the Haguenau site in 2005 and never left, working over this time as a methods department technician. When asked about his experience at SEW, Blum unhesitatingly calls himself 'a child of SEW-USOCOME, meaning I'll never say anything bad about the company. The best period most recently was 2014 to 2017 when I took part in a project getting more than 100 people involved in the new site's creation. Something like that doesn't happen every day. Haguenau was a great experience and Brumath will be a wonderful new chapter.' Beyond the project itself, Blum also speaks about the uncertainties and joys associated with his new profession as an AGV piloting process coordinator. 'At first we thought we needed two staff members but soon realized that wasn't enough. Five of us work there now, I'm the coordinator and there are two people in each team to do the

maintenance work and operate the machines.' Two of the five employees are former methods specialists, two others were manufacturing-line operatives and one is a recent external recruit. This shows a real change in the profession, since the parcel handling that used to be done with forklifts is now being managed with much more technical resources. According to Blum, 'The problem is that we had been trying to integrate cutting-edge technology that we were just getting used to.' Collaborating with the holding company headquarters has played a crucial role in this respect. 'We were trained by our German colleagues and learned things step-by-step starting from scratch.' Blum also feels that integration is key to any industry 4.0 project – to such an extent that he regrets today that he never acquired all the competencies required to control the system. 'To change the programmes, I always have to call in a control technician who has to get here quickly so our flows won't be disrupted.'

Both men agree on the future of the industry. According to Blum, 'Operatives' main tool from now on is no longer a toolbox or a notebook but a PC', with Reverdell adding that, 'The future means working more and more closely with our customers to manufacture adapted products, sell innovative services and offer quality advice. But we can only do that with highly qualified staff. Yannick and his upgraded competence levels shows us how the industry can evolve in the future.'

Principle 3

Software hybridization

Leveraging digitization to innovate disruptively, improve system efficiency and achieve end-to-end benefits

SUMMARY

- Software hybridization refers to an evolution in industrial IT involving the introduction of software at all levels in an attempt to hybridize the world of physical transformations with the digital world.

- Software hybridization can involve design, production and customer relationships, making it possible to accelerate the 'development–industrialization–production launch–after-sales service' loop.

- Tesla shows that cars can be designed to become computers that drive.

INTRODUCTION TO SOFTWARE HYBRIDIZATION

Alongside hypermanufacturing and cross-integration's acceleration of the organizational process, one of the main goals for a 4th Age operational model is to capitalize upon human, machine and product hyper-connectivity. Our daily lives are being invaded by apps and social networks. They simplify transactions, amplify connectivity and do a great deal to create 'use' value: they provide access to services that did not exist before; and they improve service quality by hybridizing everyday tools with digital tools. The number of internet users rose from 1.6 billion worldwide in 2008 to 4.1 billion in 2016 – 2.5 billion of whom use, according to the International Communications Union, mobile internet solutions.

The number of social network users has risen by more than 100 million to reach around 3.3 billion. Personal data scandals have had little effect on these platforms for the moment. Note, for instance, that notwithstanding the Cambridge Analytica affair, the total number of Facebook users grew by a further 3.2 per cent in 2018 (Figure 3.7).

The software world is not only impacting daily lives but also slowly penetrating all economic sectors. By so doing, it has helped manufacturing and distribution chains to revolutionize from within to offer greater responsiveness, better execution efficiency and value creation (in one form or another) for end users' benefit. A 2016 Deloitte survey of 500 industrial leaders showed that the main technological challenges respondents expect Europe and the United States to face over the next few years include the industrial internet's proliferation throughout the world of factories; product connectivity; and process digitization. One of the more momentous phenomena to have sprung up over the past decade or so is called software hybridization. This latest avatar of industrial IT has appeared in the form of programme and digital software and started to penetrate every nook and cranny of

FIGURE 3.7 Digital around the world in Q2 2018

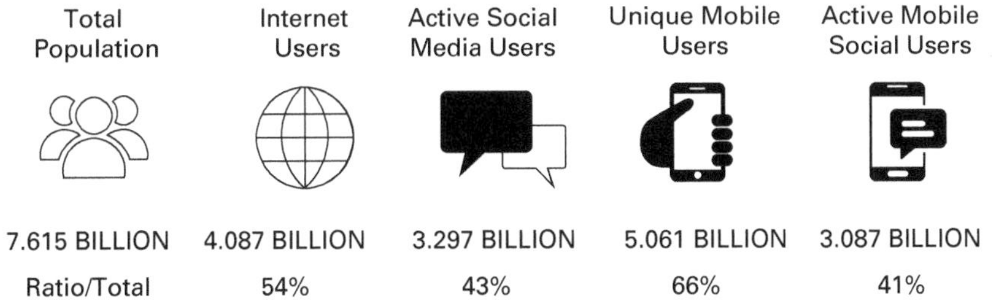

Total Population	Internet Users	Active Social Media Users	Unique Mobile Users	Active Mobile Social Users
7.615 BILLION	4.087 BILLION	3.297 BILLION	5.061 BILLION	3.087 BILLION
Ratio/Total	54%	43%	66%	41%

SOURCE OPEO, adapted from Hootsuite (2018) We are social, digital report modern economic life. The enormous computers that dominated the 1970s – machines where data entry was performed using perforated cards – were quickly replaced by graphics interface monitors. Then came laptops. Then came smartphones with increasingly sophisticated embedded functionalities reflecting three main changes: cloud computing; more interfaces and accelerated connection speeds enabling remote data storage; and much greater calculational power 'centralizing' complexity and leading to more intuitive interfaces. The smartphones that people carry in their pockets today are the embodiment of years of R&D and billions in GAFA investments.

What digitization (in the broadest sense of the term) has concretely achieved in the industrial sector has been the automation, robotization, acceleration and enhancement of industrial processes' learning capabilities. It did this by using both hardware that has been exponentially improved (internet of things, cobots, 3D printing) and software whose greater agility and routine user-friendliness creates endless connectivity by hybridizing the physical transformation world with the digital sphere. However, before further detailing software hybridization's business-wide impacts and opportunities, it is worth revisiting the birth of industrial software, one of the pillars underpinning the 3rd Age of Industry.

THE BIRTH OF INDUSTRIAL SOFTWARE

The first outlines of today's cutting-edge technologies appeared towards the start of the 3rd Age of Industry at the same time as globalization was beginning to spread everywhere. The first industrial robots emerged from the manufacturing industries to replace human beings doing tasks that were repetitive or required a high degree of dexterity. The automotive sector was one of the first to go down this road, with businesses like sheet metal working, painting and even certain assembly operations leading its modernization charge. At the same time, 3rd Age of Industry robots struggled to make headway in other sectors or indeed in smaller companies. The reason is that top-notch competencies were needed to programme and maintain these machines, which were prohibitively expensive and relatively unwieldy given that the robots had to be both completely isolated inside physical barriers and make great use of sensors to prevent accidents. From a digitization perspective, these were the early days of industrial IT, with process industries being the first to benefit from automation's potential. Progress tended to occur in isolated increments within each production flow stage, however, meaning it had no real connection to a factory's other departments. Human–machine interfaces were rudimentary and designed for the benefit of expert users – meaning that one substantial barrier to entry was people's competence in installing, running and maintaining the systems.

Beyond the local improvements generated by these new technologies, there were also the first enterprise resource planning (ERP) systems, whose scope far exceeded mere operational execution to also enable structured corporate data and better communications with the outside world (customer or purchasing orders). Once again, these systems' installation was complex, requiring input from many professions company-wide plus top expert resources. Most groups founded departments dedicated to system settings and maintenance. Installation efforts often failed in smaller structures that could not afford to acquire such competencies, translating into frequent under-use of these powerful but rigid machines' functionalities. Hence the steady dissemination of lean management thinking advocating a return to 'reality' by partially disconnecting local manufacturing floor IT systems and encouraging teams to refocus on real physical flows. Methods such as Kanban-driven flows (basic paper labels offering a very practical way of monitoring manufacturing orders) or else visual management helped to make companies less dependent on these big systems, which people started to dislike, viewing them as black boxes that were often set wrongly and generally stifled frontline initiative.

Ultimately, cross-functional project piloting would suffer from an ever-worsening silo effect caused by the actions of different business departments that began restructuring themselves specifically to cope with technological progress and accelerated market change. Product development became a critical marker ensuring good ties to the industrialization and production functions, and indeed to all of a company's cross-functional processes. Serving as a safety net meant to protect the business from a natural tendency to expand silos. A prime example of this phenomenon was the professionalization of industrial planning through processes such as sales and operations planning (S and OP).

SOFTWARE, THE SYSTEM'S NEW DNA

The growing digitization of people's daily lives completely shook up this 'mastodon' vision of the economy, one in which the big players were always expected to dominate their smaller counterparts because it was easier for the former to move operations abroad and scale up output to amortize fixed costs. On one hand, digitization would accentuate the emergence of a use-based economy, with manufactured products now being associated with a stronger demand for services. On the other hand, the proliferation of intangible flows would accustom consumers to purchasing acts being concomitant with the provision of services. Little by little, this new imperative would be transposed onto physical goods that everyone wants delivered nowadays in less than a day (or hour). The good news is that although digitization has caused this great upheaval in the industrial sector, it is also the remedy. In a world where every customer uses their mobile phone 200 times a day, industry has adapted to ensure that its processes capture all the data that can be extracted from this addictive behaviour even as it continues to accelerate its product development loops; further increases the efficiency of its manufacturing and distribution operations; and decompartmentalizes its end-to-end data flows to get customers the best possible service while taking advantage of the company's own competencies.

SOFTWARE HYBRIDIZATION IN THE DESIGN FUNCTION

For several decades now, development professions have experienced a software-driven acceleration in parts design, based on three-dimensional tools offering increasingly accurate representations of physical objects. Modelling capabilities are supported today by simulation tools that test products' dynamic specifications and thereby save time on testing. In parallel to this evolution, today there are also virtual reality tools that make it possible to visualize an object in its environment and interact directly with it. Not only can customers visualize how they might use a product but they can also help prepare this very same product's upstream production phases, notably its working ranges within a constrained environment.

In addition, and thanks to the connectivity between workstations, between businesses and between companies and their customers or suppliers, these very local gains are now being accompanied by other gains that have a much more structuring effect and relate to the ability to collaborate on complex projects. In a world where cutting-edge technological competencies are more and more precious, being able to work remotely without any versioning difficulties is essential – as is the ability to design products with great agility by integrating the specification modifications that customers demand, even when this occurs very late in the development process.

When considering physical technologies, the emergence of 3D printing has been an interesting bridge between traditional manufacturing and the digital world. The starting point here are 3D files that spawn physical objects capable of being manufactured simultaneously worldwide using networked machines. 3D printing enables a rapid acceleration of prototyping phases by supplying marketing teams with a quick physical brief. This fosters discussions and adjustments that are much more precise than would be the case with a simple 3D plan.

SOFTWARE HYBRIDIZATION IN THE PRODUCTION FUNCTION

Digitization plays out at different levels in manufacturing. At the workstations level, dematerialization makes it possible to reduce value less administrative tasks for operatives who sometimes spend up to 10 per cent of their time filling papers and monitoring compliance, flows and traceability for either control or piloting reasons. It also saves money and time for certain other support functions, exemplified by planners who sometimes spend 20 to 30 per cent of their time printing manufacturing orders. The same for product pickers who spend a great deal of time printing plans or task lists. When combined with these greater efficiencies, dematerialization also furthers the fight against non-quality by avoiding any versioning of the different tools that a workstation might require. This makes it easier to track single units while capitalizing on any important information that could be used to solve problems associated with a particular product or type of production.

Digitization also accelerates training thanks to the use of simulations and virtual reality. Further, its augmented reality aspect helps improve people's ability to avoid making mistakes.

More broadly, digitization helps to accelerate and improve process operational modes by enhancing understanding of particular phenomena and their causes. With artificial intelligence, for instance, it is easier to learn continuously (and increase quality and efficiency) by linking certain settings to certain outcomes. Similarly, machine learning algorithms help to take advantage of defects in such a way as to avoid future breakdowns through a better anticipation of weak signals.

Lastly, thanks to digitization, operational leaders can execute their routine functions much more fluidly using digitized frontline visits, IT-connected performance monitoring scoreboards and generally much quicker information that makes it possible to react sooner to unforeseen problems via structured workflows. Moreover, insofar as piloting systems exist to ensure robust interactions between all functions, the ensuing increase in sharing also facilitates monitoring.

SOFTWARE HYBRIDIZATION IN THE CUSTOMER RELATIONSHIP FUNCTION

Connecting products has three advantages:

- This allows end users to better understand how a product is used, thereby improving future products' design.
- It also becomes possible to sell product-associated services (such as maintenance or targeted expertise), all of which helps people to make better use of the product or system that is being manufactured.

- Lastly – and this has been a huge revolution in the world of physical objects – upgrading has become a normal part of product lifecycles, with all customers benefiting today from serially produced improvements.

'Disconnected' products always lose technological value over time whereas 'connected' products are enriched by natural technological change, which they embed through ongoing software upgrades.

END-TO-END SOFTWARE HYBRIDIZATION

One of the best things that digitization enables is the end-to-end decompartmentalization of all value chain functions and businesses, from upstream suppliers through downstream end users. Having a virtual data chain that offers end-to-end transmissions sidesteps the many intermediaries who offer little value-added; increases transmission accuracy from one link in the chain to another; and augments supply chain transparency to improve planning and balance physical flows. It also accelerates the 'development–industrialization–production–after-sale service' loop by churning out manufacturing programmes and task lists almost instantaneously, based on 3D product plans and on after-sales teams receiving remote spare-parts supply files. Decompartmentalization also helps leverage competencies up and down the value chain by encompassing the collective memory of each business involved. This supports the transmission of know-how as well as problem solving (Figure 3.8).

FIGURE 3.8 The impacts of software hybridization

Product innovation

- End-to-end collaboration
- Protoyping speed-up

- 0 paper
- Leadership digitalization
- IA process improvement
- Training speed-up
- Anti-error
- Predictive failures

- Usage capitalization
- Innovating services

De-silotization   Real-time communication   Product life-cycle improvement

Digital continuity

Knowledge continuity

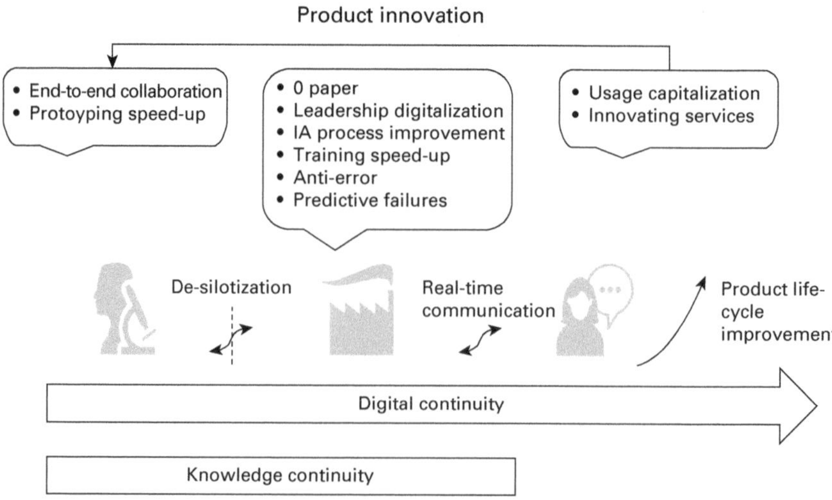

SOURCE OPEO

LESSONS FROM TESLA

An approach that consists of always trying to massify, connect and refer complexity to the highest layers of an information system architecture constitutes an important ingredient in understanding the thinking of Elon Musk, who grew up in a coding culture. It is in these terms that Musk himself conceptualizes his products as well as his factories and organization. Software hybridization assumes different forms at Tesla, in particular where products are concerned, with vehicle design being conceptualized in the form of a robust information system architecture. The advantage for Tesla as a new entrant in the automotive market is that it is free to start from scratch when designing its platform. Tesla models are designed first as computers that also possess a mobility function. This architecture, which enables the interconnection of all components from powertrains to inside functions, offers the enormous advantage of making the vehicle perfectible over time as upgrades arrive, much like a piece of software. Tesla's Model S is one of the few vehicles in the marketplace to have improved during its lifespan (braking systems, energy consumption, driverless system, etc). Even more recently, Tesla teams were able, within a few short weeks, to solve braking problems affecting its entire Model 3 stock. This incredibly empowers the maker, since they can react to customer requests almost instantaneously. A number of customers recently asked Musk, for instance, to create a function so that the steering wheel rises and the seat lowers whenever the car is switched off. The requisite code modification was included in the following upgrade – only one week later – but also worked on all Tesla vehicles currently in service thanks to the car's 4G connection, which operates almost as if it were an iPhone on wheels.

In addition to the direct customer relationship, development processes have also fully benefited from the digitization of the product and operating procedures, combined with a 'testing and learning' mindset. Simulation is so extensive that Tesla only requires a minimum number of physical tests when validating, for example, its crash technology. A design engineer named M Javidan has spoken, for instance, about Toyota teams' surprise when they noticed, while undertaking a cross-benchmarking exercise, that Tesla was only using around 15 beta vehicles for testing purposes, versus more than 250 at Toyota (Fabernovel, 2018).

Another aspect of software hybridization at Tesla is the way teams are constantly judged on their ability to develop products or solutions offering an excellent user experience (being a key principle for the leading players in the digital world). When the Model S was designed, for example, a decision was taken to have it include a central console featuring a tablet of a size that was nowhere to be found in the automotive market. Musk turned to computer equipment suppliers for help in overcoming certain rigidities in the automotive market, characterized by traditional suppliers who thought about innovation in a more iterative manner.

Lastly, and in addition to purely technological aspects, this enthusiasm for software has been largely driven by the leader's personal mindset. As aforementioned, Elon Musk started coding when he was very young. His various entrepreneurial experiences with PayPal followed by Space X, Solar City and Tesla taught him how to combine bits and atoms to get the best out of both worlds. This ability to operate as an architect wearing both a mechanical and an IT hat is a formidable advantage in an environment defined by the 4th Industrial Revolution.

QUESTIONS FOR LEADERS

- Have I been personally sensitized to the different digital solutions that exist in the market for my company's core businesses?
- Do I understand the IT coding principle's hidden logic as well as the link between system architecture, software layers and programme and application language?
- Do my development teams use 3D computer-assisted development tools, or augmented reality, or virtual reality?
- Do my frontline operational managers use digital solutions to manage their frontline visits, motivate performance, monitor alerts and resolve problems?
- Does my operating system integrate digital solutions to avoid quality problems, accelerate training and predict breakdowns?
- Do my teams make sufficient use of collaborative digital tools to pilot cross-functional development, industrialization and supply chain processes? Have I started thinking about an end-to-end digital chain?
- Do I make sufficient use of digitization's potential for leveraging competencies and operational standards?
- Do I have enough internal competencies to integrate innovative software solutions?
- Have I done at least one proof of concept (POC) incorporating an artificial intelligence dimension?
- Does my strategy include a digital component to gather data from my end users, reflect upon innovative services or better understand how the products I sell are being used?

SOCOMEC INTERVIEW

'Using a global vision of software hybridization to improve customer service'

Socomec is one of the great unknown entrepreneurial adventures. Specialized in providing and supervising safe low-voltage electricity networks, the company is remarkable in many ways. Founded in 1922 by a family that retains a capital stake, by 2017 Socomec had more than 3,000 employees and exported product through around 30 subsidiaries all across the world. Operating in a niche characterized by extreme expertise, Socomec is global leader in several fields, including energy controls on the systems that it sells. The current Director for Group Strategy, Roland Schaeffer, is a key player at Socomec, which he joined more than 20 years ago. Formerly Head of IT at another company, Vincent Brunetta works as Socomec's Chief Digital Officer (CDO), a position that he has more or less shaped as he saw fit ever since it was first created in 2014. The two men offer a vision of what software hybridization means in a fast-growing group that has proactively decided to capitalize upon the digital revolution by revisiting its strategy, product offer and organizational modes.

A RESOLUTELY FUTURE-ORIENTED DIGITAL PROGRAMME AFFECTING THE WHOLE BUSINESS

Schaeffer has gone through some big changes at Socomec, including the building of a new factory in France, internationalization and a reinforced production system. But the transition he guided over the past two years is clearly one of the most important turns that the company has ever had to make. In a sector accustomed to frequent self-scrutiny, Socomec's management decided in 2014 to launch a digital programme furthering its leadership in its areas of expertise while also uncovering new growth drivers. According to Schaeffer, 'At first we wanted to push digital continuity within the company and make sure we weren't duplicating data. The goal was to achieve end-to-end coherency, reliability and efficiency, and improving customer services in this way.' This explains why the first workstreams were so customer-centric, focusing on digital connectivity, service innovation and how to improve the treatment of (and extract more value from) whatever market and product data it could find. The plan was quickly supplemented by two other streams that completed the system loop and culminated in an in-depth transformation of the company. One of these streams was a cross-functional effort addressing Socomec's various competencies and professions. The second was more operationally oriented and launched 'Industry 4.0' actions. In Schaeffer's opinion, Socomec's ecosystem has contributed greatly to the company's general understanding and more structured thinking today – exemplified by the value derived from its visits to local benchmark companies or to centres of expertise dedicated to the technologies of the future. 'At first we were unclear about this concept. We joined the community of local leaders and I met various companies like Bosch, SEW-USOCOME and PSA. We also visited the Commissariat à l'Energie Atomique and studied cobots and virtual reality. It was all very helpful.'

SOFTWARE HYBRIDIZATION DRIVEN BY THE CREATION OF AGILE INDEPENDENT SUBSIDIARIES

Brunetta feels that the approach's success is largely explained by the strategic decision 'to found an entirely independent energy branch. Choosing to create a standalone structure has done wonders for our agility.' Schaeffer thinks the same. 'The energy branch has clearly accelerated the entire company's transformation by showing us that other ways of working are possible. Being more responsive and a lot more flexible, this has been very important psychologically.' The performance of the energy branch, which is only three years old, has been encouraging and counts as one of the overall programme's main successes, having generated revenues of €36 million and employing more than 200 staff members. Brunetta also stresses the vehicle subsidiary's impact on Socomec's market. 'We have offered a perfect response to the market's current needs. Energy storage is one thing but knowing how to optimize energy use at the right time is something else. Our solutions, which mix product-related technological know-how with an optimal use of data imported from different systems, are widely praised. We've even started conquered a few new markets, including data centres in the United States, because of our reputation for excellence in the field of energy efficiency. The subsidiary has bolstered this reputation.' Above and beyond the economic aspect, the most promising thing for the future is the synergy between the company's new and its traditional activities. Again according to Brunetta, 'We have created new ways of selling online so that, in the years to come, it is the products themselves that will evolve with an increasingly substantial digital element.' In his opinion, digital support for customer relationship management should be broken down into three complementary objectives: offering customers new functionalities; improving product use knowledge to provide more adapted data services; and closing the product life management (PLM) loop to ensure that the different businesses always track needs. With respect to this latter aspect, Brunetta spontaneously cites two examples to explain its concrete translation into internal operating modes. 'The quality department has benefited from information about how products work and can now offer process adaptations and even remote interventions. The engineering department gathers data about product obsolescence and integrates it into specifications so it can develop products that will be more reliable in the future.'

AN ALREADY SOLID INDUSTRIAL ORGANIZATION AND IT PLATFORM EVEN BEFORE THE SOFTWARE WAS DEVELOPED

In total, software hybridization has gone well beyond any simple product development framework. According to Brunetta, 'The first level involved embedding more software into products. Materials became cyber-physical with communication functions helping to transfer calculational functions from silicon chips into the actual coding. The second level involved customer services with, for instance, a massive use of cloud computing as well as energy efficiency-based value proposals. All of which has made our offer more configurable and flexible. Then, the third level involved greater agility and frontline efficiency, based for instance on production lines becoming configurable and the elimination of paper.' Schaeffer notes that operational improvement was a precondition for this latter aspect. 'The time was right for us since we had already deeply transformed our production system by implementing lean management principles, and because we decided to renew our ERP system. We didn't fully understand this at first but both elements have been key to our shifting successfully to operations characterized by software hybridization.' At the same time, Schaeffer also expresses concern that the company had yet to achieve a robust standardization of components and sub-assemblies. This has slowed down product differentiation, causing operational inefficiency and delaying the development of a customer interface that uses a configurator capable of producing customized products at the lowest possible cost.

LEARNING AS A DRIVER OF PROFESSIONAL DEVELOPMENT

The idea behind the digital programme has been to gradually drip each of these transformations into the company's different professions. In Brunetta's words, 'Once a technology has been invalidated, and the teams working in a given area have attained sufficient maturity, we move on to the next profession. We started with the business application department that prepares our product offers. Today they are autonomous so we can now focus on operations and sales.' In addition to this tactical aspect, Socomec has expended an enormous amount of energy on learning. 'We have created training programmes replete with dedicated digital tools and learning platforms... but it's not enough since we also need to work within each profession to identify what competencies are needed for the future. Our strategy is to use technology to do this. For instance, our historical R&D professions focus on mechanics and electronics. What we want to do is supplement these competencies with data science and digitization to supplement our traditional know-how.' Note that this technology-oriented analysis goes much further than the normal evolution of competencies. It is also a way of understanding market trends and leveraging opportunities to 'disrupt' the market and/or avoid being 'disintermediated'. Brunetta uses a blockchain example to explain the group's thinking. 'We try first and foremost to understand end users' uses and connect them to new technology. For instance, a blockchain may well be able to completely reshape the landscape for players in the energy sector. It is a technology that we must understand to see if it is useful for acquiring competencies helping us to capture future markets.' Schaeffer, on the other hand, focuses more on the physical side. 'We have created a separate learning and customer centre to change things completely.' In effect, Socomec is reproducing the same strategy as when it founded its energy subsidiary, hiving off the disruptive activity to get traction that is then applied in the more traditional activities. Brunetta analyses this in light of the company's total investment over the past three years. 'Our training and product innovation tools have won several awards. They more than pay for themselves, even if it sometimes takes a while.'

Schaeffer's vision of the sector in 10 years sounds very optimistic: 'You'll get data that is structured, coherent and updated in real time, based on automated processes, with management concentrating on work teams' sense of serenity... without forgetting increasingly cutting-edge competencies, maximum product customization and a software layer that is omnipresent in customer relationships and in operational activities.' In short, Socomec is very much on the move and intends to take advantage of all the self-renewal opportunities that the 4th Industrial Revolution has to offer.

Principle 4

Tentacular traction

Approaching markets with a tentacular trans-sectorial vision and operating in network mode to gain commercial traction

SUMMARY

- Tentacular traction is a traditional form of commercial traction augmented by a network effect. Digital platforms work like 'tentacles' to aggregate markets and facilitate a 'disintermediated' relationship between producers and consumers, leading to market faster growth than traditional markets might achieve.

- With digitization, traditional unidirectional flows are replaced by star-shaped flows where the parties intervening during a value chain's initial upstream phases are in direct contact with their downstream counterparts.

- A new type of flow piloting involves a 'pulsing' principle where production is no longer done solely on-demand but also in a way that maximizes customer participation, thereby enhancing the network effect.

- The effect characterizes a platform logic. Without taking anything away from this approach, it is also crucial that industrialists learn to implement (and take advantage of) network effects.

- Tesla teaches that the best way to build platforms in the industrial world is to create one's own network through a product.

INTRODUCTION TO TENTACULAR TRACTION

The previous chapter showed that software hybridization is a basic foundation for connectivity both within a company and with its clients. But, to truly leverage the power of digitization as a driver destined to revolutionize markets and business models, the most interesting approach consists of companies disrupting their own sectors by using digital platforms to take more of a trans-sectorial vision of products. The ensuing tentacular traction is akin to traditional commercial traction augmented by a network effect.

Digital platforms that operate like 'tentacles' aggregating markets and facilitating 'disintermediated' relationships between producers and consumers are growing much faster than traditional markets. Google's market share exemplifies this tentacular phenomenon, with 92 per cent of all internet searches in 2017 using the platform daily to browse 20 billion websites and 30 trillion indexed webpages – all of which explains why it is so important to discover the characteristics of these new tools that have had such a strong effect on flows and growth models.

STAR-SHAPED FLOWS REPLACING LINEAR FLOWS

As noted in the chapter on cross-integration, the 3rd Age of Industry witnessed certain very large structures organizing themselves in such a way as to focus on their core businesses while delegating large swathes of their value chains to subcontractors, many of whom were working out of low-cost countries. Players in these chains became increasingly interdependent in the late 20th century, reflecting end users' growing demand for responsiveness.

Then came digitization, combining two effects that would perturb this production model: the chain's different players could connect directly to another; and IT data speeds and volumes increased exponentially, in line with Moore's law. Interconnectivity and instantaneous exchanges became the norm. Little by little, the first networks were created, producing a mathematical phenomenon known as the 'network effect', in which the power of one network is proportional to the square of its members. More recently, researchers have shown that the main influence in a network has always been the number of connections.

A new, so-called star-shaped flow would be born in the form of a platform (Figure 3.9). One strength of this type of biface platform is that producers could also be consumers and vice versa, increasing the scale effect on demand. The probability that a transaction could be done using such a platform was much greater than it would have been in a world of linear flows characterized by limited connections and much slower response times.

This new type of flow would supplement (or sometimes deeply modify) traditional unidirectional flows from producers to final consumers. This new vision of the supply chain with its traditional mode of operating between customers and suppliers would soon be considered disruptive. One widespread effect of the change was the disintermediation of various players in the chain, with those operating towards its most upstream side now being able to connect directly to those working at its more downstream levels, and

FIGURE 3.9 Star-shaped flows replacing linear flows

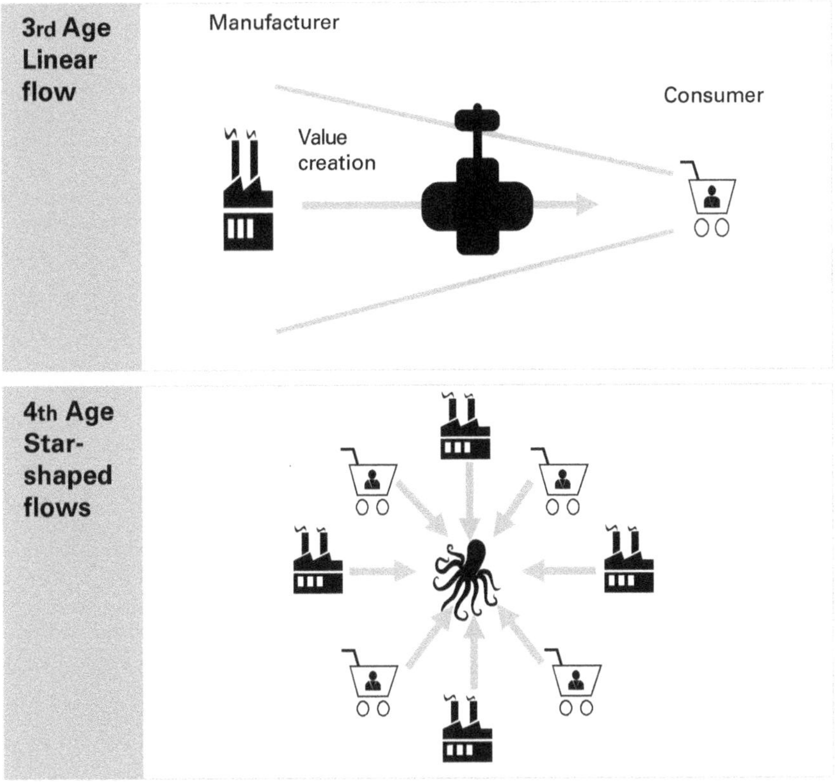

3rd Age Linear flow

Manufacturer

Consumer

Value creation

4th Age Star-shaped flows

SOURCE OPEO. Adapted from Parker, Van Alstyne and Choudary (2016)

even with end users. This was very different from a world where customers traditionally had no contact with industry.

PULSED FLOWS REPLACING LEAN FLOWS

In addition to value chain interaction modes' quantum leap ahead, a new flows piloting logic would be pursued, one based on lean flows. This had been an essential component of the just-in-time system, enabling thousands of companies to save a great deal of money over the past 40 years by drastically reducing the working capital they needed. The basic principle was simple – to avoid over-consumption, never produce without first receiving an order.

In the new paradigm, product renewals speeds, the level of customization required by markets (and the degree of innovation required to succeed) has led to the rise of a new way of piloting flows, one called a 'pulsed' flow.

FIGURE 3.10 From lean flows to pulsed flows

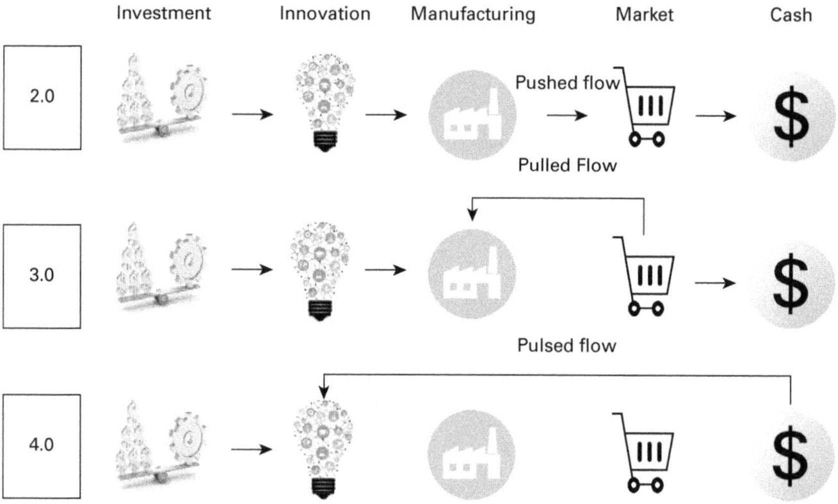

SOURCE OPEO. Adapted from Fabernovel (2018)

The principle is no longer only to produce on demand but to get potential customers to help fund future product innovation by asking for pre-orders. This has the benefit of turning customers into short-term investors since they are now supporting the company's development and benefiting in exchange from exclusivity by being one of the first to own the new innovative product (Figure 3.10). Similar to the 'beta' approach used by many pure digital players to get users to test and improve their new products, the new approach comes with several preconditions, however. In the industrial world, it is impossible to test a product that has not been a least partially completed – unlike the software world, where customers can download beta versions instantaneously (in one click).

One of the main prerequisites at this level is to have a sufficiently powerful community of believers while pursuing ongoing communication with the new network of potential customers. This can be done by means of an inspiring story that encourages customers to play a fuller role in the project and not only buy a product because it is fashionable. The other prerequisite is also crucial, namely the need for products that are connected and that can improve over time. The idea here is that the initial customers must not feel at a disadvantage compared to those who come later, something that would be particularly frustrating since they had supported the innovation by investing in it and waiting patiently for months until the product was ready.

TENTACLES: A NEW TRANS-SECTORIAL GROWTH MODEL

The new flow (star-shaped, pulsed and tentacular) offers four major advantages to users and to the parties running the networks created in this way:

- Price optimization. Enabling market price arbitrages' instantaneous adjustment via massified real-time connections.

- Magnetism. Optimizing capacities by balancing different network stakeholders' workloads and capacities.

- Exponential growth. Almost zero marginal cost when acquiring a new user.

- Intimacy. Familiarity with users' data helps to customize their experience and leads to their being offered an integrated vision of the services they might enjoy.

Historically, IT service sectors were the first to test this new flow mode, based on work done by pioneers like IBM and Microsoft. Initial tests were followed by a creative wave embodied in the emergence of social networks such as Facebook, Twitter and YouTube, among others. The concept then spread to business-to-consumer (B2C) sectors epitomized by Uber or Airbnb, respectively disrupting the travel and hotel markets. Today, this type of flow dominates entire sections of the economy, including B2B and manufacturing industries, based on transactions that are no longer only intangible or service-related but also involve physical goods.

The operational system associated with this new flow type is very different from its predecessors (Figure 3.11). As aforementioned, the growth models associated with the first industrial ages were characterized by asset aggregation; larger companies; a better coverage of overheads; and more control over profitability. Of course, the operational systems in use during these periods were also enormous structures consuming huge quantities of labour and capital. Today's new platforms, on the other hand, do not own the assets they use to create value. Instead, they rely strongly on users to perform tasks that had traditionally been performed by a company's expert resources. One example is provided by 'conservation', which is akin to controlling platform flow quality. Another comes from marketing, which nowadays often involves users constantly offering their opinions and providing in this way data that helps to predict future trends (thereby intimating to the company which products it may wish to develop). In other words, digital platforms are like information factories that do not own their own inventory. Unlike their traditional competitors, staff in these new

FIGURE 3.11 From pipeline to platform – a new paradigm

Market and value

- Value added, at lowest cost
- Know-how, agility
- Technical barrier to entry
- Uni-directional flow from producer to consumer

→
→
→
→

- Collaborative value
- Connectivity, user experience
- Data
- Star-shaped flows, possibility of alternance between consumer and producer roles

Business strategy

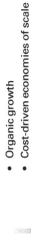

- Organic growth
- Cost-driven economies of scale
- Ownership of assets
- Aggregation of assets

→
→
→
→

- Growth driven by network effects
- Demand-driven economies of scale
- Value decoupled from ownership
- Aggregation of markets

Execution model

- Complex and extended supply chain
- Internal resources
- Quality control expertise
- Marketing run in-house

→
→
→
→

- Disintermediation
- Ecosystem
- User-driven conservation
- User-conveyed marketing

SOURCE OPEO

companies are often 'decorrelated' from their production capacities and therefore find themselves in a relatively weakened position. One striking example is Airbnb, which had 3,100 employees at year-end 2017, compared to the 240,000 people working at AccorHotels, even as the former company had a market capitalization two and a half times higher (€31 billion versus €13 billion).

In financial terms, one effect of this use of 'tentacles' to exploit networking modes is that different methods can also be used to value a company. Platforms' market multiplier (the ratio between the market's assessment of a company's value and its price earnings ratio) is around 8.2 versus 4.8 for 4th Age Industry suppliers, 2.6 for traditional service providers and 2.0 for parties producing traditional product manufacturing assets (Parker, Van Alstyne and Choudary, 2016).

INDUSTRY PLATFORMS REMAIN A VAGUE CONCEPT

Despite the markets' enthusiasm for platforms in the digital sector, the concept has yet to spread widely across all industry activities. This is despite the fact that most large industrial groups possess tools that can create network effects at their corporate interfaces, for instance, by developing purchasing platforms run according to a reverse auction logic to get the possible best price or offer from a network of suppliers. Notable examples include the automotive and aviation industries, both when they procure parts and consumables but also when they allocate new products to different markets. On the other side of this flow, these same groups have also been acquiring e-commerce sites enabling them to supplement their sales channels while facilitating the user experience (or exchange quality, in the case of B2B). This means that customers increasingly have an opportunity to tailor-make their own products from a catalogue. Like the kitchens that buyers can design themselves using an online portal before ordering, many equipment suppliers' websites offer online configurators selling products adapted to their customers quickly and virtually.

All in all, these tools continue to be entirely geared towards unidirectional flows. Digitization is only used to accelerate exchanges and generate traffic, meaning that the full potential of bi-face platforms remains under-exploited. One of the first places where this type of disruptive platform has started to emerge is the machinery supply market. Currently there is a competitive battle for leadership in machine-to-machine connection platforms. The stakes are high since the company whose platform becomes the benchmark technology will then be able to impose its communication and connectivity

FIGURE 3.12   Four business models for the 4th Age of Industry, plus their market
multiplier

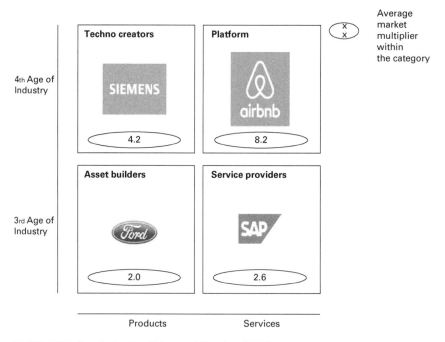

SOURCE OPEO, from Parker, Van Alstyne and Choudary (2016)

standards, its apps and its preventive maintenance and machine piloting
solutions. Such platforms will become indispensable for machine purchasers
and suppliers, turning the winning company into a kind of Google for the
world of industrial equipment manufacturing. For players in this sector,
owning a platform is therefore not only a question of which new service line
a company should be operating but also a key factor in acquiring leadership
in its traditional business. Moreover, the danger does not only come from the
usual rivals since the player disrupting the market is always operating at the
intersection between its market's traditional businesses and the digital world.
The machine manufacturing sector features a wide variety of suppliers,
including GE (machinery), Siemens (assistance and components), Bosch
(systems and industrial resources) but also SAP (integrated information
systems) and even Dassault Systèmes (software and applications).

INTER OPERABILITY, THE CORNERSTONE OF INDUSTRIAL PLATFORMIZATION
One factor facilitating the creation of platforms is the definition of applicable inter operability standards. This is an area where the digital world is

decades ahead of the manufacturing world. A number of charitable foundations, in conjunction with the giants of the internet but operating on a non-profit basis, regularly agree standards enabling total inter-connectivity to free up value creation by all the players in a chain. One of the best-known protocols of this type is tcp/ip, which was partially responsible for the rise of the internet. However, the principle also applies to every layer in the IT world, like website graphic interfaces written in html or coded using API. These interfaces are governed by norms that are very explicit in terms of the kind of information being exchanged but also in the way this is done. At the same time, each player is totally free to manoeuvre between the different interfaces. It is largely thanks to this that the platforms actually work. The two sides (supply and demand) can connect almost instantaneously because of the standards governing the interfaces. But each can also organize themselves as they see fit within these interfaces and innovate continuously without endangering the whole regime. The software world has even established automated testing that tests all new code proposals continuously and automatically to ensure they respect interfacing standards.

The parallel with the factory world would be if the way parts are industrialized, ordered, planned, launched, manufactured and delivered were subject to standards so explicit that each supply chain participant could subcontract one of these functions without having to engage in any particular exchange with the subcontractor aside from setting the transaction price. A few functions have started to adopt these kinds of standards in both the world of information flows and the world of physical flows. One example is the supply chain success of materials resource planning (MRP), which makes it possible to use electronic data interchange (EDI) to connect a need with a resource. In the physical world, industrial logistics is the business that has made the greatest progress along these lines. Historically, the creation of containers with standardized sizes led to an explosion in maritime trade volumes. Today it is the parcels that are starting to have certain standardized specificities (weight, size, etc) facilitating product shipments whether they are measured in kilogrammes or cubic metres. Parcels have been commoditized and this has translated into an explosion in the volume of small package shipments.

Aside from a few businesses and sectors that are starting to change, however, such transformations remain confidential. The explosion in manufacturing values and uses will therefore require a revolution in the way interfaces between different parties are viewed.

PLATFORM REASONING, A WAY OF THINKING THAT TRANSCENDS THE NORMAL BUSINESS MODEL

Without going so far as to create digital platforms that are by their very nature disruptive hence complicated to implement, in an industrial environment several preconditions must be satisfied before network effects can be achieved. The lighthouses currently showcased in industry 4.0 have all created product family platforms allowing them to be much more responsive and agile in developing new products. They do this by commonalizing as many components and sub-assemblies as possible. Towards this end, close integration with supplier and subcontractor networks is necessary, as is the establishment of joint part nomenclature, design and monitoring systems.

The creation of communities of customers or believers offers another example of network thinking. This is a very powerful lever for creating natural traction in the marketplace; for designing in a way that gets the end user involved via methods like design thinking; and for getting end users to pre-finance project phases through targeted crowdfunding.

Beyond the economic impact of these new business models, tentacular traction has caused a radical change in ways of thinking about companies and their vision of society; their mission vis-à-vis their staff, customers and suppliers; their relationships with actors in their ecosystem; and their operational model. The incentive here is to sell integrated solutions focused on consumer uses to try and get as close as possible to final consumers so as to sell them services that are as specific as possible – while, of course, sharing resources throughout this process.

In short, goods and services production can also be conceptualized as something 'networked' involving the search for extra brainpower and muscle on demand. Work here becomes liquid, characterized by production capabilities with maximum flexibility to respond to market needs. The aim for business leaders is not only to get a new sales channel but to achieve a complete cultural revolution affecting the whole of the economy, even if the speed at which the tentacular traction advances (and the form it takes) vary markedly from one sector to another.

LESSONS FROM TESLA

In today's industrial world, the best way to build platforms is to create one's own product-based network. Elon Musk understood this very early on, which explains the whole stock of connected cars and houses that he has built, all of which have become platforms capable of sharing energy and services. The strategy's ultimate goal is to create the conditions for an ecosystem that encourages value creation by enabling parties to gain commercial leverage from assets they do not own.

There is the example of Apple with its Apple stores relying on a network of Apple products connected everywhere in the world and also via iOS. The objective over time is to enable an energy transfer between Tesla cars and the homes that Musk has equipped, transformed into solar energy generation plants thanks to his Solar City solar roof slate manufacturing subsidiary. The connectivity between cars and homes will create a huge self-regulating network smoothing out electricity consumption peaks and troughs by replacing fossil or nuclear fuels with solar energy. Defending his vision, Musk's simple explanation is that the amount of sunlight shining on Planet Earth in one hour is more than enough to cover all of our annual energy needs. In this way, he has positioned himself in a chain that goes much further than simple carmaking. He also aspires to create a car-sharing platform enabling any Tesla owner to rent out their vehicle whenever they feel like scheduling this. The advantage is threefold: rapid amortization of car acquisition costs (similar to what many homeowners do with Airbnb); fewer vehicles in service (hence a radical transformation in urban architecture with less need for car-related infrastructure like roads and parking lots); and a response to urban mobility's real-time needs, something that platforms like Uber are also working on at present.

The next step includes the rapid development of driverless cars that can pick up users as arranged then take them to their destination before driving back to the car owner without the latter having to make any physical effort. Of course, this also requires the development of high-performance digital platforms, efficient GPS systems, robust transaction systems and, possibly, funding solutions tailored to amortize the vehicles quickly. Lastly, it is also worth noting that Musk has gone far beyond car use to look at cars' lifecycle, having created an insurance company for Tesla brand vehicles and devising plans to create a vehicle resale platform that would make this market more liquid. All these preconditions have an extremely structuring effect because they encourage the company not to hide behind the traditional vision of the automobile but to expand its scope of possible intervention in line with Musk's global vision. The automotive sector would then become a sector for mobility, energy, collaborative economics, funding, etc (Figure 3.13).

Musk's customer relationships also operate in network mode to achieve continuous product improvement through upgrades and vehicle use data recovery. This disintermediates the traditional relationship between vehicle purchaser and carmaker. Normally there needs to be a sales network that is

FIGURE 3.13 Tentacular traction at Tesla: from carmaking to car use and mobility

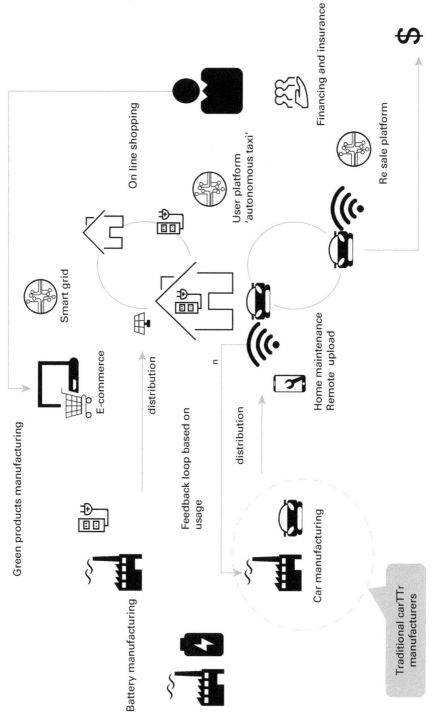

SOURCE OPEO. Adapted from Fabernovel (2018)

more or less loyal to one make, together with a repair network whose players, on the other hand, be completely independent. Tessa operates differently by offering, from the purchasing act onwards, direct online sales that do not necessarily involve a dealership. The same applies to vehicle maintenance, with Musk having created a roadside assistance service that even visits owners at home when the interventions cannot be done remotely. Lastly, the customer experience is viewed as central to the strategy, incentivizing Tesla to position itself as something bigger than a mere automobile production and sales company. Along these lines, it also offers a network of charging points to service its vehicles, proposing interfaces between cars and homes as well as a whole range of online services intended to simplify users' lives. In simple terms, it is as if Ford at the beginning of the 20th century had started to develop a service-station network offering to maintain customers' cars at their homes in order to retain their business.

QUESTIONS FOR LEADERS

- Can I integrate more with my network of trusted suppliers to improve responsiveness?
- Have I thought strategically about standardizing my systems or basic components to create product platforms?
- Is it possible within the value chain to which I belong to disintermediate my relationship with end users?
- Can I network with current competitors to create new services offering customers added value?
- What use data helps improve the design of the future products we are developing?
- Is it possible to generate product data through either connectivity or social networks?
- Is it possible to expand my sector of origin's scope using digital platforms?
- Have I tried to build a network of loyal customers?
- How can I best use my customers to achieve continuous product improvement?
- Have my teams been sensitized to the concept of platforms and trained in this? Are these platforms there to facilitate purchases or to disseminate information?

GE DIGITAL FOUNDRY INTERVIEW
'Using an open-mode platform strategy to create tentacular traction'

Observing the gradual digitization of the industrial world, GE has set up a number of 'Digital Foundry' units across the world to support large industrial groups' digital transformation. The focus here is on critical machinery like gas turbines or airplanes, and on critical systems such as electrical networks or production lines. Today, GE Digital offers a range of solutions based on technologies like cloud computing, data science or artificial intelligence, mainly rolled out via its Predix platform. Vincent Champain is Managing Director for Digital Foundry in Europe and explains below GE's strategic choices in this domain plus the ingredients of its success in the New World of the 4th Age of Industry, with a particular emphasis on network modes and tentacular traction.

AT GE DIGITAL, PLATFORMS ARE ONLY ONE COMPONENT OF TENTACULAR TRACTION
Limiting the definition of GE Digital to a simple platform would be very reductionist. The strategy clearly involves proposing end-to-end solutions. These can include selling a use (based on access to a standard brick platform); developing new tailor-made applications; offering ancillary services (like maintenance tasks); and/or monetizing performance improvements. In this latter case, GE Digital has promised customers to raise the performance of one of their critical resources and be remunerated on any gains – turning the entire effort into a win-win situation.

OPEN-MODE INNOVATION, ONE OF THE GE DIGITAL SYSTEM'S MAIN STRENGTHS
Implementation is not simple, however. Customers' perceived risks can become major stumbling blocks: cyber-security, data privacy, information being used for commercial purposes, etc. To overcome these barriers and compete with GAFA (Google, Amazon, Facebook, Apple) or other rivals, GE has made the highly structuring strategic choice to offer an open mode platform. This approach has several advantages First, customers can develop their own tailored applications, which they can subsequently sell via the platform. Second, it enables agile innovation with a wider variety of partners. Third, customers tend to be reassured when they are able to retain full ownership of their data and not have to pay (if need be) for its use or removal. Alongside this, GE Digital guarantees that data will be completely confidential and protected from the outside world. To illustrate this open state of mind, the company has even started to sell its system on machines competing with the ones that it makes itself.

A CULTURAL AND ORGANIZATIONAL CHANGE

Because these choices, which are anything but self-evident, could have been perceived internally as counterproductive, the decision was made to support them with some major organizational changes. Each of GE's business units hired a chief digital officer (CDO) with a direct reporting line to the managing director. Otherwise, teams built around specific objectives (eg critical machinery improvements) would prioritize the recruitment of top talent, whether externally, internally or from another GE Digital business unit. According to Champain, 'Resources like data scientists are so rare that we needed to prioritize adaptation to the new way of working.' In the end, new organizational approaches would lead to relatively different working methods. 'The project is ongoing and far from finished' but cultural adaptation is progressing due to increasing connectivity inside and outside the company.

HYBRIDIZATION, A KEY PRINCIPLE IN THE NEW WORLD

The duality between openness and internal know-how is far from being the only area where 'hybrid' thinking has had to replace Old World rigidities. This starts with products, which are by definition a hybrid of standard and customized bricks developed by customers or partners. Everything depends on where the cursor is pointing, however. For instance, a more 'centralized' emphasis at the organizational level would tend to favour synchronization and development cost savings. Conversely, allowing teams to innovate locally without any central control could encourage innovation but also runs a risk of solutions being duplicated. From a broader perspective, value creation will increasingly reflect the hybridization of physical with digital flows. Champain feels that contrary to received wisdom, physical flows will continue to be the company's main driver, accounting for at least 90 per cent of the value it creates, but that those actors who will succeed are the ones who can differentiate themselves with respect to one of these two flows. The same applies to artificial intelligence, which will be only one of many factors leading to success, with others such as professional know-how or simple natural intelligence remaining indispensable foundations.

CREATING A VISION, AVOIDING THE INERTIA TRAP THROUGH PLANNED UPSCALING

Champain feels that the best way for a leader to take advantage of a New World in which hybridization is the norm would be to create a helicopter view of new technologies' potential impact on business. Thinking in this area should see leaders asking themselves four questions, namely whether they are sufficiently well-equipped to engage in relevant data science; if their teams are agile to design products and solutions; if the infrastructure (especially cloud computing) is robust enough for rapid upscaling; and if enough thought has been given to interconnections with existing systems. Following this, it is crucial to plan future upscaling actions even if it is clear that things will change along the way. Inaction is never the solution, or, as Chamain jokingly says mirroring a funny quote by Lino Ventura, 'My main rival is the status quo. In the New World, two smart people sitting on their backsides are less useful than a stupid person who is at least trying to get something done.'

Reasoning on an end-to-end and an open-mode basis, adapting the organization and culture to the system's inevitable hybridization, being visionary but acting quickly by developing the resources enabling upscaling – tentacular traction has clearly become a central part of GE Digital's DNA, embodied in a very clear vision of the right strategy for maximizing its benefits.

LUXOR LIGHTING INTERVIEW
'Tentacular traction is first and foremost a catalyst of further growth'

Luxor Lighting designs, develops and industrializes products and functions (including automotive LED technologies) that it either sells directly to carmakers or to the main Tier 1 suppliers in this sector. After a crisis between 2012 and 2015 when company revenues fell by 30 per cent, there was a total turnaround with exceptional growth of 100 per cent between 2015 and 2018. One reason for this recovery was the company's ability to position itself in promising market segments and engage in joint thinking with customers and partners (thereby pursuing a tentacular traction logic). Patrick Scholz is current CEO at Luxor, which he took over nine years ago and ran throughout the transition period. He explains the foundations of this success.

WINNING NEW MARKETS BY ADOPTING A 'TENTACULAR' APPROACH
TO CUSTOMERS AND SUPPLIERS
Scholz, who first started to invest in Luxor after departing from a large German industrial, begins the explanation of his new entrepreneurial adventure by observing that, 'Customers had lost confidence.' Several work streams were therefore inaugurated in a bid to return to growth. The first was strategic and involved greater connectivity with customers through a better integration of product design. Scholz invested massively in a digital simulation system that responded better to what his end users (carmakers) wanted. 'Tier 1 suppliers were already focusing on big front or rear headlights so we positioned

ourselves in the market for internal automotive lighting, plus a few small ones on the outside. For carmakers to get a full light signature, however, we needed digital integration.' This was implemented via a daily EDI system. Towards the other end of the value chain, there was similar thinking as to how suppliers and solution providers might be better integrated. The company started working with a local partner with expertise in robotics and who helped it design special machines. Scholz saw this as 'important because it helped us to go quicker and trust in ourselves'.

A VIRTUOUS ECOSYSTEM EFFECT AND LOCAL TENTACLES
Scholz also notes the crucial role that the ecosystem beyond his company's branch played in its recovery. 'Tentacles also stretch out into the local fabric.' On one hand, the local authorities helped Luxor to acquire a new industrial site. On the other, the group's corporate social responsibility (CSR) policy got him to start looking at things differently. On top of this, he became aware of the 'Made in' labels' usefulness as a sales argument. 'Carmakers have changed their attitudes in this respect. For years, all that mattered was delocalization. But today we've reverted to a more progressive view. What companies look for now is greater responsiveness, meaning that price per se has become relatively less important in the decision-making process. Proximity effects are working in our favour.'

INTEGRATING STRATEGIC BUSINESSES TO GAIN IN AGILITY AND AUTONOMY
Alongside these more strategic projects, there was also a transformation of practices in a bid to increase agility. This started with the implementation of lean manufacturing principles. 'We rolled up our sleeves and started to question everything we were doing.' As a result, the company would redefine its flows, launch a quick-response quality control (QRQC) and improve management's visioning of everything happening out in the field. The next step would be to digitize flows to finally eliminate all paper from the production floors while increasing competitiveness. To increase its agility, however, the company needed to gain control of its core lighting-system design businesses. Luxor Lighting gradually acquired the requisite know-how in optics and mechanics. 'This was fundamental since it helped us to move more quickly during the first development phases and start picking up a few contracts... Having said that, if we had had competencies in electronics, we could have also controlled every aspect of the product and further strengthened our ties to customers.'

CREATING TRANSPARENCY TO GIVE TEAMS MORE RESPONSIBILITY

Tentacles do not stop at the borders of the firm. Scholz pays particular attention to communications with his teams, sending out monthly briefings that go as far as to provide detailed financial information about company accounts. 'It wasn't easy since at first many people in our teams found it pretty dry. But over time, this helped us to create real trust – with teams subsequently agreeing to take on greater responsibility.' Scholz feels that the company is far better equipped today to deal with any crisis that might arise. Everything – the connections with customers and suppliers, the ecosystem, the teams – is more robust. 'A network mode works. The key is to get smarter every single day. I'm 54 years old and struck each and every time by how much the world of factories is modernizing. Yes, there will be fewer humans working in factories in the future but there will always be room for people because progress only happens when collective intelligence drives it.'

Principle 5

Story-making

Inspiring the world yet keeping one's feet on the ground

SUMMARY

- Storymaking refers to the ability to energize people using an inspiring objective, both within a company but also in society and with customers and investors.

- Constructing this kind of vision involves much more than simply wanting to conquer a market. It means transforming an activity based on the very reasons that it exists.

- This way of communicating is often paradoxical, requiring total oversight and control of the communications' timing and channels, remaining highly transparent all the while. It also implies the leader's full-throated commitment.

- This way of communicating offers major benefits in terms of being able to attract top talent and build up fan clubs.

- Tesla is driven by Elon Musk's vision of promoting a 360-degree energy transition enabling humankind to survive both on earth and in space.

INTRODUCTION TO STORY-MAKING

Boosting and connecting the industrial system were two preconditions for the Teslism rocket's launch into space. The four technical and organizational pillars detailed in the preceding chapters may have been necessary but they would had had no chance of effecting lasting change had the model not been based on a vision folding the company and its mission into a gloriously inspiring project based on more than mere business considerations. Story-making refers to the ability to create energy around a motivational aspiration, be it within a company or vis-à-vis the rest of society, including customers and investors. The idea of telling stories to convey ideas is nothing new but has only recently started to inundate the economic and political spheres, a trend not unrelated to communications increasingly being portrayed as a key factor of success. In 2017, 1 billion hours of video were watched every day on YouTube (amounting to 114,000 years in total); 500 million tweets were sent; and 1.4 billion users connected to Facebook, including 1.2 billion to its mobile version.

The concept of story-making derives from storytelling. The novelty is that instead of merely talking about good stories, the new construct contains the fact of doing something, ie showing the way by actually being part of the action – offering a kind of authenticity that not only runs through everything being said but also through the company's values and what it (notably its management) does on a daily basis (Figure 3.14).

FIGURE 3.14 The four facets of story-making

 Story   **Making**

An inspiring story for clients, employees and citizens

 A CEO who is himself media-cool and direct in communicating with the outside world, but very strong and directive with the inside communication channels

A trans-sectorial, long-term-oriented vision without focusing on 'return on investment' only

 A technician CEO, trained to new technologies, able to lead and execute most of the projects and operations of the company

SOURCE OPEO

FROM PRODUCT PROMOTION TO A STORY THAT INSPIRES EVERYONE

The 3rd Age of Industry started with product customization followed by greater emphasis on customers and their needs. Products would ultimately acquire real statutory value. In the automotive business, for instance, brands would highlight performance and quality to attract male customers; elegance and use for women; or humour for younger generations. Despite this general trend, however, the fact remains that all the many things happening outside of a company would involve contacting only a few of its functions, usually sales, marketing or after-sales. Things happening inside the company (like lean manufacturing) kept artificially connected to the outside thanks to the constant efforts of the managers to remind everyone that the customer should be at the heart of the factory.

Most real customers had very little if any contact with the factory itself. With today's hyper-connected frontline teams, machines and products, however, companies' internal and external worlds are no longer hermetically sealed from one another. The communications mode that consisted of defining one marketing strategy for customers, on one hand, and one for the employer brand, on the other, has become obsolete. Explanations for this shift include younger generations' growing demand for meaning as well as the exponential change in technologies, all of which has started a war to attract the best talent – which has itself become a new key factor of success. The most successful companies are the ones that have a coherent vision of the world. The goal is no longer to target a market segment or a customer but to create a coherent story, one that is accessible, understandable and that inspires everyone operating in the company's ecosystem: employees, young talents, public officials, media, partners, suppliers, etc.

Companies today must be part of something that is bigger than they are.

ROI IS DEAD, LONG LIVE THE VISION!

A disruptive mission usually requires disruptive resources. This is because a start-up is usually an organization that is in the process of seeking a business model. The initial lack of profitability is something expected, with the idea being that the company should subsequently be able to accelerate quickly to compensate for its early losses. Hence the importance during this interlude of preserving a long-term vision that will keep the teams motivated. The problem is that the industrial world's view of investment, as a concept, is culturally more in line with a bookkeeper's perspective, if only because of industry's natural proclivity to prioritize short-term outcomes. A good factory manager will spend time challenging any team member who submits an investment proposal to ensure that the payback period is no long than 18 months. Factual analyses will then be done to shore up this demonstration. To join the 4th Industrial Revolution, however, a radically disruptive mindset is required, especially from leaders. Investing for the future means forging beliefs based on a structured and coherent vision, one transcending a simple desire to conquer markets. Instead, the aim today is to transform activities by reasoning in terms of their raison d'être. The more a boss believes in a vision, the more s/he will be audacious and persuasive, getting the whole team to make investment decisions with more of a long-term outlook, often based on holistic thinking and not short-term local returns.

Most lighthouses for the industry of the future focus on the concept of confidence as an essential ingredient in helping each corporate decision maker to make the right choice, with everyone being motivated by a shared and coherent vision. The idea is not to invest randomly or become 'techno-smug' but to reason like a family shareholder preparing for tomorrow.

THE MEDIA BOSS: COOL ON THE OUTSIDE, STRICT ON THE INSIDE
Communicating a vision and doing this well is a challenge, especially given the need to create intimacy with all of the actors within one's ecosystem without revealing so much information that competitors find it easy to copy a model's differentiating forces. Tesla's communications – like so many modern executives or politicians – suffer from a kind of paradox.

On one hand, there is an external communications style that is very direct, informal and social media-friendly. On the other, there is great secretiveness regarding internal operational procedures designed to survive exponential growth's negative side effects – to wit, the disruption that will ultimately blow up the model. The real goal is to control information, timing and channels. At Tesla, for instance, Musk himself offers a media presence capable of responding instantaneously to customers who may tweet him several times a day asking about his plans and how things are going. This creates a veneer of transparency, especially given Musk's promise to be open about his innovations by offering open-source access to many parts of his software – not to mention his official statements that he hopes other carmakers will copy him. This is because Musk's ultimate objective is to contribute to the global energy transition. When trying to understand the company's internal operating modes, it is striking to note how very locked down everything seems. To write this book, for instance, the author could speak with many current Tesla employees and ex-employees but no official company interview was ever organized. Similarly, visits to Tesla facilities come with a tough-minded non-disclosure agreement specifying very strict conduct on-site, even if there is nothing confidential about the visit.

Cool on the outside but strict on the inside, Tesla's communication mode is more complex than it first seems.

THE RETURN OF THE TECHNICIAN-BOSS

In the wake of financialization and globalization trends that have swamped the economy since the 1980s, the qualities required to become a major industrial leader today seem more associated with business and political competencies than with technical or sector-based ones. Many leading executives move successfully from one country and/or sector to another, reinvigorating large groups each time thanks to their analytical and managerial abilities. Two exceptions to this pattern are Germany and Japan, which for cultural reasons have maintained the (successful) custom of appointing leaders coming out of their own national industries. Recent trends have reverted to form elsewhere, however, notably in the automotive sector. In France, for instance, Carlos Ghosn at Renault and Carlos Tavarès at Peugeot are bosses recognized for their very detailed knowledge of every topic, something they use to keep up the pressure on their teams. Similarly, at Tesla, Elon Musk is known first and foremost for regularly drilling deeply into a wide variety of topics, ranging from product development to manufacturing. Employees are often stressed by their interactions with Musk due to the challenging questions he always asks and the factual, well-argued and aspirational responses he expects.

LESSONS FROM TESLA

To understand Elon Musk's ability to focus on the technical sides of his business, analysis should start with his childhood. Vance has written that Musk is one of the first 'geeks' to learn to code at a very young age, having always been passionate not only about computers but about physics in general. This explains his 'first principle' belief detailed in the present book's hypermanufacturing chapter. The idea is simple: irrespective of the problem that needs solving, it is always worth returning to underlying physics principles to free oneself from all of the constraints or habits that tend to be found in a given sector or system.

Many of the individuals whom the author met while writing the present book referred to Tesla as an unprofitable bubble. Of course, this raised the question of why so many financial institutions have invested in it – a paradox attesting to a general misunderstanding regarding the company's status. People tend to forget that Tesla is still a start-up. Investment bankers are anything but foolish – what they are betting on is Musk's big picture, which also explains why his communications revolve around this vision, ie Musk's companies aim to accelerate the transition to sustainable energy. In other words, the mission is not solely customer-centric, in which case the product would be a mere means to an end, it is no less than the future of mankind. One key element in this discourse is the global change vision that he offers. Tesla sees itself as a carmaker but also as a player in the energy transition business. The masterplan is to revolutionize the passenger transport business by offering environmentally friendly vehicles that can become autonomous and free up time for customers (with the average American spending up to 12 full days a year in the car). The vehicles Tesla offers will also have below-average maintenance need (around 80 per cent less than for an internal-combustion-engine car); participate in their own interconnected energy network to facilitate energy storage and recycling; and be usable on-demand so that Tesla customers can, if they so desire, rent out their cars when they are not being used. The main consequence of this vision's implementation would be to make road networks and infrastructure obsolete, leading to a beneficial and complete reshaping of urban architecture and lifestyle. Extending the sharing economy to a fleet of clean vehicles would mean fewer cars on the road, less pollution, less noise and therefore a totally reconfigured city.

In addition to a vision that is full and coherent enough to convince a critical mass of talents to follow in his footsteps, Musk also likes talking about radical objectives enabling collaborations federated around a shared mission. One excellent example of this disruptive thinking is the colonization of Mars. Students looking to work for Tesla never have the feeling that they are simply taking on a new role but buying into a plan to save mankind. Hence the impression when walking through the doors at Tesla that this is a tribe of geeks, or maybe a laboratory, and not a factory or R&D centre.

This way of communicating also comes with certain very concrete behaviour that balances the 'story' with the 'making'. Musk is known for getting personally invested in every new project initiated by his many companies, ostensibly because he likes to raise the bar much higher than the sector in question usually does. It is Musk, for instance, who asked his teams to front-run customer needs by developing a product like the Tesla Model S retractable door handle; or who ordered the development of a customized digital screen of a size that did not yet exist on the market but whose central console could fit the very best video games. Everything that Tesla develops must exceed market expectations. The key is perfectionism, even for things that may appear insignificant. This was also one of Steve Jobs's characteristics. Musk's search for exemplarity means that he himself will undertake certain basic tasks where he deems this necessary. Space X's chief engineer recently talked about how Musk himself has systematically taken charge of projects after dismissing managers he thought were doing a poor job. Lastly, Musk is responsible for a large proportion of the company's external communications. He counts 12.1 million Twitter followers, or more than the world's top 10 carmakers combined. His YouTube videos have been seen more than 30 million times.

All in all, the story-making that Elon Musk embodies is a key element in Teslism and one that brings a lot of benefits. Tesla attracts Silicon Valley's top talents in an employment region where competition with pure digital players is cutthroat. It is one of the world's most attractive companies, having received 500,000 unsolicited job applications in 2017 alone. Tesla has helped make its sector attractive again – and it is always worth recalling that the last time a major automaker was created goes back to the very beginning of the 20th century.

Tesla is American students' sixth favourite company, with no other carmaker being in the top 50. Its marketing budget is 40 per cent lower than those of its main rivals. Its customers constitute a community of believers, with most models financed through customer crowdfunding even before the product development phase has been completed (being the pulsed flows principle described in the previous chapter on tentacular traction).

The other side of the coin with this method of communication is a type of management that is highly demanding, with Musk enforcing exacting work rates as well as a highly critical appraisal process. In addition, Tesla's attractiveness means there is a relatively high turnover of senior managers head-hunted by other firms. Tesla staff tend to be less well paid than the local average; they work under huge pressure; and they can lose their jobs quite easily in case of a disagreement – all of which means that new recruit training time is a real bottleneck for the company. Even a management approach rooted in energy and trust has its problems. Some 'good soldiers' can get rapidly promoted but then hit a ceiling in terms of their competencies, notably where industrial efficiency is involved. Yet the company needs expert competencies more than ever – and so has to recruit externally.

QUESTIONS FOR LEADERS

- Have I spent enough time articulating my mission, vision and operational strategy?
- Is my vision sufficiently inspiring and disruptive to attract the best talents and transform my customers into a community?
- Do I have channels (like a company social network) that are sufficiently responsive to share my vision, send messages in very short loops and ingest unfiltered feedback from any employee who wants to take part?
- Am I sufficiently clear in communicating my vision outside of the company, for instance, to local authorities, financial partners or customers?
- Am I myself active enough as a media outlet for the company?
- Do I have a Twitter account and a coherent profile across all social networks, with a regularly scheduled moderation of my online communications?
- Do I spend enough time with frontline teams and participate sufficiently in product development and manufacturing?
- Am I capable of replacing any person leading an innovative project if necessary, and carrying this to fruition?
- Have I received sufficient training in new technologies and the company's core businesses to be able to talk about this with every employee and take the right short-loop decision?
- When I'm out in the field, are my communications about the company's strategy and objectives clear and sufficiently motivational?

ALFI TECHNOLOGIES INTERVIEW
'Story-making is first and foremost a reflection of the CEO's vision and personal drive'

ALFI technologies specializes in engineering, manufacturing handling lines and designing automated production solutions. Since 2009, Yann Jaubert has headed the group, helping to shape and reinvigorate – all of which fits into the vision of 'story-making' he shares here. In a business recovery situation and in a sector undergoing rapid change, Jaubert returns to the main ingredients that allowed him to get some early wins and build up a head start over the competition. Thanks to digitizations and his own strong drive, the image of the group that he has built is steadily improving in both customers and employees' eyes. From the very outset, Jaubert has focused on his daily transformation drive's systemic aspects. 'The most important thing is that we are experiencing these great times together. It would be hard to talk about one memory in particular without telling the whole story.'

HAVING A COMMON, SELF-DEFINED MISSION: THE KEY TO SUCCESS IN THE NEW WORLD
One of the first ingredients in this change was to define a vision that is coherent and transcends simple machinery manufacturing and sales. 'If you explain to young graduates that you make machines and are just looking for a competent automation engineer, no one will come work for you', says Jaubert. In the change narrative that he has devised, three main elements explain his success in attracting new prospects, retaining long-standing customers and recruiting young talent. The first is the definition of a shared destiny, as a company comprised of different entities featuring similar operational modes and missions and as a team whose goal is to inspire by defining the branch's industrial processes of the future. After this, the important thing is to get teams to understand that they are on the road to a digital revolution, even if they 'don't notice much day-in day-out but discover this by word of mouth'. The third and key final ingredient is to front-run technological progress. This happens at ALFI Technologies thanks to a virtual factory concept enabling a much more agile design and production of handling lines, based on an integration of the various businesses comprising this activity and offering over time innovative services so that the company can differentiate itself from competitors working out of low-cost countries.

STORY-MAKING GETS ITS IMPETUS FROM THE LEADER WHO MUST START BY RECEIVING TRAINING HIM/HERSELF IN THE TECHNOLOGIES OF THE FUTURE
Jaubert is convinced that all these efforts are driven by the attitude of the leader, who has to build up a very detailed understanding of the ins and outs of the new technologies so as to be able to choose them intelligently and define the appropriate strategy. Jaubert, for instance, has trained up in artificial intelligence, choosing the start-ups with which his company would work and co-creating with them plans for testing the concept on his company's products. The leader's role is particularly important since the best way to implement a given technology – even for a company's partners – is not always the most obvious one. 'Start-ups have great ideas but rarely a clear vision of the best way of testing them. But not all data is magic. Storing data in and of itself does not suffice. Professional competence remains key to the

development of innovative and relevant solutions.' It is only subsequently that teams enter the loop and get trained. 'It would be wrong to think that success depends on first recruiting 10 data scientists. That's the wrong approach. The first thing to do is understand. Only then can individual concepts be tested.'

FUTURE LEADERS ARE ALSO RESOURCES THAT HELP TO SHAPE
A COMPANY'S ECOSYSTEM

Understanding the technologies of the future and finding the right strategy for testing them is crucial. Before this, however, there needs to be a connection with the company's ecosystem to ensure a continuous supply of new ideas and an ongoing evolution in the company's vision. According to Jaubert, there is no such thing as a corporate 'ecosystem' because this concept has to remain dynamic. Each leader creates their own ecosystem and engages in continuous trend-spotting, often using social media towards this end. 'Yes I consider myself a media figure because I do communicate quite a lot about my vision for the company. Having said that, social media also gives me some great daily feeds. It is an integral part of my role hence my agenda.' ALFI's ecosystem has evolved greatly since the group was founded. 'Ten years ago, I was mainly surrounded by robot manufacturers. Today I'm always out visiting innovative start-ups. It is through these ongoing customer encounters and discussions that we always find new ideas. It's also how we ensure that everyone is in sync with any changes in the ecosystem.'

MOTIVATING TEAMS MEANS HIGHLIGHTING EARLY WINS AS A PROOF
OF CONCEPT (POC)

Ideas are not enough, however, with the first aim of ALFI's strategic plan obviously being to ensure profitability. The teams are very aware of this. One key in motivating them is therefore to publicize concrete outcomes through a POC. In Jaubert's words, 'You need some initial successes before trying to shoot the moon.' ALFI was able, for instance, to find a new prospect (a very big German distribution group) thanks to a virtual factory POC that it had presented at a trade fair. 'This was an incredible success, they came to see us at our stand and then our facilities, where they quickly decided to work with us. We were able to do a very detailed simulation of parcel handling including things like parcels bumping into each other or being dropped. In the end, the Germans ordered a machine. People often talk about Germany as the country of industry 4.0 so our teams were very impressed that we were still able to get these kinds of customers.' Lastly, a critical mass of business drivers must be targeted and persuaded by the plan to bring everyone else along with them.

MODULARITY, DATA AND DIGITAL PLATFORMS – THE MAIN CHALLENGES
IN THE YEARS TO COME

ALFI's success today is largely predicated on digital simulation. This is the platform that allows the company to advance more quickly from the design through the distribution phases, even as it continues to sell innovative services. Jaubert explains how his team evolved from a situation where it usually took months to define and design a working line responsive to customer needs – versus the way things are at present, when the whole process only takes a few weeks and has much lower development costs. Of course, this has been accompanied by a well-thought-out modularization policy that is being deployed step by step without anyone really considering the need for a 'big bang'. In Jaubert's view, each innovation is considered as a plug-in that the company adds on. This makes it possible to do things differently, to move more quickly and to strengthen basic activities like standard components or subsystems. 'It used to take upwards of a year to install a big ERP or customer relationship management (CRM) but that is no longer the case, with things moving so quickly that projects are no longer relevant if they take a year to complete.' The main challenge in the future therefore lies elsewhere and involves the need to build a strong position in data capture and use throughout the industrial machine-manufacturing value chain. 'The sector has big players today, starting with Bosch, GE, Siemens and Dassault Systèmes. It's a war to get into the best possible value redistribution position. Everyone wants to create their own platform and become indispensable.'

THE INDUSTRY OF THE FUTURE WILL BE MORE AGILE AND INTELLIGENT. HUMANS WILL
HAVE A BIG ROLE TO PLAY, ESPECIALLY IN EUROPE

Despite everything, Jaubert keeps his feet on the ground. 'This is not a B2C sector and we should not be fighting the wrong war. There will always be noisy processes and people working in factories running machines. Disruptions don't have to be brutal but should be seen instead as a kind of permanent race to keep ahead of other players and not fall behind because you missed out on an important technology.' In this view, the factory of the future will first and foremost be agile and intelligent, with major implications for human roles. 'There will be a permanent need to train and communicate a vision that teams find inspiring. Things are moving so quickly that changes in competence and culture often struggle to follow changes in technology.' One of ALFI's main satisfactions in recent years has been its success in bringing back previously dissatisfied customers, but also (and above all) restoring teams' pride in being part of a group that is using the digital revolution to rebuild gradually its dynamic and innovative image. The end result is that old Europe seems to have a good shot in the battle for global leadership. 'We do not have the same weapons as US or Asian companies who find it easier to access capital. But we are very strong in traditional businesses and can mobilize our teams' innovation capabilities, which makes a real difference. I strongly believe that the industrial sector is key to today's high-performance Europe.'

Principle 6

Start-up leadership

Instilling a start-up mindset throughout the company to encourage initiative and team development

SUMMARY

- Start-up leadership is both a system and a managerial attitude that enables teams to assume responsibility in a way that will encourage creativity, initiative and collective intelligence.

- Getting teams to take responsibility entails a number of ex ante transformations in the management system as well as new managerial behaviour.

- Tomorrow's leaders will also be coaches assuming a greater number of roles (as cultivators, challengers, accelerators but also doers) than their predecessors did.

- Elon Musk's attitudes are a perfect illustration of these new components of management.

INTRODUCTION TO START-UP LEADERSHIP

The previous chapter analysed story-making and leaders' ability to disseminate extraordinary energy throughout their company during this, the 4th Age of Industry. If the industrial system cannot relay this impetus, however, its energy will be diluted. Start-up leadership responds to this need to create a mirror effect in the field, one representing the ambition and energy that the leader has deployed. It is both a system and a managerial attitude that encourages creativity and initiative by giving greater responsibility to teams while engaging in regular coaching so each individual can develop and be in sync with the company's mission. The idea is to instil into every team a mindset that (similarly to what happens in most successful start-ups) allows people to re-create positive energy around an inspirational project, accompanied by highly flexible feedback mechanisms.

Having a start-up mindset is not enough in industry, however. It is vital to ensure the system's overall coherence so that everyone helps to generate collective intelligence. A 2016 *Industry Week* study shows that industry leaders in the United States consider training in leadership styles, performance monitoring and competence as three key ingredients in a company's attractiveness. This implies a new managerial model (organization, roles and responsibilities, performance indicators, problem-solving methods, agenda and time management) as well as new managerial behaviour based on a renewed form of leadership.

FROM A PYRAMID SYSTEM TO KAIZENOCRACY

Modern industry largely grew up in the early 20th century around big personalities like Édouard Michelin or Henry Ford. They left a mark on their sectors with their extraordinary vision and ability to motivate big teams using 'directive' methods. It was an era of great visionaries who could lead people. The system that they ran was by its very definition pyramidal in nature, with all decisions being taken at the top echelons, engineers developing operational standards and teams of operatives applying them. The Toyota system revolutionized the model from the 1960s onwards. But unlike what the company's direct competitors often believed at the time, the things Toyota was doing that gave it a winning advantage did not involve, per se, just-in-time, standardization or a full range of concrete frontline tools. Success was based instead on managerial methods. The Toyota system relies on bottom-up improvements where all of a company's brains are entrusted with the mission of finding solutions to problems. This would later be known as kaizen or 'continuous improvement'. Managerial roles changed markedly in this system because, on top of normal hierarchical considerations and the need for vision, now there was also a need for team management competencies and for problem-solving processes to which each employee could contribute opportunistically by talking about the problems they faced and by helping to find solutions. The Toyota system involved 'blue collar' staff more or less running the whole of the company. It was rooted in charisma and in a few individuals' leadership abilities – a form of 'kaizenocracy' where everyone participates in improvement efforts.

The main points in common between the 2nd Industrial Revolution's dominant Fordism and its successor's Toyotism was that both systems were very robust and required management behaviour that was coherent with the system's basic principles. More concretely, for example, Toyotism demanded that particular attention be paid to piloting performance and frequent performance reviews at all levels; that managers spend a great deal of time out in the field to see for themselves and that sessions be organized every day for senior managers to get involved in problem solving. These system ingredients let management help frontline teams be the best they could be. But none of this meant much unless managers adopted the right attitude during these rituals, adapting their agenda to ensure systematic participation. They also had to be precise and focus on the here and now, assuming the most adapted and exemplary attitudes during these interactions so as to stimulate the participative dimension, come what may, while developing each team member's ability to nurture the best possible solution.

One notable difference between the two organizational modes is that Fordism remained very self-centred whereas Toyotism manifested much greater openness. This could be explained by the principle of ensuring close collaboration with customers and suppliers to achieve greater standardization among both models and industrial worksites, maximizing the just-in-time system's effectiveness in this way. Even so, technological and professional change forced support functions to specialize more and to operate increasingly in silos. This was a move away from their original mission, which consisted of serving the whole of the production function.

LEADERSHIP IN THE START-UP MODE: A NEW MANAGEMENT SYSTEM

THE START-UP MODE REVOLUTION

Several big changes have raised questions about some or all of the two systems that came into being during the 20th century. First, younger generations no longer feel at home in self-centred superstructures that leave little room for intrapreneurship. The digital boom has also had an effect, with most employees nowadays communicating constantly with the outside world in real time. Power used to be more or less monopolized by oversized support functions or senior management but has now been devolved to frontline teams, with information and data always going from bottom up nowadays. Otherwise, the exponential progress of technology has made it almost impossible to achieve complete control over all the different kinds of know-how held by different value chain participants, however integrated they might be. Managerial systems and behaviours have therefore had to adapt again to further accelerate information exchanges. To take full advantage of these new, faster exchanges, the only solution has been to devolve to frontline teams many of the decisions that management used to take alone. The teams are in permanent real-time contact with the company's customers, suppliers and partners. They are therefore best placed to execute things on a daily basis. Giving operative teams greater responsibility is therefore a major issue in start-up leadership, the goal being to get everyone to appropriate the leader's story-making. For this to happen, however, the measurement system must first undergo a number of transformations.

DIGITIZATION-ACCELERATED PERFORMANCE PILOTING PRACTICES

The first of these transformations involves using digitization to accelerate the transfer and incorporation of performance piloting information. Digitization means that any alerts that teams send to management or to the support function arrive more quickly. Information loops that used to take a day to signal a quality problem or the shutdown of a line can now happen in real time thanks to the Andon digital system. They can also be directed, using settable workflows, to the right person with the right competence at the right decision-making level. Managerial visits to the frontlines (rituals structuring the best systems derived from Toyotism) have also been digitalizing with the huge advantage of enabling real-time responses to the thing being detected; its sharing with different levels and functions; and a definition of the actions or decisions that need to be made. They also ensure that daily field visits are better targeted. Performance reviews (including equally important team motivation exercises) benefit from this both through a visual piloting of indicators coming straight from the frontlines and, above all, from a better tracking of actions using collaborative action-sharing tools.

Lastly, problem solving (an essential activity in any continuous improvement drive) also speeds up because information sent from machines via the internet of things is more precise. On top of this, data analysis is more efficient, leading in turn to team compositions being a better reflection of the particular actions that they are supposed to execute. Teams can be specifically warned and called to action using digital-calendar organization tools. Moreover, digitization also means better information sharing with customers who can be given access to elements relating to changes in orders or requests, alleviating some of the support functions' transactional workload. There is also a better sharing of information with partners or subcontractors, who benefit greatly from a clearer view of the long-term needs that they will be asked to satisfy – being a transparency that enhances overall flow efficiency. Lastly, process management control can be done in a very simple and visual way by applying an electronic kamishibai principle – a visual tablet with green labels on one side and red labels on the other, ensuring that each manager can check in one glance that their routine tasks have been done. Greater confidence in one's control over daily execution makes it easier to align all the actors in an operational chain, whether factories, logistics centres or the entire supply chain.

DEFINING A 4.0 ARCHITECT'S ROLE TO ENSURE OVERALL COHERENCE

The second transformation consists of setting up a coherency supervision structure with management adopting full responsibility for detecting and facilitating the deployment of successful integration solutions. 'Proof of concept' (POC) makes it possible to leverage frontline teams' energy locally and using this to launch innovative tools in something tantamount to kaizen 4.0. The downside is when these efforts are unchannelled – it is hard to replicate them elsewhere. In this case, leadership must avoid system divergences or the creation of units that no longer have anything in common. Nor is digitization a silver bullet. Digitized waste has no more value than handmade waste does. Despite the very large number of process digitizing solutions that exist today, it is not necessarily very easy to find one that is adapted to a given organization or corporate context. Quite the contrary, this is almost impossible without a substantial trend-spotting function always on the lookout for parties that can provide solutions, including ones that involve different teams' piloting, management and collaboration. All of these prerogatives imply the need for a new corporate function, namely Architect 4.0. Setting up this function will be a challenge, however, since the profile associated with it is a hybrid of digital and operational expertise on one hand, with change management, on the other.

SUPPORT FUNCTIONS' EVOLVING ROLE

The third transformation pertains to support functions and their role. Increasing teams' responsibility and autonomy requires a significant change in the role that some of these functions perform. For instance, if frontline teams are allowed to manage themselves using their own recruitment processes, it is hard to see how the end result will automatically fit in with the company's HRM policies – nor the implications for the people currently responsible for recruitment and career development. HR's role has evolved, with the function more geared today towards facilitation than prescription, guaranteeing a kind of operational unity across the organization. A second example might involve machine operators being increasingly connected via digital interfaces to all company systems, giving the operative direct access to information that used to be mediated by the engineering, methods, quality or logistics departments. Today it is possible for this person to subcontract work, for example, or receive information directly from end users – all data flows that were traditionally managed by support-function intermediaries, including departments such as sales administration, supply chain, planning and warehousing.

With this change, the support professions have lost their transactional roles of transmitting information and deploying operational standards. They are now part of the change in competencies, performing technological trend-spotting and above all continually improving the system by adding core functions to address any root problems. Problem detection may have been relatively quick to digitize but a great deal of effort is still needed to accelerate the speed at which these very same problems are resolved. This implies tools and above all changes in competencies and mindsets, notably in support functions like industrial maintenance or IT, quality, methods or engineering – functions whose problem-solving 'expert' and 'support' roles have become a bottleneck for the overall industrial system. If these two changes (in tools and in mindsets) are not carried out in parallel to one another, the functions run a serious risk of overload and discouragement.

ACCESSING RARE COMPETENCIES BY OPENING UP TO THE OUTSIDE
Fourth, companies must be more open than ever before to targeted partnerships. If, for instance, leaders really want to change their approach to become frontline 'coaches' providing 'support', one prerequisite is that they be able to understand the impact of new technologies like collaborative robotization or 3D printing. Continuous training in 'new tech' sectors is now indispensable, either involving existing learning trajectories or more often tech labs that leverage in real time the technologies that are being tested or implemented in the organization, and which offer materials, curriculum and internal shared resources that teams can use for training purposes. At this level, surrounding oneself with good local centres of competence – in conjunction with other

FIGURE 3.15 Start-up leadership system

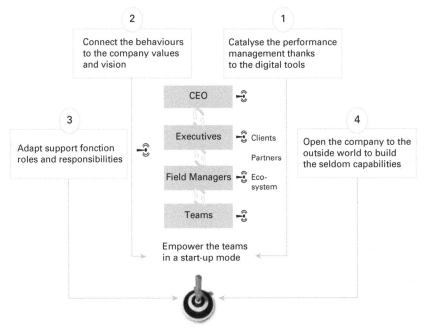

SOURCE OPEO

local companies, branches or institutions – becomes indispensable. Yet another example involving narrowly targeted technologies is the difficulty that some companies have in finding the competencies they need, either internally or in the surrounding ecosystem. One example here would be data scientists, relatively rare resources who have been broadly swept up in the digital sector. Hence the importance of finding partners who can offer ad hoc assistance as part of a long-term relationship that will facilitate the sharing of rare competencies (Figure 3.15).

LEADERSHIP IN A START-UP MODE: NEW MANAGERIAL BEHAVIOUR

It remains that the most important precondition for adapting a management system is the leader's own behaviour. Transitioning from an era of continuous improvement to one of continuous bottom-up piloting necessitates a complete shift in leaders' agendas, attitudes and daily routines. Future leaders will need to combine this role with that of being a coach, wearing at least four more hats than their predecessors did (Figure 3.16).

FIGURE 3.16 Start-up leaders' new kinds of behaviour

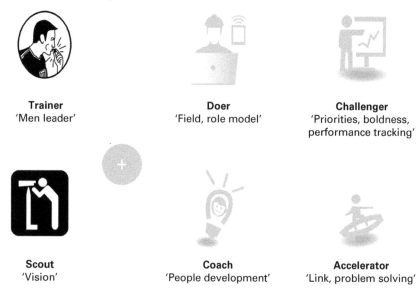

Trainer	**Doer**	**Challenger**
'Men leader'	'Field, role model'	'Priorities, boldness, performance tracking'
Scout	**Coach**	**Accelerator**
'Vision'	'People development'	'Link, problem solving'

SOURCE OPEO

The leader as cultivator   Start-up leaders use coaching to develop the technological competencies of the future as well as the human competencies needed for relational intelligence. They give teams autonomy, allowing them to blossom and reach their full potential. This starts with a frontline mindset where 'testing and learning' is encouraged and where people have the right to make mistakes. It also involves an attitude of curiosity and being supportive in one's daily interactions with teams. As coaches, these leaders use constructive feedback to provide frequent input to the parties they observe during field visits. Towards this end, they allocate time specifically to active observation of each team member, either individually or in groups. This generally amounts to 30 per cent of the time spent in the field. To ensure the relevance of the advice and feedback they give teams, coaches must be up to date with new technologies.

The leader as challenger   Start-up leaders decloister functions by piloting performance while thinking globally but acting locally. They ensure frequent performance reviews of the different value chain professions and functions, taking an active role in the appraisals while pushing all the different functions to come up with win-win solutions. They notably take responsibility for a fluid dissemination of data throughout the system so that every department benefits fully, whether this involves internal data or customer- and partner-related data. They also direct traffic to facilitate different functions' entrepreneurship and transparency to get them to co-construct the best solutions.

The leader as accelerator   Start-up leaders structure and support problem-solving. They are protagonists in the search for problems' root causes and in the implementation of systemic improvements. They ensure that decisions are rooted in facts based on robust data. They scrutinize the problem-solving methodology as well as the speed with which actions are pursued. They work daily to maximize responsiveness and ensure that no decision is ever delayed due to blockages in the performance monitoring system. More prosaically, they are extraordinarily perseverant and expend constant energy fighting sources of inertia.

The leader as doer   More than ever before, start-up leaders must give meaning to local initiatives' global aspects. Digitization is a powerful driver of bottom-up initiatives that can be fulfilling for everyone. At the same time, it increases the risk of divergence from the overall strategy. In addition to story-making, leaders must prove in their daily behaviour that they understand how their vision connects to the things they are getting back from the frontlines; and how this will help these different strands to converge. More concretely, this involves a regular observation of collective behaviour to ensure that corporate values are being correctly translated into teams' daily experiences. On top of this, the transformation programme must be permanently and systematically described to teams in light of its four necessarily interlinked aspects: strategy, technology, CSR and HRM. In the attitudes they display when working out in the field, doer leaders are open and try to educate. Their behaviour is exemplary and they support all local initiatives without compromising their values or losing long-term resilience.

LESSONS FROM TESLA

Elon Musk has the particularity of being a perfect hybrid of the Old World and the New World. As a visionary leader and coach, he always keeps his focus, regardless how bad a crisis gets. This reassures his teams but also investors, even if some of his projects regularly skirt failure, with Musk rarely meeting the timelines that he himself announces. Of course, this has always been less of a priority for him than the idea of energy and movement. Musk is always – always – pushing people to be aspirational.

He often does this by challenging them. Musk never considers 'no' to be a good answer and is incredibly stubborn at demanding results relating, for instance, to product functionality or customer journey – often after going over every detail with a fine-toothed comb. Moreover, it is precisely because he is so incredibly demanding that Tesla has done such a good job at differentiating its products.

As a visionary leader, Musk compensates for this toughness with an ability to inspire his teams. Most people at Tesla say that it is hard working with him because he is always questioning things (thereby embodying his famous first principle). At the same time, they are very proud to work for him, pursue the company mission and make top-notch products.

As a leader-accelerator, Musk has always sought to bring together into his team people from different functions. The IT department, for instance, is totally dispersed throughout his industrial facilities to enable blue- and white-collar staff members to work with one another on a daily basis. At Tesla, welders collaborate with Silicon Valley geeks who graduated from top US universities. This is how Tesla was able to crash-test certify its Model 3 in less than one year, where other carmakers would need up to four years. This ability to shorten time-to-market is bolstered by Musk's personal style and by the constant reference to his first principle. He always challenges the status quo, constraints and timelines that the automotive industry generally considers standard.

As a leader who is also a doer and a cultivator, Musk has always promoted horizontal behaviour. He is constantly walking around Tesla's facilities, visiting anything from the factory floor to the engineering department, preferring direct contact with his teams who he then challenges, day-in day-out. His direct management team is encouraged to behave just as horizontally.

QUESTIONS FOR LEADERS

- Have I spent enough time training myself in 'new tech'? Have I done any training this year in that area?

- Within my perimeter of action, do I detect problems and improvement ideas quickly enough? Do I digitize enough to accelerate information-processing flows?

- Do we digitize enough to visually pilot the shop floor in real time when performing our management rituals?

- Do I do enough to promote mutual assistance and transparency in the daily work that people accomplish at the interfaces of the organization?

- Are the teams trained in multidisciplinary approaches to problem solving?

- Do I do enough to promote a mass use of data, the El Dorado of the 21st century?

- Are my teams quick enough at addressing problems' root causes?

- Do I spend more than 20 per cent of my time in the field observing people and getting constructive feedback? When I am out visiting, do I sometimes forget to be boss and act like a coach?

- Are the company's values easy to transpose into concrete behaviour? Do I take enough time to observe group behaviour and feedback on people's adherence to these values?

- Do I set an example by occasionally running projects myself or getting very deeply involved in challenging teams in relation to a few very specific examples?

THYSSENKRUPP PRESTA FRANCE INTERVIEW
'A nugget of start-up leadership hidden in the bowels of yesterday's industry'

ThyssenKrupp Presta France runs an ultra-modern factory located in the middle of a landscape of coking furnaces and chimney stacks. A global leader in the steering column and rack and pinion business, the company enjoys a top-notch reputation as supplier to the most prestigious brands in Europe and worldwide. As a division of ThyssenKrupp Steering, which equips one out of every four cars in the world, ThyssenKrupp Presta France is a great success story that the general public knows very little about. Nestled in a region mainly known for industrial actions affecting ThyssenKrupp Steering's famous steelmaking neighbour, the factory is a prime example of industrial models' never-ending resilience when managed pragmatically and in a long-term perspective. The site itself has changed many times from its original cold-heading business, before assuming its latest avatar as a high-speed manufacturer of steering columns and racks and pinions, using lines that are ultra-modern and increasingly automated in the three factories where they run. The company employs nearly 1,200 people today and has revenues of more than €600 million. The site is often referred to internally as a benchmark for the whole group due to its efficiency and operational robustness.

A TRANSFORMATION PLAN CENTRING ON LEADERSHIP MODES

Nicolas Jacques, who manages the North factory, was hired by the company in 2004. In the transcript below and together with Mathieu Fiacre (a line supervisor) and Sandrine Trognon (a manufacturing operative), he sets the tone right away by saying that the greatest achievement for a leader is to be questioned by their own team, one example being when staff members come up with a solution different from the one s/he thought superior. Similar sentiments come from Fiacre and Trognon, who both speak about the team accomplishments they remember, with the latter saying, for instance, 'I remember our record on line 1086, when we were all rolling the same direction.'

Speaking about the project's genesis, Jacques says, 'The dynamic here is driven by permanent questioning. We have a plan to transform ourselves into an industry of the future and things are already under way. Three years ago we noticed that our manufacturing lead managers were already working too hard putting out fires, relating poorly to other service areas and had few people promoting continuous improvement. We were convinced that this would undermine the system's long-term sustainability. At first we thought that the problem was merely behavioural. But then we did a diagnostic and realized that even if behaviour could be improved and adapted, the system itself was not where it needed to be for everyone to succeed. Hence our CIBLE ('Target') initiative aimed at harmonizing how lead managers do their job while supporting them in their management role and freeing them up to take an overview.' This is a big issue for a company that wants to become the global reference for steering columns manufacturing by the year 2020. The improvement objectives are ambitious: reducing non-quality by 50 per cent; raising productivity by 5 per cent. All of which translates into concrete objectives affecting Fiacre and Trognon's daily activities. Fiacre feels that, 'The purpose of CIBLE is to solve daily problems more quickly, sorting out even the slightest issue to maximize machine performance and account for everything happening behind the scenes.' Trognon prefers to highlight teams' collaborative objectives. 'For me, CIBLE's first goal is to help people to better analyse the situation in their own team but also in other teams, understanding recurring behaviour and develop a sense of solidarity. It puts everyone on the same page.'

START-UP LEADERSHIP, A PALPABLE SHIFT IN BEHAVIOUR
AND MANAGEMENT SYSTEMS

Jacques feels that the project's main impact has been to make the teams more rigorous while achieving a tangible change in behaviour. 'At first, we tried to inject our values into the daily behaviour we observed. A value like "acting as if you were alone" meant, for instance, respecting the rest of the team by being on time for performance rituals and listening actively to everyone who speaks during the field reviews. Nowadays when I visit the assembly lines, my greatest satisfaction is to see all rituals being executed exactly as they are supposed to be, meaning we can address a greater number of concrete problems.' Beyond this, Jacques also notes that lead managers set their own rules more than ever before. 'Today they're held accountable for their sector when the boss asks about it, deciding action plans autonomously or else in conjunction with the support functions, and even with people from outside the company.' This change in behaviour has been enabled by the management system becoming more 'horizontalized'. 'The bottom-up cascading of piloting responsibilities brings the whole organization under review, particularly people's relationships with support functions like maintenance. Operatives now sense they are part of a team that solves problems; forums have been created where they can express themselves; and lead managers' changed behaviour has positively affected people's willingness to be entrepreneurial.' As for Trognon, she feels much more involved than she used to. 'Nowadays we get answers to all of the little questions that arise regularly, for instance, why a machine breaks down, where the maintenance teams have gone, the next thing that people are planning to do – all of which means that you get less irritated.' Similarly, Trognon also mentions a shift in lead managers' engagement. 'When senior managers engage, things get solved that much quicker.' Fiacre also refers to different functions' expanded collaboration and culture of sharing. 'Today, if we have a problem, it's visible and something that everybody shares in. In the past, things moved much more slowly.' In his view, the best way to measure the impact is through the production unit's basic indicators. 'There has been real improvement in quality, delays and above all in safety.'

FUTURE LEADERS WILL BE A MANAGERIAL JACK OF ALL TRADES AND NO LONGER NECESSARILY A GREAT LEADER OF TROOPS

For Jacques, in the 4th Industrial Revolution it will be extremely important that leaders know where they are taking their troops. 'Leaders who are doers lead in the same way as someone heads an army – riding ahead to scout out any ambushes and keep the troops safe – but also as someone communicating a vision that ensures that people's daily actions are meaningful.' In his view, the main quality for becoming a leader is empathy or 'being able to step into someone else's shoes and predict what is going to happen in most cases...

making it easier for people to accept the things they are being asked to do. In the past, for instance, lead managers struggled to find anyone to volunteer for overtime because they were never very good at explaining why the company needed this. It's much easier today.' Otherwise, Fiacre and Trognon both feel that the company's senior management team is doing its best to behave well and communicate a clear medium-term vision. 'Our big boss tells us every year the things that he expects to happen, which clients we will be serving in the future and the production lines they expect to build.'

For this vision to translate into concrete outcomes, however, the leader must also be able to energize the system. Jacques muses wistfully about how people will procrastinate if given the chance. 'Human beings all tend to rebel against constraints. A team without a leader to energize people and accelerate things may do okay but not excellently. Very few teams have a real ability to work completely autonomously without being challenged.' For Fiacre, leaders serving an accelerator function are first and foremost people who want to solve problems as quickly as possible. 'They must be capable of prioritizing very quickly and escalate any major problems so obstacles can be overcome as soon as possible.' For Trognon, who has other thoughts about what should happen in the long run, making 'acceleration' part of the new leadership models is a natural reflection of how everyone feels after 20 years of a non-stop upheaval. 'In the past we used to simply assemble parts on the production line, now everything is done a lot more quickly so the job has really changed. It is much more interesting, which is good because I enjoy work more when I learn something.' The main issue at this level is a person's mindset. 'I always say that I'm ready to go, to do whatever is needed to succeed, which usually means accepting change. It's the same thing for the bosses.'

There is less of a consensus within the team about personal development, however. In Fiacre's opinion, the company does an enormous amount (and much more than most of its counterparts) to prepare future competencies. 'For instance, we have the ADAPT training programmes, which are really good and use role plays to accustom us to future changes. That must cost the company a pretty penny.' In leaders' cultivator role, they also help teams to question themselves and accept change. Trognon is on board with this trend, although she feels that the main change in the years to come will be the arrival of new generations with a different way of looking at work. For Jacques, on the other hand, cultivating teams is mandatory, not optional. 'I spend around 20 per cent of my time on team development, giving out feedback. But clearly more is needed.' He also has a special way of describing the leader's role in the factory of the future. 'Ultimately I should no longer be indispensable to the system because my role is to help everyone else develop.' Jacques also regrets the site management team's generally insufficient involvement along these lines, be it in terms of time spent or methodology applied. 'It takes a lot of listening and we're not there yet.' His general sense is that the model of a great leader of troops has gone past its sell-by date, if only because the factory of the future will be much more automated hence require experts and leaders who know how to listen, adapt, see the big picture and help teams take the right decisions.

In short, the leaders of the future will be challengers. Still, according to Jacques, 'They will be there to open up people's chakras.' To achieve this, however, it will often be necessary to break down silos while adapting mindsets. 'Some will act as facilitators for their team alone but I think that the leaders of the future will have a global vision and always make the best decision for the company by facilitating everything from A to Z.' Fiacre agrees. 'I had an excellent leader who was able to work with all the support functions, the outside world and his own reporting line to ensure that things advanced.' Trognon avers that a facilitator is also someone's direct manager, being the person who takes responsibility for team problems and helps define the best compromise allowing the company to progress. Jacques ends the discussion by talking about one of the things he finds most satisfying in the project. 'We are now dealing with problems where they are supposed to be handled, discussing them at the right level.' To do this, however, people have had to abandon certain responsibilities and delegate them to their teams. 'The authoritarian leader is finished. The managers we need today will have responsibilities but not wield any real power. Power is obsolete.'

All three are optimistic about the future of industry. Trognon has seen so much change in her time that she simply predicts, 'We will continue to adapt.' Fiacre thinks that in 20 years there will be screens everywhere but also humans doing the thinking. 'We will be thinking robots.' Jacques speaks about factories having flatter reporting lines but also being reinforced due to new technical competencies that are less labour intensive – and where his own role may no longer have much meaning. 'There will be fewer managers leading the troops since that won't make much sense any more. Yes, I know, I'm talking about my own job! But there will be other things for me to do so I'm not worried.'

Principle 7

Human and machine learning
Continuous training and short-loop learning to marry human intelligence with machine intelligence day-in day-out

SUMMARY

- The intelligence of an industrial system is always a collective adventure driven by people's ability to develop, to capitalize quickly upon opportunities and to optimize machinery. The human and machine learning construct includes all these dimensions.

- Learning must be lifelong, since its regulating role has become increasingly important in industrial organizations seeking overall coherence and, towards that end, transforming their training methods.

- 'Testing and learning' methods help produce a mindset where it becomes possible to use short loops to learn and capitalize on things quickly and collectively.

- One of Tesla's greatest strengths is its ability to learn from its mistakes and change direction quickly to avoid running into walls or any other unexpected obstacles.

INTRODUCTION TO HUMAN AND MACHINE LEARNING

The previous chapter showed that start-up leadership is necessary to create system disruption by encouraging initiative. It remains that the intelligence of an industrial system will always be a collective adventure based on people's ability to develop, leverage advantages quickly and optimize machinery to accelerate everything that might be automated. This is summarized in the concept of human and machine learning (Figure 3.17). In an environment that is highly geared towards artificial intelligence, machines are omnipresent and cause deep transformations in peoples' way of working, their roles and the competencies they need in order to be successful. Just as software products improve throughout their lifetime, humans must learn to learn continuously. This is because the role they perform as regulators has become increasingly crucial to industrial organizations' overall coherence. The corollary of this new approach to human development in companies is the right

FIGURE 3.17 Human and machine learning, the reactor core

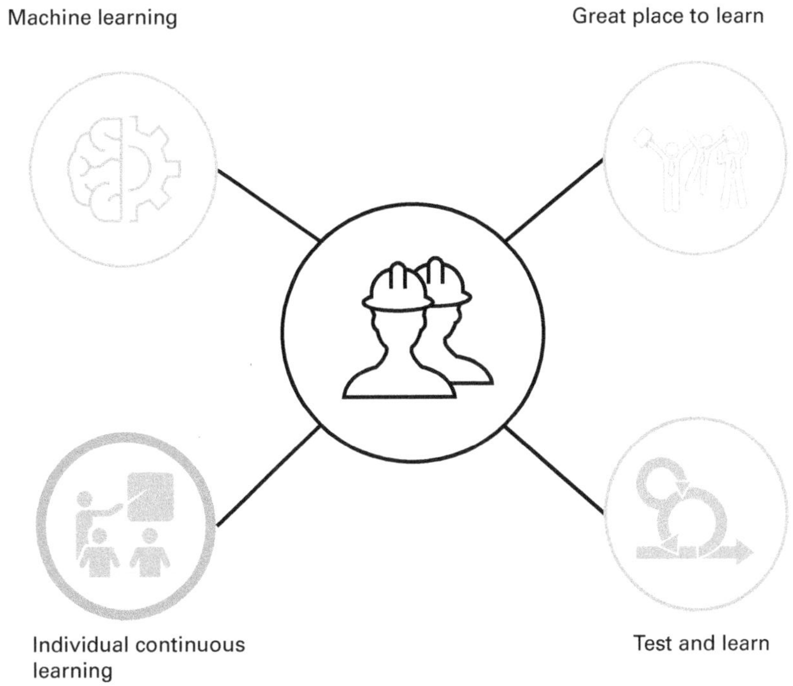

Machine learning   Great place to learn

Individual continuous   Test and learn
learning

SOURCE OPEO

to make mistakes, given the imperative of moving quickly and also because action constitutes in and of itself a great source of learning. This is a major change calling for a mindset that completely disrupts previous models. According to a 2017 Dell and Institute for the Future study, 85 per cent of all jobs in 2030 have yet to exist. A similarly surprising statistic shows that 74 per cent of today's industrial companies consider themselves poorly or not at all equipped in data analysis, despite everyone agreeing that this is a paramount competence (PwC, 2016). All in all, the challenge is enormous.

THE LINK BETWEEN HUMANS AND WORK CHANGES WITH EACH INDUSTRIAL REVOLUTION

Working methods have evolved dramatically from one industrial revolution to the next. With the introduction of mechanization in the late 18th century, machines gradually appeared in factories, making simple laborious tasks easier but also progressively alienating workers who were being steadily subjugated by machine speeds imposing high work rates. The 2nd Industrial

Revolution saw the rise of Taylorism and more specifically the specialization of tasks. Productivity gains were impressive but work became cyclical hence much more repetitive. Work organization was largely dictated by engineers who defined product ranges and task lists, with frontline teams being paid to apply these precepts, often on a one-piece flow basis. In other words, improvement efforts at the time tended to be top down. It was an era famous for having a 'foreperson' who was there to ensure that a very large mass of people were able to meet their daily production targets.

This pyramid was then turned upside down with the 3rd Industrial Revolution, where the system largely revolved around frontline technicians' competence and ability to react quickly and improve processes continuously. The aim for each employee was no longer to simply produce but also to improve things. The arrival of robots and industrial IT also helped spark the early automation of repetitive and arduous tasks in the production area and in certain support functions. Lastly, polyvalence spread, helping the system to adapt to fluctuations in market demand.

LIFELONG LEARNING

In the 4th Age of Industry, the exponential nature of progress will provide great impetus for a new relationship between humans and work. This will have numerous practical consequences in the industrial sphere in terms of the professions that people exercise and the ongoing development of their competencies – largely because of the need to train permanently to keep abreast with this exponential and combinatory rate of progress. In turn, this will cause major changes in the systems used to manage people and human know-how. Initial training is often insufficient when market needs change so quickly that the academic curriculum cannot keep up. Most lighthouses for the industry of the future have therefore started to build their own tech labs to help teams gain familiarity with the new technologies and train in them. With lifelong learning, classroom attendance – a mainstay of traditional learning – no longer suffices to cover the full spectrum of know-how that people must appropriate. Digitization accelerates learning trajectories via remote e-learning or MOOC tools that can be used to access contents prepared by top experts while accelerating training in basic gestures and task lists thanks to video and virtual reality.

This new form of learning also comes with new forms of team appraisal. Traditional individual evaluations based on performance objectives are being supplemented or replaced nowadays by competence-based evaluation systems. Beyond these new competencies, new professions have also started to emerge, often resulting from a hybridization of traditional professions with new professions coming out of the world of digital industrial robotics. One concrete example involving a factory characterized by its highly automated product throughput system is the way that internal logistics are increasingly being managed by intelligent machines directly connected to the production planning system and therefore 'on-line' with the process. Stacker cranes in logistics warehouses, AGVs transferring products from warehouse to the shop floor, automated conveyor belts moving product along the assembly line, forklifts located underneath machines to automate loading tasks and save time... Production and logistics are functions that can be hybridized, with former warehouse staff or forklift operators now working as equipment controllers. The competence that companies are looking for is no longer human dexterity but the ability to understand industrial planning, manage flows, repair automation problems, dialogue with technological solution providers, etc. The logistics role has been transformed into a hybrid of production, planning, maintenance and industrial IT systems.

A GREAT PLACE TO LEARN

Despite the enthusiasm sparked by this professional evolution, a number of problems have also arisen, notably in attracting the increasingly expert hence rare talents capable of mastering cutting-edge technologies. Companies either operate in dynamic zones characterized by severe competition with other players (notably ones operating in non-industrial sectors) or else they do not, in which case they may simply lack the talent needed for certain competencies.

To succeed in this context, it is paramount to have a good support system comprised either of local institutions whose help will be crucial in finding useful partners and in supporting competence development, or else an ecosystem comprised of partners, customers and colleagues operating within the same branch, all of whom will be precious in developing the innovative solutions of the future while sharing rare resources. From a team perspective, it is essential to make people feel safe in showing initiative in a world where there are many things to be afraid of. Work is becoming increasingly 'liquid' and with growing volatility in markets and competencies there is a temptation to only work on-demand to expressed specifications, hence to build ultra-flexible systems whose adjustment variable is their capacity, calculated in terms of time and industrial teams' competence. So-called extended social dialogue has become a necessity and a true key success factor.

This new way of conceptualizing social connections transcends the business framework alone since it seeks harmonization and win-win operational modes at the level of the ecosystem as a whole, and/or the particular industrial branch concerned. Many initiatives have arisen with a view towards mutualizing this market volatility risk. These include multi-company learning programmes; having individual working times calculated by (and divided between) two companies operating in markets characterized by countercyclical seasonality; the mutualization of competence centres or tech labs; branch-wide CSR agreements, etc. Nowadays, discussions about modes of work no longer only happen within one professional branch. The system has been decentralized and organized to be much more agile depending on geographic location, the branch and the profession. In addition to this extended social dialogue, the lighthouses of the industry of the future also have in common that everyone is thinking deeply about the roles that humans are meant to play in the system. This starts with the organization of work space, being undoubtedly the element that is most tangible for teams in their daily activities. Ideas here include well-tended relaxation hives, the organization of extra-professional leisure activities (like after-work events or sports), good-quality catering, etc. Similarly, shared workspaces are being conceptualized as living spaces, which has implications for things like lighting, acoustics and how people move around their place of work.

MACHINE LEARNING: HYBRIDIZING WITH MACHINES

So-called 'connected devices' are omnipresent nowadays, including in factories. Like the smartphone – the emblem of modern living – frontline operatives are equipped with a large number of systems and machines. These can be more or less agile and mobile, supporting people in their daily jobs and training them to be better at anticipating, planning and executing work, without overly fatiguing themselves. The end result is an improvement in manufacturing, maintenance and logistics tasks. Examples of these kinds of systems or machines include virtual reality, which accelerates training 'in an online and risk-free' environment; augmented reality, which anticipates machine movements in advanced programmes; advanced planning interfaces that bring planning as close as possible to frontline realities by integrating all production constraints (thereby offering customers agile responses); intelligent robots and exo-skeletons capable of automating repetitive or arduous manufacturing and logistics tasks; and 3D printing, which reduces the number of manufacturing phases, thereby accelerating the process without any additional efforts having to be made.

Lastly, cutting-edge data analysis methods mean that the whole system can be 'self-learning', with thousands of setting values connecting to a given outcome and encouraging a permanent search for optimal system performance. Learning to work differently using all these tools will be a major challenge in the years to come. Those who succeed will have a competitive advantage by being better at exploiting data and by making sure that their systems are actually self-learning. Machines and humans will no longer compete in the same fields of excellence. Machines will always be better than humans in calculating or doing repetitive tasks. Humans, however, have a greater capacity for empathy, creativity, complex multi-actor problem solving or simply making deeper use of human senses. System optimization will therefore come from complementarity between the two forms of excellence.

TESTING AND LEARNING, A MINDSET FOR LEARNING AND BENEFITING COLLECTIVELY

Teamwork and responsiveness are the modes that will be most impacted by these new challenges, especially in a use-based economy. End users will expect that this permanent novelty makes their lives easier, something that will be more important to them than taking possession of statutory goods. This will make time-to-market even more important than it was in the era of 'right first time'. The 'digital natives' philosophy says that customers are the best people to get involved in the development process to ensure that products correspond exactly to what they want. Modern approaches like 'design thinking' are entirely based on empathy with final users, ie not making decisions in their stead but asking them questions as directly as possible. What is relatively straightforward in the pure digital world – to wit, rapid launches of beta versions that can be subsequently improved – is much more complicated in physical product development.

To respond to this dual need for rapid time-to-market while adapting to customer preferences, the 'testing and learning' method has progressively entered the world of industry through two separate doors. The first involves product innovation where teams try different agile work methods in order to launch a prototype and 'zero' series as quickly as possible, even as the ultimate improvements are being planned together with end users. The second door is the factory where teams accustomed to continuous improvement methods, like kaizen, have discovered something analogous with 'testing and learning', an approach also driven by gradual improvements but this time involving a wider circle of actors – if only because it is almost impossible to test anything in the New World without including at least one person from IT or engineering. The great advantage of 'testing and learning' is that it makes frontline teams take the initiative for launching new ideas. Each unit, if it so desires and where this is deemed useful, has the power to test potential innovative solutions. The risk is divergence within the system, with everyone launching their own innovations by themselves. Hence the need for coordination and traffic control overseeing all these innovations. This will come from a function assuming the role of transformation architect, as noted in the previous chapter on start-up leadership.

LESSONS FROM TESLA

Finding funding for the automotive market – which is already mature and saturated, and where financial returns are expected to be low – can be very difficult. To overcome this obstacle in an environment requiring frequent investment in R&D and new models, Elon Musk has used his company's attractiveness to detect new talent and recruit particularly motivated teams ready to work flat out on inspiring projects while undertaking continuous training to stay ahead of the competition. According to Musk, this makes it possible to internalize innovations that many other large carmakers devolve to their main suppliers. At Tesla, it is Musk's 'story-making' that drives talent recruitment efforts. Everyone can contribute to a greater, more meaningful cause – and the ancillary professional benefits are legion. For instance, three-quarters of the recruitment website for the Gigafactory – where Tesla manufactures its batteries – highlights the aspirations underpinning the project plus the fact that the facilities are located in a great area offering wonderful amenities for young persons or families thinking of moving there. Similarly, Tesla facilities are designed to offer workers living spaces that feel like labs, not factories. Walls and floors are painted white, there are green plants everywhere, cafeterias are attractive, all the different functions and management levels share the same working spaces, production floors have an open-space design, giant digital screens are deployed everywhere, the food truck service is great and the patios are cosy. Everything is done to make people feel that this is a 'great place to learn'.

The human–machine relationship is deeply embedded in Tesla's DNA, which is first and foremost a software company that manufactures vehicles. There is a particular focus on newer production lines replacing manual operations with robots or using mechanization to make human labour easier. Similarly, the R&D department's digital simulation tools operate at 100 per cent of their potential to shorten development times, notably via crash test simulations or rapid prototyping phases. Digitization is used to help humans enhance their know-how.

As for learning itself, Elon Musk has encouraged his teams to always apply 'testing and learning', irrespective of any obstacles, by doing everything possible to accelerate innovation loops. He recently demonstrated again, if need be, to what extent he considers learning speed paramount. Notwithstanding an initial strategy that consisted of massively automating the Model 3 production line to rapidly ramp up output and dramatically decrease the automotive sector's customary 'takt time' (the gap between two vehicles coming off the line), Musk reversed himself after only a few months because he felt that the line was not reliable enough and because his teams were unable to maintain the 2,500 unit weekly output rate he had set for the month of May 2018. Instead of being pig-headed about it, he simply reverted to more manual operations. What was remarkable about this story is the speed at which Musk moved (a total of three weeks whereas most carmakers would have probably taken several months to react) as well as his personal involvement before the actual decision was taken. According to staff members, Musk worked night and day for three months on the production floor analysing the problems that frontline operatives faced. This helped him to energize everyone and get them on board with his decision. The following month, Musk went as far as to create a third line underneath a 'tent', eliminating 300 out of the car bodies' 5,000 welding points, despite series production having already been started a few months previous. By the end of the month, he hit his target of 5,000 vehicles per week (New York Times, 2018). No other carmaker had ever tried to do this, if only because the sector's paradigm had always tended to promote stability as a basic principle. The key for Musk, on the other hand, was the willingness to take a risk, be responsive and learn quickly, without any dogma at any level. During this entire period he was unsurprisingly criticized by many observers. But most were wrong about the real lesson to take from this episode (Liker, 2018). The point was not to choose between lean manufacturing (more focused on human labour) and hyper-manufacturing (more focused on automation), but to understand that in the New World the real currency is learning, allowing oneself to think disruptively while being pragmatic and leveraging opportunities as quickly as possible.

QUESTIONS FOR LEADERS

- Do my frontline teams know how to collaborate with machines or robots? Have I personally tested the piloting of a collaborative robot (cobot)?

- Do I put enough energy and investment in collaborative digital solutions that facilitate, accelerate and/or decloister the work that teams do?

- Are there new professions that I should expect to arise over the next few years and organize training programmes or adapt our recruitment?

- Do I give my teams sufficient encouragement to develop early solutions to problems and improve them en route? Do I work on this myself from time to time?

- Am I sufficiently connected to my ecosystem (partners, industrial colleagues, local institutions, competitors, branch, schools and universities, etc) to develop and share training paths building the competencies of the future?

- Over the past year, has every member of my team trained in digitization or another new technology?

- Does everyone in the company have a formalized continuous learning programme?

- Do I regularly encourage teams to train in different innovative tools (MOOC, e-learning, etc) whenever feasible?

- Do our end-of-year appraisals include competence appropriation evaluation?

- Do I spend as much energy defining pleasant work and leisure spaces as I spend on efficiency processes?

BOSCH INTERVIEW

'A 4.0 project centred on human and machine learning'

Bosch's Rodez site is part of this famous automotive equipment supplier's mobility division. Specialized in diesel-engine injector manufacturing, the site – with around 1,600 employees – has undergone major changes in an attempt to develop its future plans. The Head of Digital Development Solutions, Grégory Brouillet, explains how the 'industry 4.0' solution discussed earlier in the book – and which the group did in fact initiate – supports future transformations. Brouillet has a particular technical background, having joined the company very young and continuing to train up all throughout his career.

A great enthusiast for new challenges, it is only natural that he accepted the offer made to him in 2014 to promote the sector's 'Maintenance 4.0' initiative. Operating in a group that has a relatively mature vision of technological issues, Brouillet agreed to deliver his vision of 'humans and learning', a key factor in the approach's success.

ANY VISION FOCUSING ON RETURN ON INVESTMENT (ROI) ALONE
IS BOUND TO FAIL

Surprisingly, Brouillet talks about the aims of his '4.0' site maintenance project in terms of its being 'very people-focused, because we want to make things simpler for everyone'. Management is clearly looking to improve efficiency in general, specifically by enhancing overall equipment efficiency (OEE). This would be impossible to achieve, however, if the approach were not people-centric. According to Brouillet, a top-down culture shock is key to starting the process. 'Our CEO is not only a strong believer in this way of doing things but even more importantly has pushed a change dynamic that goes well past simple financial aspirations like a quick return on investment.' The main issue locally, beyond performance and working conditions, is how to bolster the site's reputation vis-à-vis the rest of the group. One of Brouillet's great satisfactions is fielding requests from colleagues on other sites, some of which may be bigger than Rodez yet are interested by the solutions it develops or tests.

SIMPLE MARCHING ORDERS FROM THE CEO: 'TRAIN, TRAIN, TRAIN'

Communications and training have been crucial to the initiative's launch. They take time to organize but are indispensable, with Brouillet highlighting one of the traditional fears associated with industry 4.0, namely that humans will be replaced by robots. 'I'd always been convinced that this is a win-win proposition. We have 71 robots in operation and they help us to maintain our activity levels, not kill them off. But we have to be able to explain this using language that our frontline staff finds credible.' Nor is communication by itself enough. The Bosch group CEO – with his mantra of 'train, train and train' – and the local 4.0 initiative pilot spend a great deal of time training all 1,600 people on-site, getting everyone to think about the new direction, especially given plans to build a 4.0 mini assembly line training teams specifically in the operating procedures of the future.

TESTING AND LEARNING, A DISRUPTIVE MINDSET

Training is also necessary to understand the new technologies and ease their implementation, which could be very challenging since they are so different from what happened in the past. The idea here is to use the digital world's 'testing and learning' method, which consists of creating very short loops to speed up iterations even before a perfect solution has been developed. This requires a very specific mindset, accepting the possibility of failure and the fact that solutions are never perfect. In Brouillet's view, 'Testing and learning have become a little harder given how accustomed technicians got to doing big, chunky things that were expensive but long-lasting.'

USING DESIGN THINKING TO INTEGRATE USERS
One way to overcome this obstacle is to get end users involved in solutions very early on. Brouillet explains that people sometimes come 'off' the production line for a few weeks in order to immerse in the project team. 'They are there to speak on behalf of the end user, which makes everything more relevant and means you can iterate very quickly and lose much less time.' The aim is to get the whole site to empathize with the final user – a key precept in design-thinking methodology, albeit one that Brouillet feels 'has yet to break through', with much more having to be done to fully incorporate users' needs and ideas as early as possible in the solutions. Hence the importance of getting workers to accept the new tools.

QUICK CHANGES IN EXISTING PROFESSIONS RATHER THAN NEW PROFESSIONS
Brouillet does not think that the factory professions have been revolutionized so far. Instead, he thinks they are evolving, a trend he wants to support. The main goal at this level is to homogenize as much as possible the solutions being proposed for the different production lines and professions, because this lets people move from one environment to another seamlessly and with maximum agility. Hence the need to limit the number of concepts being developed while channelling the innovations. 'Operatives used to push buttons to run a machine. Nowadays they have a touchscreen tablet or smartphone. In the future they will probably have augmented reality visors. It will take a while to happen, especially if nothing is done beforehand to define the solutions that have to be tested.'

PROJECT 4.0, A WAY TO CONQUER MARKETS WHILE CREATING MORE OPENNESS
TO THE OUTSIDE WORLD
In addition to aspects like reputation, efficiency and working conditions, Brouillet also sees the project as an opportunity for the site to strengthen its bonds with its ecosystem, notably the local Mécanique Valley automotive and aeronautics clusters. The site is fairly isolated, '200 kilometres from anywhere'. The idea of opening up internally developed training programmes to other local companies has traction. Generally, site managers are very pragmatic and

interested in any service ideas that might come out of the approach, whether this involves training or selling the solutions that teams have developed. The site could easily be viewed as a trailblazer in the hybridization of the industrial and service worlds, creating significant opportunities for new growth. Brouillet cites the example of a successful start-up, mobility work, a kind of social network for maintenance specialists created by an intern working at the time for an industrial company. 'If this young man was able to develop a platform of this sort, that means it is possible to do fantastic things that will get people to question themselves. In the end, the whole of the industrial sector will benefit.'

SCHMIDT GROUP INTERVIEW
Automation and man's role in industry

Schmidt Groupe is one of the most advanced middle-size companies in digitization and automation for a so called 'traditional business'. Anne Leitzgen, President, launched the project 10 years ago to manufacture a top-quality kitchen in one day and deliver it 10 days later. In this project, the seller creates a 'virtual' kitchen with the client; the order is then handled by exchanging computer data; manufacturing is carried out by robots.

Therefore, a standard order can be made without almost any human intervention. Despite the use of robots, the Schmidt Groupe makes sure that its employees are not overlooked: not only have they managed to keep their jobs, but they have also become operators of complex installations. This project required time and a great deal of training and trust, but it was made easier by the fact that the company is family-owned.

The Cuisines Schmidt brand was created in 1989; then a second brand, Cuisinella, was launched in 1992, which was aimed at younger clients with a smaller budget. 'After 2004, we specialized in the production of custom-made furniture for every room. At the present time, digitization allows us to make considerable progress with this approach', says Anne Leitzgen.

The Schmidt Groupe is currently the leading manufacturer of kitchens in France, and number six in Europe. It has a turnover of €470 million. It has five production sites covering a total of 160,000 square metres (including one in Germany and four in Alsace), and employs 1,500 people. The investment has grown from €20 million in the past few years to €40 million in 2016, and should reach €60–80 million in the near future. These sums cover industrial investment and also the development of brands and digital business, and investments for consumers and industrial sites. In 2014, the group made a joint venture with Suofeiya in China.

In this age of the internet and social networks, everything is visible, and if a company wants to continue to exist, it has to be recognized as the best in its sector. This is why Schmidt Group aims to become in 2025 the group with the most preferred European brands in terms of custom-made home planning.

The programme 'Consumer Connect', launched in 2015, aims to coordinate all the digital initiatives to improve the customer experience. 'Originally this experience began when the consumer walked into one of our shops. Nowadays it begins much earlier, when a person says "I'd like a new kitchen", and starts looking on the internet. It is important that we attract this client to our brand and then convince him or her that if they walk into one of our shops they will have a much more interesting experience with us than with any of our competitors.'

The quality of this experience is based on the quality of the relationship. People often make the distinction between business to business (B2B) and business to consumer (B2C). At Schmidt Group, they prefer talking about 'H to H', human to human. Anne Leitzgen explained: 'When a customer buys a kitchen from us, he or she is helped by a pleasant and competent salesperson. In order for a salesperson to have these qualities, their boss must also be pleasant and competent. We too have to be pleasant and competent with their boss. Thus, the entire relationship is about quality. This is the most important factor for the relationship to be long-lasting because, having installed the client's kitchen, our hope is that we could also sell him or her a walk-in closet or a bookcase in the future.'

In practical terms, when a customer visits the company's website, he or she is asked if they would like to create their own account in which they will be able to start putting down ideas about their dream project. The website enables the sales staff to access all the work the customer has done on his or her online account, with the customer's consent. Consequently, the sales staff are immediately able to make suggestions adapted to the customer's budget and taste. For example, if the sales staff notice that the customer has been looking mainly at modern white kitchens, they will not suggest considering a country-style kitchen.

The customer will also be able to make an appointment online, which will help the sales staff to prepare the meeting. Staff can use various ways of enhancing the customer's project, particularly by presenting him or her with a 3D version of their future kitchen. Previously the customer used 3D glasses, but the sales staff explained that paradoxically this did not help 'close the deal' and even tended to lessen sales. This illustrates the fact that technology is of no interest in itself if it does not bring any value to the customer or the sales staff.

Once the quotation has been made and the kitchen ordered, the customer can track the manufacture of his or her kitchen online and know when it will leave the factory and be delivered to their address.

At the end of the process, the customer is asked if he or she wants to stay in touch with the brand, talk about it to their own social network, be invited to meetings (for example, to cooking lessons organized in the shops), or even to introduce their friends. Of course, the brand also respects the choice of the customers who would rather not hear from the company again once their kitchen is installed.

Digitalization has greatly changed almost all the professional activities within the company, from marketing and sales to production.

MARKETING, SALES AND COMMUNICATION: GOING DIGITAL

First, digitalization has transformed the activity of the sales staff. It also changed the way in which the company communicates about its products. 'We have moved from communication marketing (making the brand known in order to encourage consumers to walk into our shops) to digital marketing (determining the support to be used in order to sell products; the management of our customers' opinions; and activity on social networks). We have also moved from one "single-channel" sales relationship to a "multi-channel" sales relationship, which raises new questions such as: To whom does the prospective client "belong"? Does he "belong" to us via our website, or the shop he visited? What did he buy on the website? What did he buy in the shop?'

MANAGEMENT OF DATA

The digitalization process also transforms the way in which data is managed. Originally the company had several decentralized databases. The emergence of the internet forced them to create a centralized database both for products and for consumers. This change is also qualitative: the company must progress from a very technical database essentially designed for salespeople, to a presentation of products aimed at consumers with relevant content and pictures.

The choice of made-to-order production and customized manufacturing involves a considerable volume of data. Schmidt Group never make the same kitchen twice, and they have no stock. All the components are produced specially for each customer, some in two hours and others in several days (such as lacquered fronts, which require a great deal of time to dry). All the various components come from different factories and must arrive together on the loading dock at a specific time. With approximately 1,450 orders per day, this represents 4,000 pieces of furniture, 18,000 parcels and, in total, 5 million pieces of information to exchange daily in order to ensure that the information arrives at the right time and in the right place so that the entire operation runs smoothly. In fact, Schmidt Group's profession is no longer the manufacture of furniture, but the management of logistics associated with information and components.

Nonetheless, diversity is still a risk. The company has to make sure that there is a balance between diversity that earns money and diversity that costs money.

AUTOMATION OF PRODUCTION

Automating a large part of manufacturing enables not only to control quality, but also to limit the burden of work, and to maintain ageing staff in their jobs by reducing their workload both physically and mentally.

Above all, automation allows the company to avoid relocation. Knowing that the direct wage share only represents 7 per cent of the turnover, it is not in its interest to delocalize production to countries with lower costs, especially since the jobs require more and more qualifications. In the past, people used to say to children, 'If you do not study hard at school, you will have to go and work in a factory!' Today, it would be nonsense: industrial jobs require increasing degrees of skill. But the company supports the people who have been there for a long time so that they can make progress and keep their jobs.

Nonetheless, it is true that automation generally destroys jobs. Fortunately, the company has grown, and so can continue to create jobs even though Schmidt is increasingly resorting to the use of robots. In 2009, a 23,000 square-metre factory was opened that employed 200 people; 70 in the workshops and 130 in support sectors. Today, the factory that the group is currently building will employ only 120 people for a comparable volume of production.

THE CORPORATE CULTURE: 'BE SCHMIDT'

Schmidt Group promotes both the art of living for customers in their homes and also its own art of living within the company. A few years ago, with a group of willing colleagues, they laid out the 'Be Schmidt' company culture. This is represented by a five-pointed star with the idea of pleasure in the middle. The five points of the star represent five characteristics that contribute to the pleasure of working together. These are kindness, responsibility, cooperation, trust and flexibility. Of course, working at Schmidt does not mean that everyone does enjoyable things every day, but that what each worker does is relevant and meaningful. 'About 10 years ago, when I started talking about this concept of pleasure, people often replied "Industry isn't a caring environment!" Today, this concept is starting to gain ground, and many people agree that pleasure is what drives us, and that working in industry can be a source of pleasure', says Anne Leitzgen.

Additionally, the digital transformation of the company can only be successful if all the employees 'give their best', in other words that they are able to take initiatives and decisions at all levels of the company and assume those responsibilities. On the other hand, this implies that the management must trust them, and consequently managers must allow their teams to test new ideas knowing that mistakes may be made. 'With digitalization, companies are going to undergo major changes, and it is crucial that the workforce seizes this opportunity and incorporate these changes', says Anne Leitzgen to conclude.

SOURCE Report by Elisabeth Bourguinat. Translation by Rachel Marlin. Released in May 2017. With kind permission of Ecole de Paris du management: https://www.ecole.org/fr/seance/1195-automatiser-en-renforcant-le-role-de-l-homme

Note

1   Physical logistics, which makes it possible to move parts around both within factories and externally. Traditionally done using forklifts, nowadays this is often automated.

04

Onwards and upwards for the 4th age of industry

SUMMARY

- We would be wrong to believe that we still have time to adapt. The 4th Industrial Revolution is already a reality.

- The seven dimensions of the Tesla Way constitute an integrated system: if one were to go missing, the system itself would lose in efficiency, become unbalanced and risk its long-term survival, which is why the term 'model' is appropriate here.

- The model is not specific to Tesla. It is already relevant to a number of companies and may serve one day to inspire many further still.

The 4th Industrial Revolution is already here

It would be wrong to believe that there is still time for all these things to play out. As evidenced by a number of observations and projects, the 4th Industrial Revolution is already under way.

The first thing to note at this level is the density of connections worldwide, something that materializes relatively precisely in the volume of data being generated and exploited. Idate estimated in a 2017 report that the quantity of connected devices in the world will surpass 36 billion by the year 2030, versus 4 billion in 2010 and 15 billion today in 2018. This exponential growth in a leading data catalyst is clearly a good explanation for another telling statistic relating to the amount of data available in the world. International Data Corporation (IDC) has estimated that required storage capacities will rise from 20 Zettaoctets in 2018 to 44 in 2020 and 163 in 2025, versus 4.4 Zettaoctets in 2013. Volumes are rising so rapidly that 90 per cent of all data available at present is less than two years old, with the world generating each and every day in 2018 as much data as mankind produced between the dawn of time and the year 2003.

The second observation relates to the exponential rise in actual or planned investments in future technologies, attesting to the business world's enthusiasm for this field. In robotics, for instance, global investments were US $7.4 billion in the year 2000. By 2015, the number was $26.9 billion, with $66.9 billion projected by 2025 (BCG, 2015).

Hyper-concentration has turned into tangible and measurable data in both the economic and geographic sense of the term. A few good examples of this can be found in Pierre Veltz (2017).

At present, just 10 economic clusters account for 40 per cent of global GDP and 75 per cent of global R&D. The GDP of the cities of New York and Tokyo would be the same as Spain and Sweden were they independent.

Value creation analysis is just as instructive at the product level, starting with the iconic iPhone. One-third of all jobs associated with this product are located in the United States, meaning two-thirds are elsewhere (mainly China). Yet two-thirds of the total wages paid in this branch go to the United States, with China only accounting for 3 per cent of the total.

The magnitude and speed of these phenomena make it indispensable for all industrial companies to consider their business models, value creation drivers and overall industrial systems. This is especially true seeing as everyone is talking everywhere about how to embed small and medium-sized companies' productive fabric into the movement – an idea for which analysis of the Tesla model can be a great source of inspiration.

Teslism and its three concentric circles: a systemic model

Teslism's seven dimensions form a coherent and indivisible entity. If one dimension were to go missing, the system would become inefficient and unbalanced, risking its long-term survival. The systemic dimension is largely predicated on the three concentric circles that characterize it (Figure 4.1).

Human and machine learning is Teslism's core dimension. Industrial systems' performance in this 4th Age of Industry mainly depends on the connection between their heart and backbone. Humans are more central to

FIGURE 4.1 The three circles model

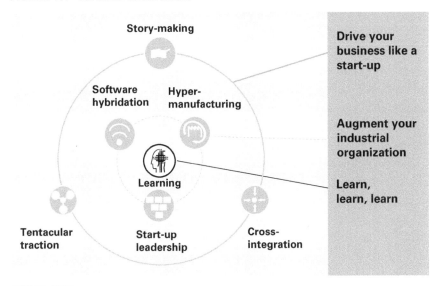

SOURCE OPEO

the system than ever before but it is mainly their ability to learn quickly that has become paramount. Irrespective of the topic, the most important thing is to capitalize on opportunities as quickly as possible by always adapting strategy and operational tactics. Hybrid humans, in constant contact with machines characterized by increasingly perfect digital interfaces, are steadily hybridizing with the technologies that surround them while learning to work with artificial intelligence in such a way as to take full advantage of the possibilities and ensure that each corporate unit is self-learning. This is a fundamental development since it is by constantly acquiring new competencies that each member of an industrial team can help the system to become self-learning, as per the 'testing and learning' paradigm that allows individuals and groups to make mistakes, as long as they are corrected rapidly. Otherwise, to ensure that the system remains balanced, it is essential to reinforce social dialogue and even to extend it to all stakeholders in a company's ecosystem.

The first circle surrounding this core is largely focused on the company's organization and technologies. It is comprised of three complementary and indivisible dimensions in the industrial company of the 4th Age of Industry. The first is start-up leadership, a new management mode adapted to the necessary horizontalization of organizations so that each manager and function within the company provides service to frontline operatives. The second, hyper-manufacturing, refers to the system's ability to renew itself rapidly and review its physical and information flows with minimal friction, in line with the company's ecosystem (while getting as close as possible to the final consumer to maximize the user journey). The final dimension is software hybridization, an indispensable technological driver that helps inside the company to drive major improvements in efficiency, better leverage end-to-end opportunities and, above all, improve understanding of customer uses, either to design products that are more adapted or else to invent innovative new services.

All of this is supported by a second circle that is even more disruptive. This circle is strategic in nature and largely geared towards what is outside a company. It is also comprised of three dimensions that make it possible to disrupt the market by thinking differently. The first dimension here is story-making, or leaders' ability to energize by means of a vision that largely supersedes the company's customary business vocation to attract talent and create a community of believers. Such energy is best channelled when leaders behave in an exemplary fashion by doing as much as possible together with the teams to show them the way and teach them how to overcome constraints that can be difficult to decipher in today's world. In turn, indispensable leadership vision relies on two weapons for conquering markets. The first is cross-integration, enabling a much quicker response to volatility by maximizing integration (whether through acquisitions, the development of internal know-how or better connections between a company's different business lines or with its partners). The second is tentacular traction, which maximizes the benefits of newly networked commercial channels – notably thanks to digital platforms – and creating in this way commercial traction by thinking outside of the box that traditionally frames a company's sector of origin.

The three circles model is not specific to Tesla

The Tesla model is undoubtedly one of the most disruptive ones that industry has ever known but that does not necessarily make it an isolated case. Teslism is not limited to Tesla, quite the contrary, since each industrial company will have to adopt its model to the new paradigm that comes with the 4th Age of Industry. A number of traditional industry's big players have already started to develop systems that can be assimilated with forms of Teslism due to their proximity with the Tesla model's three circle structure.

Examples include Michelin and Mars, both pursuing disruptive strategies and, in this way, ensuring their overall system's coherence.

MICHELIN INTERVIEW
'The first global strategy for an industry of the future lighthouse'

As the world's leading tyre manufacturer and a company benefiting from its leadership in the market for human and product mobility, Michelin has completely transformed its strategic, industrial and commercial approaches to take full advantage of the benefits of the 4th Age of Industry. The company is more than 100 years old so this is not the first time that it has invited change – quite the contrary. Michelin has always questioned itself and is seeking to do the same with this new industrial revolution, in the hope of coming out of it even stronger than before. Global Engineering Director Jean-Philippe Ollier discusses below the main implications of this momentous change. After working in the branch for 20 years and having managed the engineering department before serving as Factory Manager and Director for Industry, Ollier spent the previous 10 years of his career in different company entities, including Michelin's Global Aircraft Tyre Sector and its Latin America Business Unit. Wearing this double hat, he explains the ins and outs of the dual 'business' and 'competitiveness' opportunities that the 4th Industrial Revolution offers the company.

A GLOBAL VISION OF INDUSTRIAL/DIGITAL HYBRIDIZATION,
ONE IN WHICH TYRES BECOME ASSETS

'Digitizing means exploiting data to make better use of company assets while improving general understanding of customer uses and offering increasingly adapted services.' This definition of Michelin's strategy for the industry of the future is a good starting point for apprehending how the transformations might impact the company and its customers. Tyres have become increasingly connected and intelligent and can be sold for a given use instead of on a per-unit basis. In the aircraft tyre sector, for example, Michelin has started invoicing by number of plane landings. In the truck tyre sector, invoicing now depends on journey length. The first effect of this major change is that tyres are now seen as assets by the company that owns them, making innovation even more crucial to performance improvements over the course of the product lifetime. The change has also helped to cut product use costs while optimizing the costs being charged. By extending product use and ensuring sustainable performance, recycling costs are also lower.

SUPPORTED BY AN INNOVATIVE RESPONSIBILITY POLICY, OPERATIVES BECOME CENTRAL FIGURES IN DIGITAL TRANSFORMATION

Beyond this one advantage, the new approach also implies very close connections between the data that production operatives exploit on a daily basis and the data that customers then use throughout the product's lifespan. Hence the importance of equipping frontline factory teams with adapted digital interfaces guaranteeing digital continuity.

All of this underpins the group's decision to get teams as involved as possible in defining concrete solutions facilitating the communication and exploitation of production-floor data. Interfaces and tools are defined together with operatives, who acquire in this way competence and new roles – one by-product of this is a need to assume greater responsibility. To facilitate this change, the company has launched several initiatives reinforcing teams' autonomy in a number of areas that used to be covered by senior management or support functions. These include industrial planning, recruitment and holiday planning. 'Of course, the factory of the future will be comprised of people who are more responsible', according to Ollier. To get there, solid foundations will have to be built, requiring a robust production system. The name given to the approach is the 'Michelin Manufacturing Way', the idea being that if tyres are considered assets, it is important to optimize their lifelong performance by ensuring the robustness of operational and managerial practices in the group's factories and supply chains.

A CLEVER PARTNERSHIP STRATEGY AND CUSTOMIZED INTEGRATION POLICY FOSTERING LONG-TERM GROWTH

To drive this production system, Michelin relies on a dual strategy of integration and highly specific distribution.

As a company that was historically very integrated, Michelin has decided to pursue this policy while promoting a 'customized' tactic reflecting assets' strategic dimension. This means that it continues to develop machines that are differentiated from the competition. Alongside this, Michelin also has partnerships through which it purchases machines for more traditional businesses offering no process-related competitive advantage.

Regarding sales and distribution, Michelin again opts for a clever partnership policy allowing it to maintain relations with end users even as it leverages the strength of its distribution network. When, for instance, the company invoices airline customers based on the number of times a plane lands (or truck companies based on how far a vehicle has driven), it asks partners to undertake field analysis and ensure the tyres' maintenance. The work is often done by a local distributor, enabling Michelin to access markets where the company would not have been competitive pursuing a use-based strategy. 'A transport-company customer might find it difficult to pay for a premium Michelin tyre but, if you sell them based on the number of kilometres travelled with retread tyres, it changes everything.'

THE INDUSTRY OF THE FUTURE IS ALSO (AND ABOVE ALL)
A COHERENT STORY ABOUT SOCIETY

Beyond these business aspects, Ollier also highlights the company's ideas for interacting with society. 'Reducing product deterioration by 20 per cent means consuming 20 per cent fewer tyres; reducing production capacities by 20 per cent means consuming 20 per cent less energy and raw materials while having 20 per cent fewer tyres to recycle. That is a net gain for all of society.' As an important factor in Michelin's brand image, this economic advantage also attracts young talent, as do the company's digitization efforts, which make it seem like a modern structure where people would be happy to work.

Focused on humans and learning; supported by a robust production system and a management policy of allowing people to assume greater responsibility; driven by a use-oriented digitization strategy and by a tactic of customized integration; and strengthened by a track record of interacting coherently with the rest of society – the organizational model that Michelin has created to take advantage of the 4th Age of Industry exemplifies a coherent system redolent of the strategic, technological and human circles that typify Teslism.

MARS AND MY M&M'S INTERVIEWS
'A start-up with 4th Age of Industry DNA'

My M&M's has experienced a singular adventure. As a new start-up in one of the agribusiness sector's most structured groups, this around 40 employee-strong organization is a rising star in the 4th Age of Industry. The company has achieved the exploit of making M&M's that end users can design themselves, and doing this at breakneck speed. Value Stream Manager Valérie Metzmeyer is responsible for flows management and operational development. As dynamic a start-up manager as can be, she enthusiastically explains the strength and specificities of the My M&M's model, one characterized by deeply systemic operational methods.

DIGITIZATION HELPS START-UPS TO BE QUICK OUT OF THE BLOCKS

Even after 30 years of career, Metzmeyer still gets excited talking about My M&M's European kick-off. 'Our CEO discovered the concept in the United States and fell so deeply in love with it that we were already launching in France in December 2006, despite it only being nine months since we first decided to deploy there!' Everything went very quickly after this. With the printing technology already being widely deployed in the company's US business units, the start-up's new host factory could start manufacturing chocolate-coated M&M's immediately. The concept has been a great success, with customers being recruited through channels that are very different from the ones associated with normal in-store impulse purchases. The e-commerce website offers additional traction. 'The product has a high emotional charge since customers can customize their M&M's any way they want to celebrate important events in their lives.' Consumers play a full role in the product creation process, tailoring the product however they like in terms of colours, graphics, packaging and even associated goodies. The closeness of their relationship to the company creates a true sense of accomplishment. In 10 years, the start-up has increased its revenues tenfold.

RADICALLY NEW MANUFACTURING PRACTICES

To achieve this extraordinary growth, one of the main arguments that the brand uses is responsiveness. M&M's can be delivered extremely quickly. This is not something that can be improvised given everything involved in terms of industrial organization, planning practices and teams' operational modes – all of which are very different from what is done in the rest of the company. In high season, for instance, production-line capacities have to be tripled, requiring additional operatives who need to be upskilled very quickly. To achieve this, everyone must be ready to serve as an information source and transmit their know-how. Processes must also be as simplified as possible. 'Lean thinking was very useful to us but it is not enough. The New World also requires a strong mindset, based on the transmission of robust values and ability to question oneself non-stop.' A further complexity is the implication of changing employees' work patterns on their private lives. Hence the need for managerial relays who are prepared to listen to people, to explain things to them and to facilitate their relations with support functions or other parts of the factory.

STRONG VALUES AND AN INTEGRATION THAT CREATES OPENNESS
TO THE OUTSIDE WORLD

In addition to its leadership modes, the company's long-term differentiation is mainly rooted in a value system built around quality, responsibility, mutuality, efficiency and freedom. Each of these seminal Mars group values is central to the start-up's own culture. They guide daily decision making by highlighting people's sense of responsibility and respect for all the colleagues and partners involved in a particular activity. It is an operational mode that has energized the company in a way redolent of Teslism's three concentric circles. Workers are encouraged to use new technology and learn continuously. The company is organized and piloted by means of a flexible and collaborative 'hyper' manufacturing tool supported both by an extremely robust digital e-commerce platform and by professional integration in line with the general start-up model.

Thanks to its different activity segments, Mars is considered a very attractive employer in France, coming third in the country's 2018 Great-Place-to-Work rankings. Interns also voted it their favourite company in France's 2017 Happy Trainee classification.

The group has been very interested in communicating about its activities and development opportunities, raising the question of whether My M&M's might in the future alter the rest of the Mars group. However things turn out, there is no doubt that this has been a successful experience, one further demonstrating the fact that the 4th Age of Industry is already up and running, even if for the moment it remains limited to a few small pockets of growth.

05

How can you implement the Tesla way in your organization?

SUMMARY

The first step towards understanding the Tesla organization's transformation is apprehending the company's business model.
The transformation's implementation, however, requires the framing of a broader canvas.

This chapter, with its more operational focus, should help every company director, industrial engineer or analyst to apprehend the bases underpinning the Tesla model's organizational implementation. By identifying the main diagnostic phases needed to assess a company's 'degree of Teslism', the present section will reveal the levers that people must pull to achieve overall system improvements.

Diagnose hypermanufacturing with a 4.0 VSM

As was the case for lean manufacturing, most of the ingredients for hyper-manufacturing can be translated to companies other than Tesla. To launch this approach in your company, you should first leverage an augmented 4.0 version of value stream mapping (VSM). As with traditional VSM, this mapping should be done in the field but in reverse of the value flow, starting with the clients and then mapping at the same time the information flows with the physical flows. For example, in a typical plant, this mean starting the journey at the expedition area; then walking through packaging, assembly, machining and so on; and finally ending at the procurement area.

To map the collaborative value, you should track at each step the eight types of waste of the 4th Industrial Age, which are broken into two categories: visual waste and virtual waste.

Visual waste

Some wastes are quite visual and easy to detect when walking through the value stream: over-consumption, waiting time, repetitive or cognitively painful tasks and bureaucracy.

To track over-consumption, you should look for an excess of inventory, scrap, active leaks (typically air or water over-consumption or oil) and, even more important, the way these wastes are measured and monitored on a daily basis by the teams in the field. If these wastes are under control, there should be key performance indicators linked to them, with clear objectives. They should be managed by the frontline leaders and challenged by the plant management during every plant tour.

Waiting time is probably the easiest waste to track: walking through a workshop you will see machines that are not busy, which could be caused by planning inefficiency, improper changeovers, breakdowns, absenteeism and so on. The key performance indicator (KPI) to measure machine efficiency is the overall equipment efficiency (OEE). There is an easy way to get a proxy of this OEE when walking in the field: every minute, look at every machine in your visual area and point out which of those machines are running versus which of them are waiting. Counting the waiting machines typically shows that they are pausing between 5 per cent and 70 per cent of the time. If the machine is not the master of the pace of the process, the workload–capacity balance can explain a certain proportion (5–10 per cent) of this waiting time. Waiting time also depends on the manufacturing environment. In asset-intensive workshops, the focus should be on making sure that the main processes constantly run and so the percentage of machines waiting is generally low (10–20 per cent). In machining environments, the product mix has a large influence on machine workload, and so 20–25 per cent of machines could be idling during certain time periods. In assembly or manual/semi-automated environments, there are fewer constraints apart from skills, and so the waiting time of the workstations should not be more than 5–15 per cent. But machines are not the only ones waiting in a manufacturing environment: materials, work in process, and even people generally spend a part of their time waiting. Operators in the field usually wait for a tool, a part or information, which generates discussions. The best way to measure the impact of waiting on people is to frequently sample workers' activities when you walk through the workshop: are they creating value for the final client or doing anything other than waiting for something or someone? Waiting or inefficient discussions can represent 5–25 per cent of wasted working time, depending on industrial activities. The best way to address this waste is to design a structured performance management system and implement collaborative solutions to share information in a very reactive way.

Repetitive or arduous tasks are a bit trickier to detect. You should pause at a fixed station and observe the same activity for a few cycles. Repetitive tasks are becoming easier to automatize. Overall, our observations show that 10–30 per cent of current tasks performed in a manufacturing workshop could be automatized within a medium-range future, depending on the sectors or processes. Nevertheless, some tasks, even if they are not repetitive, should be automatized to make sure that employees keep a high level of motivation and believe in the company mission. There is nothing worse for people retention than a gap between an inspiring official mission for the company and very bad work conditions for the teams within the company. The best way to estimate the comfort of a workstation is to look for gestures and motions that are difficult to do and measure their frequency together with the required intensity. For example, if you raise your arm above the level of your heart once per hour to push a button, it will be safe. But if you do it 10 times per hour carrying 10 kilogrammes or more, it starts to become very difficult for your muscles and can lead to permanent injuries. Last but not least, in the digital world, you also should take into account cognitively painful tasks, for example, frequent interruptions: most managers are frequently interrupted during their daily tasks. Our brain needs at least two minutes to focus again when interrupted, and it gets much more tired when multitasking. In an office environment or with a management team, this king of waste should be taken into account when measuring painful tasks or conditions.

Bureaucracy is also a type of waste that is easy to see. When walking through the workshop, just look at the quantity of paper on each desk or at each workstation. Generally, managers spend 5–20 per cent of their time dealing with administrative tasks, and frontline operators still spend 5–10 per cent of their time on paperwork in most manufacturing environments. Nevertheless, to assess bureaucracy it is also necessary to interview the main support functions about their daily tasks regarding their core processes. For instance, an industrial planner spends most of his or her time preparing an efficient, client-centric plan. But to do so he or she generally needs a very large amount of information: forecasts are supplied by sales or marketing; manufacturing constraints are provided by the production managers; inventory level and the various plan parameters (lead time, etc) can be extracted from the system, although they are supervised by supply chain leaders and so on. This amount of information is more or less digitalized. So the time required to evaluate the synthesis depends on the organization's 'hyper-ability'. But beyond the process itself, there are important considerations when the planning cannot meet the target (for example, client service level, inventory level, manufacturing efficiency). The decision process also will be more or less reactive depending on the organization and its ability to take risks and/or empower people. This is the most intangible part of bureaucracy: that you should assess the complete process duration (lead time in days) versus the effective process workload (total amount of work people contribute to the process).

Virtual waste

As with the example of bureaucracy, some wastes are not visual and so it is necessary to spend time mapping information flows and interacting a lot with the teams to capture the data about these kinds of waste: indecisions, silos, lack of user friendliness and unexploited data.

Indecision seems to be one of the most difficult wastes to measure. However, there are at least two methodologies to do so. First, attend key meetings of the organization to detect micro indecisions. This can be done at various levels (for instance, one in the field with operators and one with the plant leadership). You should listen to the discussions and list all the actions that are mentioned during the meeting or details of any conflicts. Note then the percentage of actions or debates that lead to concrete decisions with a clear owner and a firm deadline. Generally speaking, the time spent in meetings adds less than 20 per cent of value to the company. This is caused by various factors: lack of a clear agenda, lack of a clear leadership, lack of tools to formalize the actions and the decisions, stakeholders being unprepared or a lack of discipline (late arrival, two discussions at a time, phone discussions during the meeting and so on). But even when all the attendants are focused, a low level of acceptance of risks and a lack of empowerment over the different functions can lead to indecisions. Have you ever been in a room where, after two hours of meeting with 20 brilliant people, no one knows what to do next?

The second method to assess indecision is to measure the efficiency process, which can be accomplished at a workshop, plant, supply chain or company level. Coming back to the example of plan processes, the key is to understand the total lead time the teams need to make a decision in the real work context. For instance, at the company level, sales and operation planning is a very important process to balance workload and capacity in the mid-term. You should involve between 10 and 50 people to obtain adequate information, with each person working one hour on average. At the end, if the organization is hyper-efficient, key decisions should be made within one hour, consulting with 5–10 people. The total amount of work is a maximum of between 10 and 60 hours. If this process lasts one week, its efficiency is nearly 100 per cent (the lead time of the process is five days and the workload is about five days for one person). But if the lead time is one month or longer, the process starts to be inefficient. This type of process is iterative, with the lead time depending on the number of loops that should be done before a decision is made. Unfortunately, the consequence of a long lead time will be increased inefficiency, because when the decision takes too long the inputs will vary, requiring another set of loops. It can become a vicious circle.

To avoid this type of pitfall a good choice is to agree on a decision process with a clear timeline and a clear definition of roles and responsibilities: when will the leader consult and listen? When will he or she make their decision? What criteria will influence their decision? Most people think that a good decision is necessarily one that satisfies the majority of the stakeholders, but in the 4th Industrial Age, a good decision is first a clear decision made with a transparent process after listening to all stakeholders and in accordance with the company mission. But most of all it is a leadership act, and the main leader should be accountable for it, no matter if the majority of stakeholders agree with it or not.

Similar to indecision, silos are not easy to see when walking in a plant. There are three ways to assess the ability of an organization to avoid silos. The first is to observe teams in the field on a daily basis: do people help each other easily? Is the workload well balanced among the different areas or functions? Agility in balancing workloads and capacity on a daily or hourly basis is one of the key elements of a hyper-organization. To do so you need not only to have a good planning and monitoring system but also a very good level of collaboration among functions and a very good level of trust: if I am a shop-floor manager and I agree to send one of my teammates to your unit today, how can I be sure that you will do so tomorrow when

I need more arms? The same can be observed at a workstation level: if the balancing process is not perfect (and that is the case most of the time, especially with the explosion of product diversity), why would I help my neighbour if the system does not encourage it or if I do not trust that I will be helped tomorrow when I may not follow the proscribed pace?

The second way is to observe behaviours outside the core activity. In hyper-organizations, all teams have the same dress code (except for those guarding security equipment), work in the same area, without dedicated offices, have lunch in the same area, and mix with workers doing other functions or with other levels of the organization. The 'blue collar versus white collar' paradigm is over. Listen to the way each individual introduces himself or herself and assess how people feel about the rest of the organization: are they collaborative or driven mainly by a 'you and us' mindset?

By observing these daily details you quickly will assess if people really feel that they belong to the same organization. It is generally very instructive. This can seem superficial but it is a very important ingredient to achieving hypermanufacturing when collaboration is key and status becomes highly unproductive.

Last, silos can be detected with an organization chart and team objectives. Hyper-organizations are generally quite flat and foster quick decision-making. Take any team leader in the field and assess the distance in number of organizational chart links between this person and those who are sitting in the same office space. This will be a good proxy of the organization's ability to avoid silo mindsets. Another way to highlight silos is by reviewing the annual objectives of a service – for instance, purchasing – to see if it is in accordance with general end-to-end or local, functional objectives. For instance, a desiloed purchasing service would buy equipment to improve the total cost of ownership or select its suppliers not only for costs but also for reliability and industrial performance.

User friendliness is a feeling before being a measurable specification. A lack of it can cause problems. There are two opposite but complementary ways to diagnose a lack of user friendliness in an IT interface or, more generally, in an industrial workstation. The first is to assess the environment of the workplace, observe it, and then interview the user about specifications that need to be adapted or improved. This also can be done using a quotation methodology to assess the painfulness of the job. After creating a list, improvement ideas could be segmented to decide which ones should be implemented first (the most easy and impactful).

Another way to understand user friendliness is to think with a '0-based' approach. Start the process again as if the workstation or systems do not exist. Focus on the key specifications for the user. Then perform a sensitivity study to understand which specification will lead to a bigger 'amazing' effect for the user. App design experts use a famous framework to make sure that users get hooked (from Nir Eyal's book *Hooked: How to build habit-forming products*): trigger, action, variable rewards and investment. The idea is to make sure that every user gets a sufficient reward at each use of the system so that he or she will be prompted to use it again the next time they are 'triggered'. These principles from app designers are important to leverage when implementing a 0-based approach to improve the probability that the user really will use the system regularly. How many times have you invested in machines, robots or IT systems that were not used at all because the basic functionalities were not thought through for users? Reconcile approaches to design a good customized workstation/ system for users.

Data are the new source of value, so unexploited data should be tracked on a daily basis by every manager. Unfortunately, this waste is a little bit difficult to track because it is totally intangible and even difficult to understand: everyone knows that a good leader should be able to decide and see the implications of a good decision about the agility of an organization. But having data available will never prevent anyone from working. It is just a missed opportunity for value creation. Therefore, this waste should be tracked a bit differently. First, all the teams should be informed about the stakes that depend on a good use of data. Then a diagnostic can be performed using three different steps: collection, management and exploitation. To determine data collection, the assessor will need to find some of the information in the field (for example, manual and automated controls, manual and automated monitoring processes, performance management information, key machine parameters and so on) and some of the information should be tracked on systems (ERP, MES, PLM, CRM and so on) or through machine automates and interfaces. Data management should be assessed with the IT service through data stream mapping of each key process in the company. This will highlight the potential issues linked to system connectivity, cybersecurity and more generally with the IT architecture. Data exploitation is easier to diagnose: it should be done by first generating ideas on how to improve the key performance indicators and then checking if the available data are leveraged enough to help the teams monitor, improve the process and capitalize.

Diagnose cross-integration with an augmented version of the Porter Forces:

To assess the level of integration in your organization, it is useful to leverage an augmented version of the five forces of Porter. Use new technologies to do the following (see Figure 5.1):

- Improve the value proposition for your clients and disrupt your value chain if needed.

- Reinforce any barriers to entry in terms of platform threats.

- Review the level of connection with your network of suppliers and disrupt some of the upstream activities.

- Assess new opportunities of partnership with your ecosystem.

- Revisit your core value proposition to focus on the more important business lines and speed up the level of collaboration among your key internal functions.

Improve the value proposition for your clients and disrupt your value chain if needed

Having access to final customer data is key to understanding their motivations and willingness to pay for new services. The goal of challenging the

FIGURE 5.1 Augmented Porter Forces

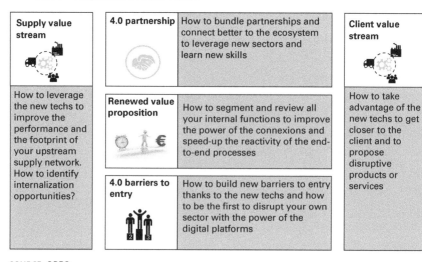

client side of your value stream is to determine how to leverage technologies to get closer to the final customer. There are various levers, from connecting the product to getting data directly from it to a radical change of the sales distribution approach or even a reinternalization of the downstream steps of the process. In any case the idea is to think differently about the value proposition and to get to know your client's needs much better to make sure you can propose adequate services. For example, the testimony of the previously mentioned Roland Schaeffer of Socomec reveals that the company has decided to propose energetic monitoring services to their client when they used to sell only electrical material. This led them to get data from their industrial clients and to propose or adapt solutions to save costs through better energy consumption.

Reinforce any barriers to entry in terms of platform threats

There are two ways to reinforce barriers to entry in your sector and two ways to diagnose opportunities for improvement regarding these barriers.

The first way is to spend time on the existing barrier and see if you can go further using new technologies. For instance, in the aeronautical sector, there is a huge requirement of traceability all along the supply chain, and at the same time there is increasing pressure on delivery punctuality. Dassault System took advantage of these requirements to propose to Boeing a unique contract stipulating that Boeing and all the players in its supply chain should be connected through its product '3D experience'.

The second way is simply to think out of the box when trying to disrupt your own sector. You can create internal innovations or obtain a stake in start-ups that are disrupting your sector with new business models. This is, for instance, what Suez did in the waste sector thanks to a defensive equity investment in Rubicon, a fresh platform in Canada that started to 'uberize' the waste market.

Review the level of connection with your network of suppliers and disrupt some of the upstream activities

To assess the supply side of your value stream, there are two main questions to speed up the agility of your industrial organization: are there any core parts or subsystems of the product that would develop faster if I did it internally? Are there any suppliers or upstream supply chains lacking reliability or reactivity? In both cases, there are three levels of reaction. First, explore how the new technologies can lead to a better connection with those suppliers, for instance, in accelerating the scheduling or forecast processes through electronically automated orders. Second, find out if there might be technologies that can disrupt the supply chain. For instance, some of the traditional machining workshops can be replaced by 3D printing with subsequent savings in cost, lead time and supply reliability. This is true in both prototyping during the R&D phase and also for manufacturing with parts, such as accessories in the luxury sector and even plastic components in the automotive industry. The third level of reaction is to buy your supplier, but of course this is not always possible and depends on your financial health.

Assess new opportunities of partnership with your ecosystem

In the digital era, the ability to collect data is vital to scale-up new value propositions and take advantage of the network effect. The industrial companies are often too small or isolated to manage this scaling effect. So there is a real substitution threat coming from the digital pure players. Nevertheless there are a few ways to diagnose your organization's ability to deal with those threats. First you can assess your geographical potential partners. The companies in your area might produce totally different products but have a concrete interest in collaborating with you on bottom-line topics that are very often common to all industrial companies: How can we develop new tech skills? How can we save energy? How can we improve the performance management system? How can we improve the scheduling process, the quality-control process, the supply process and so on? How can we make the company and the area attractive for young people? The good news is that a lot of these topics are often already discussed in local entrepreneur clubs or public initiatives. The first thing to do is to map all existing networks. For instance, a tier 1 supplier in the automotive industry in France decided to create a lab to build its capabilities using new technologies and then opened it to the local SMEs to improve the ROI of the project and contribute to local economic development at the same time. Another way to improve your network opportunities is to leverage your industrial sector. In most countries, there are existing institutions that aim to structure the sector to influence state decisions and help companies with common problems. If existing initiatives are not interesting enough, join efforts with your suppliers, clients or even competitors to design collaborative initiatives and propose them to the sector governance. Eventually, to build your skills and capabilities, review your connections with the local universities, schools and colleges and, if required, propose joint programmes to enhance the initial skill level and adapt continuous training courses. Most basics are now available online thanks to MOOCs or e-modules. It can be a good way for your managers and technicians to get trained and continue learning without leaving work.

Revisit your core value proposition to focus on the more important business lines and speed up the level of collaboration among your key internal functions

The best tool to diagnose the agility of your internal processes and functions is a function-function matrix (see Figure 5.2). On both axes, position the

FIGURE 5.2 Function-function matrix

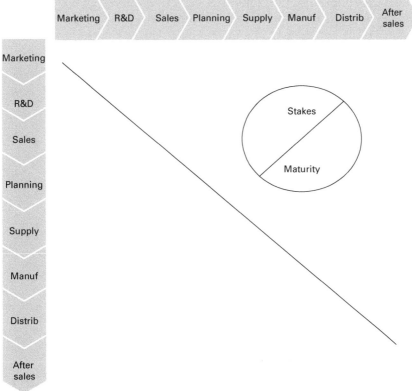

SOURCE OPEO

different key functions of the company. Then assess for each case of the matrix the stake and maturity of the connection: is the connexion vital for the growth or reactivity or the company, for the efficiency of the key processes? Are both functions reactive enough with each other? Are they able to solve complex problems together? What is the typical duration of a problem-solving session at the interface? Do leaders of the functions collaborate and manage to make common decisions when required? The idea then is to reinforce the links where the stakes are large and the construct is weak. This can be done with performance management routines, KPIs or structured problem-solving sessions. Collaborative tools and other digital solutions will help increase the speed of sharing information, capitalizing on key knowledge and work standards and making it possible to create a real-time dialogue among the key stakeholders. For example, a company in the electronics sector specializing in customized systems diagnosed a very strong need for the connection between its engineering service and the production workshop to improve the total lead time and eliminate quality rework. The initial situation frustrated both sides because the production plant felt that the engineering service did not solve problems and was unable to deliver reliable product plans, and the engineering service complained about the production process quality of service and punctuality. Thanks to a daily loop and a real-time collaborative dialogue, they managed to collaborate on product plans and a shared, prioritized action plan. This solved the tension between the services but also made the defect rate and lead time decrease significantly.

Diagnose software hybridization with a smart matrix

Software and new technology classification

Before assessing your software hybridization potential, you should address a classic pitfall: dealing with the abundance of new technologies. That is why we classify the useful technologies for hypermanufacturing in four key areas, following the natural flow of the data: collect the data with the internet of things; analyse the information with machine learning and big data; transform the data into a visual of a concrete order with digital applications, systems and simulation tools; and, finally, use the data to convert the information into physical orders with robotics, 3D printing or new processes.

Methodology

To diagnose your potential of improvement regarding software hybridization and those four key technological foundations you need to assess both the opportunities in each function and the end-to-end opportunities. For that purpose, the smart matrix is a useful tool that provides an understanding of the impact of each technology on each part of the value stream: reliability, efficiency, quality, reactivity, traceability, agility and so on (see Figure 5.3). There are lots of potential improvements using technology, but it is necessary to use methodology to avoid dispersion. The first step should be to define your stakes in the strategy, context and mission of the company. Then identify which parts of your internal value stream should be affected by these stakes, from end-to-end processes to individual functions. Last, use a smart matrix to identify which technologies you can leverage to launch proof of concepts (POCs) and then capture the potential of improvement. For example, a famous luxury watch company regularly missed sales because of a poor supply chain process that lead to stock-outs in the sales network. They decided to launch a diagnostic on their end-to-end process in order to reduce the time to market and to improve the reliability of the forecasts. Two technology basics were identified: they started to leverage the internet of things to detect customer behaviours inside their shops and get a proper daily sell-out; then they analysed the data to predict future sales and fed the master schedule planning of the different plants. This was done using a big-data algorithm.

Diagnose tentacular traction with business segmentation

Centricity-dynamic segmentation

The best way to diagnose tentacular traction is to segment your business lines and internal functions with two axes: one side represents the function of the core business line for your mission and strategic road map (business centricity) and the other is to identify what you need to fulfil it: incremental progress (typically less than 20 per cent improvement) or disruption (business dynamic) (Figure 5.4). The functions that are not core and need only incremental progress can be improved with traditional continuous improvement programmes or could get platformed, as we will see in this section dedicated to the diagnosis of tentacular traction.

FIGURE 5.3 Smart matrix

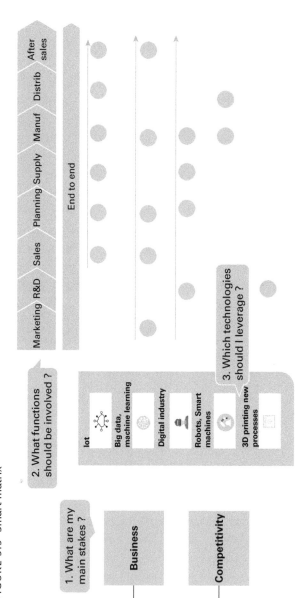

FIGURE 5.4   Business dynamic, business-centricity matrix

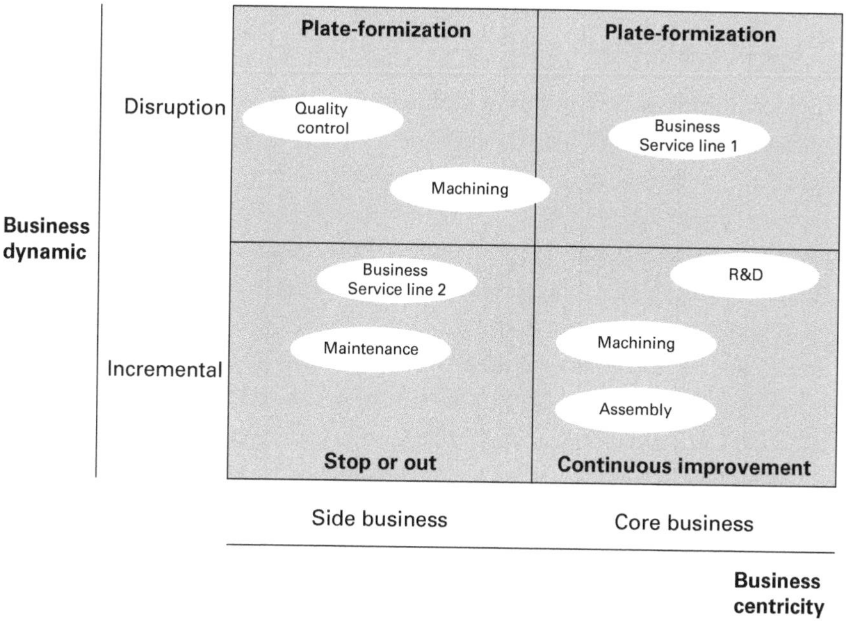

	Plate-formization	Plate-formization
Disruption	Quality control / Machining	Business Service line 1
Incremental	Business Service line 2 / Maintenance	R&D / Machining / Assembly
	Stop or out	Continuous improvement

Business dynamic

Side business   Core business

Business centricity

SOURCE OPEO

Top-line opportunities

To identify opportunities of tentacular traction, first look for top-line opportunities. The idea here is to leverage the power of the platforms to speed up the market pull, the ultimate goal being virility, which is the ability to leverage all existing assets to exponentially develop your own assets. For instance, if you are a machinemaker, one way of becoming virile is to leverage the machines that are used in all factories in the world, including those of your competitors, to deliver your own services. Coming back to the centricity-dynamic segmentation, once you have assessed all your service lines, the following steps should be taken:

- Leave and sell the business lines on the bottom left side (low business dynamic and centricity).

- Go for a continuous improvement programme for the business lines on the bottom right corner (high centricity but low business dynamic).

- For business lines that can be considered to have a high level of dynamism (a good candidate to get disrupted), you should think about opportunities to create a platform and leverage the digital network effect. Keep this initiative purely internal if the business line is core business (top right corner) and outsource the platformization initiative if it is not core business (top left corner).

In the manufacturing equipment sector, for example, there is currently a huge business dynamic regarding the internet of things. Most machinemakers have launched initiatives to connect their systems and upload data to then sell services such as repair, predictive maintenance or energy consumption. In each of these companies, there are core business lines that could be disrupted at any time: if one of the key players on the market manages to take the lead, it will be able to get most of the data and capitalize on the clients' use to sell more and more services. Other players will become only suppliers of this 'main integrator'. The idea here is to be the first to move and then see where the best strategy lies: build alliances with other competitors, build alliances with digital pure players, leverage the start-up ecosystem or build capabilities internally.

Bottom-line opportunities

The same approach can be used for internal functions: quality, maintenance, planning, supply chain, R&D, production and so on. Functions that are not part of a huge business dynamic can be outsourced if not core, or improved with a classical continuous improvement programme. But for functions subject to an important business dynamic, the next step is to think about a way to create a platform effect, either with an internal new service line (if a core business) or with an outsourced initiative (if not a core business).

For instance, in the process industry, maintenance is a core business because of the intensity of asset investments. Improving the OEE of the key assets is a basic daily preoccupation. At the same time, with the incredible progress of the internet of things in the machine sector, the rollout of manufacturing execution systems (MESs) and machine learning, maintenance is a very good candidate for disruption. So, if you are one of the big players in the process industry, you should think about ways to develop side business lines internally in order to propose remote maintenance and predictive applications.

Design a customized story-making strategy

Story-making should be assessed in two ways: 1) make sure that your vision is consistent with all actors and drives energy to your teams and ecosystem; and 2) adapt your personal leadership style to foster organizational consistency (Figure 5.5).

FIGURE 5.5   Story ingredients

Founding elements	What are the key positive elements of your history that have led to the current culture and DNA and what are the main components leading to a feeling of pride?
Major perspectives	What are the main challenges and what would you like to keep as essential components of your DNA no matter what happens?
Evolution dynamic	What is the horizon of the company to better serve the clients, ecosystem and the society and what are the key strengths to do so?
Governance modes	How do the main company stakeholders interact and decide to create more value and what are the key mindsets that are required to make it work?

SOURCE OPEO

Make sure that your vision is consistent with all actors and drives energy to your teams and ecosystem

Building a good vision is not easy and first requires some introspection. A good way to do this is to assess four aspects of your company's DNA and then align your teams on a common vision.

The first task is to understand the foundations of the company. Review your history to assess key strengths and shared grounding of the company culture. For instance, if you are a company designing and making products to improve air quality, you will need to capitalize on this very aspect of your value proposition to turn it into a common inspiring message for your teams. For example: 'Since the beginning of our company we have helped dozens of clients improve the air quality in their facilities. We have a strong belief that working in good conditions is an essential element of success for our clients and for the health of their employees.'

The second task concerns the major perspectives of the company. List the key challenges of the company in its specific sector and context. Then learn how to face these challenges and at the same time keep the foundations that are at the heart of your culture. For instance, you may want to take advantage of the data revolution to build new service lines and services, but at the same time make sure to respect individual rights, because you believe that your clients' privacy is a core element of your DNA.

The third task is to determine the evolution dynamic. You should set inspirational and ambitious objectives for the company and then collaborate with your teams to list the strengths that will enable the company to meet its targets. For instance, targeting huge growth in a niche-emerging market can be a good way to set aspirations but at the same time you should be able to list your key strategic and operational strengths to do so. Growth could be fuelled by the empowerment ability of the team, technical ability, agility and so on. There are numerous ways of capitalizing on existing assets, but it is important to highlight how.

The fourth task is to assess the governance mode. Reflect on how power is to be shared among the executive team, the shareholders, the management, the team and even the outside partners in the ecosystem. This exercise requires describing how the company makes its decisions internally and externally, and what mindset is required to sustain the governance mode. For instance, if the governance mode is assumed to be bottom-up, you need to insist on trust, respect and listening as fundamental elements of the mindset of all actors and stakeholders of the company and its ecosystem.

Adapt your personal leadership style to foster organizational consistency

Story-making is about communicating regularly with the world outside the company, especially clients, and about making sure to create a role-model attitude inside the company and in the field. You can accomplish this through your external review and communication and field behaviour.

EXTERNAL REVIEW AND COMMUNICATION

The first task here is to determine your agenda as an executive. How much time can you spend on a weekly basis reading outside content about your competitors or improving your expertise (eg digital, new tech, functional content, etc)? A good average benchmark is 10 per cent. But of course there are no one-size-fits-all solutions. The important action is to continuously explore knowledge creation outside the company. Social networks, conferences, sectorial newspapers, dedicated newsletters, professional books, MOOCs and consulting firms are typically good sources to leverage external content.

The second task concerns identifying which channels to use to communicate directly with clients and the media. What type of content would you like to keep as a leader and what type of content should be delegated to your internal communications service? How would you like to communicate that content? Would you like to dialogue directly with your clients or leave it to the sales network? These decisions depend on your sector and your clients. B2C and B2B strategies require different approaches.

FIELD BEHAVIOUR

The first task here also concerns your agenda as a leader. How much time would you like to dedicate to a concrete field tour on a daily basis? What are your concrete activities once you go in the field? There are typically two types of possible activities: 1) process management control to make sure that what you see when you walk along the industrial area is consistent with what your team says and what the key performance indicators say; and 2) observing individuals or groups and providing structured feedback to make them progress and develop themselves. These activities also help you receive direct information so you can make sure that your priorities are understood and that your strategy makes sense. You can also look for ways to improve and hunt for the previously described eight sources of waste: over-consumption, waiting time, repetitive or cognitively painful tasks, bureau-cracy, indecisions, silos, lack of user friendliness and unexploited data. This last activity can help solve complex problems (dedicated time spent by industrial teams to solve problems in the field, together with a very strict methodology) by participating personally with some of the group sessions. A good example is a plant manager with a typical 1,000 FTE span of control who spends one hour per day helping teams by simply attending a problem-solving session. He chooses a different area every day. This helps to develop the teams and maintain a level of intensity, which will prove the value of the exercise.

The second task concerns the behaviour during all the exercises that we mentioned previously. A good way to assess the ability of a leader is to rate his or her attitude on her typical management routines (performance reviews, field tours, one-to-one discussions and so on). Is the leader behaving as a doer, going regularly into the field and sometimes leading some of the project himself or herself to role model? Does he or she challenge their team by asking questions, constantly elevating the level of commitment and forcing priorities to emerge? Does he or she behave like a coach, providing structured feedback to develop people and groups, or like an accelerator, consistently challenging the speed of problem solving, adherence to the planning and process agility?

Diagnose start-up leadership systems and behaviours

Start-up leadership refers to the ability of middle management to transmit the vision and at the same time empower teams so that they develop the company. It is based on a robust management system and adapted behaviours.

A robust management system

The first brick of a start-up leadership system is the digitalization of management routines. A good way to assess the potential of digitalization is first to measure the time spent by managers on various activities. Shadowing is a good way to accomplish this. Digitalization provides more time to create value and kills administrative paper waste, reworking and uncomfortable systems. Usually, administrative tasks take up between 15 per cent and 25 per cent of the working hours in the 3.0 era, but they should fall below 5 per cent in the new era. The real power of digitalization is to speed up the connection between individuals and teams. That is why a heat map of the different relationships between functions and organization level should be developed to focus the energy on digitalizing the most impactful connections. For instance, if production and engineering are tightly linked – and this is often the case in hi-tech sectors – a collaborative solution should be tested to speed up the discussions and make shorter loops leading to a better reactivity and eliminating rework. At the same time, it is interesting to check the typical time horizon required to monitor performance. Most industries should move from weeks to days, from days to hours or from hours to minutes in order to beat competition. This is often supported by agile communications tools and a good alert system. Finally, you should check that action tracking and more general problem-solving is accomplished digitally: this clarifies performance monitoring and team engagement to get things done and drastically improves the capitalization of knowledge.

The second brick concerns the ecosystem: checking that the company leverages external skills. A way to diagnose the ecosystem is again to spend time with core and support functions, splitting the time between internal and external teams or skills. What happens when there is an obvious lack of internal knowledge on a topic? Which channels are leveraged? Typically there are four possible sources of external inspiration: institutions (eg government, local authorities and sectorial associations), start-ups, partners (eg consulting firms, tech experts) and other actors in the sector (eg suppliers, clients, competitors).

The third brick concerns support functions. A good way to check the 4.0 ability of your different support functions is to measure the split of working hours between transactional and supporting tasks, to measure their ability to standardize their own support and, finally, to automate it, taking the role of coach with a high level of attention directed towards the outside world. For instance, most scheduling of transactional tasks, such as ordering, sequencing, printing paper, entering data in the MRP and so on, will disappear. A productive scheduling function of the future should focus on finding the adapted outside agile application, defining the adapted standard operating procedure and training the production team on how to use it. Then any operator should be able to do part of the transactional work because the rest has been automated.

Adapted behaviours

Assessing behaviours can be done when observing executives. These observations should focus on support and core functions at all levels of the hierarchy. The key questions then concern whether the executives' attitudes are in sync with the company values. Are they good role models, action oriented, challenging, supporting the development of the teams and so forth? A good way to form an opinion on this is to be involved with the three main types of managerial exercises in industry: a performance review when the leader is supposed to be directing the discussions, reviewing the action and giving the vision; a field tour when the leader should check if the situation is under control and so can assess what could go wrong; and a problem-solving session when the leader should behave horizontally (in a participative manner) to help the team find the root causes of problems using the right methodology.

Diagnose people and machine learning with skill-centric assessment

People and machine learning are at the heart of Teslism. To diagnose your organization's ability to learn, you need to analyse three main ingredients separately: you should assess 1) the current state of your teams' skill set in comparison to the manufacturing skill set of the future; 2) your current transformation skill set in the organization; and 3) your capability-building system to make sure that you have the adapted processes to grow.

Manufacturing skill set of the future

There are two types of skills needed to prepare for the future of manufacturing: 1) technological skills; 2) soft skills.

- Technological skills: to assess these critical skills, first identify the key technological bricks that are relevant to adapting your business model and improving your competitiveness. It is quite impossible to acquire the entire skill set of the industry 4.0 internally, and so prioritization here is very important. Once you have identified the key technology that you would like to develop internally, you should assess your organization's main business units and functions and find out if you have the needed people or teams to showcase for the rest of the organization. It is quite common, for instance, that a factory or a production unit is ahead of the rest of the organization because one or two persons are techno-addicts and tried to launch 'proof of concepts' (POCs) on their own. It would be a pity not to capitalize on these efforts. If this is not the case, then you should get your capabilities reinforced by an outside party in your ecosystem: academic trainings, techno providers or specialized freelancers.

- Soft skills: a recent study commissioned by World Economic Forum (2018) proved that machines will have a growing importance in the total amount of working time: from 29 per cent of total working hours in 2018 to 52 per cent of working hours in 2025. This will require a totally new skill set for workers. For instance, empathy, creativity, analytical skills, complex problem-solving or programming will be increasingly needed whereas manual dexterity, memory, perfunctory writing or calculation will become obsolete. The earlier you adapt your teams to this important change, the better. Before assessing these skills in your organization, you should make sure that your hiring process and your individual evaluation process integrate this new skill set. The purpose here is not to pretend that current skills should be replaced all in one shot but that the transition should be anticipated as soon as possible.

Transformation skill set and organization

Like all major changes, a 4.0 transformation should be led and supported by a dedicated team and programme. If you would like to implement Teslism in your company, you need to focus on at least three major levers of actions:

- Top management awareness: first you should assess the top executive team's ability to understand the stakes and the maturity of the organization regarding the 4th Industrial Revolution. Is there a constant effort to benchmark and sometimes visit showcases? Do executives attend dedicated conferences and training? Is there a dedicated programme with a direct report to the top management team? Are executives clear regarding the strategy to take advantage of new technologies?

- Mixed IT/ops change teams: in the 3rd Industrial Revolution, thousands of change teams were created to design production systems inspired by Toyotism. Most of the time these change teams were composed of employees with a technical background (industrial engineering, production, quality, etc) and were trained to achieve continuous improvement through the Toyota Way. To implement Teslism, the recipe is still the same, but there should be also IT and digital skills added to the core transformation team. Software has become so important that it needs to be part of the production system DNA. Therefore the change team should not implement kaizen only but also lead POCs in the field and be able to code or at least use an adequate application programming interface (API) in order to be independent and reactive to field users.

- 4.0 architect: most of the Teslism benchmarks claim that an important factor for success is to hire or train an internal resource to coordinate and ensure the governance of the programme. Of course this is not specific to Teslism. In this new era it can be difficult to find someone who has an IT and operations background. Once again the key is to hybridize both worlds. This new type of job requires people who are able to design and communicate a clear vision with the top executive team, drive energy into the organization and make sure that the executive team is aware of the main stakes regarding the programme. That person should be able to leverage the top team and the outside world to find the adapted skills and orchestrate the drumbeat of the programme. One of the first things to do when you launch your programme is to find this architect, either on your IT team or your operational change team. It would be ideal if you have the opportunity to identify a person who can wear both hats. The CEO of a big machinemaker recently claimed that it had been the major key for success during the construction of a greenfield: the project leader, or chief of digital industry officer (CDIO), was a former plant manager and IT director in the company.

Capability-building system

Once you have completed a clear skills assessment and defined targets, you need to make sure that the organization has the ability to build its own capabilities. You should assess the system itself and its ability to transfer new skills to the workforce (Figure 5.6). There are three different aspects to diagnose:

- Training content: is the list of internal trainings up to date? What is the process to update it? Is it linked to the continuous improvement loop?

How does human resources leverage outside trainings and expertise? Are e-learning and MOOCs sufficiently promoted and accessible to the teams? Is there a good mix between classroom and on-the-job training?

- Training processes: is there a personal target for every employee? Is there a KPI to measure the capability improvements regarding the identified key skills? Has every manager identified a specific target in his or her area and designed a specific training plan for their team? Is there a continuous evaluation process to make sure that capabilities are built and employees are satisfied by the training courses and methodology?

- Management time and coaching skills: on top of receiving classic types of trainings (how to lead a performance meeting, learning to see, how to lead an individual skill review), direct management needs to develop skills for the future, most of which are soft. These skills are better taught by getting feedback and coaching based on real situation observations, but this requires deep changes in management's attitude: first, field managers should allocate time every day for this specific purpose; second, they should adopt the behaviour themselves to coach their employees. This means that management also needs soft skills training to provide good feedback and adapt their agenda on a daily basis, even before starting the programme. You should diagnose management's ability in these skills as early as possible, as we mentioned in the start-up leadership section.

FIGURE 5.6   Skills evolution

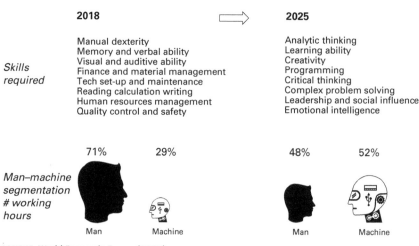

	2018	2025
Skills required	Manual dexterity Memory and verbal ability Visual and auditive ability Finance and material management Tech set-up and maintenance Reading calculation writing Human resources management Quality control and safety	Analytic thinking Learning ability Creativity Programming Critical thinking Complex problem solving Leadership and social influence Emotional intelligence

Man–machine segmentation # working hours

71% Man   29% Machine   48% Man   52% Machine

SOURCE   World Economic Forum (2018)

Implement a new way to drive your business like a start-up

Implementing a strategic change in your company thanks to digital is clearly one of the most impactful levers but not the simplest. You need to invest yourself a lot personally and be the best ambassador of the approach and objectives of the journey.

Real change starts at the top: adapt your own agenda and behaviour

As an executive, there are three things that no one should challenge you about or impose on you: your agenda, your mindset and your direct team members. First, story-making requires adapting your agenda to spend more time in the field. This means on a weekly basis you need to identify the key projects, group or problem-solving sessions that you would like to dive deeply into. This also means deciding which places in your organization you would like to observe and which teams you would like to coach on a daily basis. The second decision requires aligning the organization to your values and level of ambition. If you would like to convey a Tesla mindset, you should promote learning everywhere and at every moment: this means having the courage to take risks, refusing the status quo, accepting the possibility of failure, having the humility to get challenged, being pragmatic and being obsessed with the speed of progress more than the efforts required to do it. Of course, if you would like to convey this culture to the rest of the organization, you should also make sure that your direct team is eventually driven by the same mindset.

Create a massive external need for change

As we explain many times in this book, defining an inspirational vision and communicating it to the outside world is a key element of success, because it drives energy into your teams, your clients and also from your ecosystem. As we also saw in Chapter 4, this can be developed through four axes (founding elements, major perspectives, evolution dynamics and governance mode). If your vision is robust enough and your company flexible enough, then you should be able to trigger a massive change. But in most existing large organizations there is a lot of friction that will lower the speed of transformation, especially if the project cannibalizes part of traditional activity.

To avoid this trap, there are two different ways to react: the first is to hire a bunch of highly motivated talents from digital pure players and transfer them a very high level of responsibility to think differently. The other way is to take a defensive investment in outside competitors, and the sooner the better, because the ratio of investment to risk will be lower. For instance, the executive team of Suez, a leader in the waste management sector, decided to invest in Rubicon, a start-up that managed to create a platform to aggregate demand and the opportunities for very small businesses' waste in Canada.

Be obsessed with user experience and reactivity

Why does integration matter so much? Elon Musk is obsessed with reactivity and independence because the heart of his company is to create increasing value for the final customer. User experience is the key objective at Tesla. That is probably why the company has one of the best evaluations in the Net Promoter Score (NPS) classification (96 per cent when Apple is 72 per cent and Amazon 69 per cent), according to the 2017 index NPS.com. NPS is a customer satisfaction metric that measures the degree to which people would recommend your company to others. How can you achieve such an outcome?

User X is not a marketing concept: to convey Teslism throughout the organization, you can align all teams on one common objective: to ease the life of your direct clients, at all stages of the processes. This means, for instance, that engineering will focus on developing ergonomic workstations but at the same time everyone in the company will focus on creating a unique and distinctive user experience for the final customer.

Buy or build internal capabilities: to be really reactive, you need to acquire the ability to execute most of your key processes internally instead of buying them from suppliers. To achieve that you should first identify your core functions that create value for the users versus the need for reactivity or innovation as a competitive advantage in your market. This will lead to a matrix (see Figure 5.7). You should then internalize (make) the functions that are core for the users and need reactivity; create or buy subsidiaries for functions that are not core for the clients but key for business reactivity; outsource (buy) functions that are not core for user value and do not need reactivity; and eventually decide if you should buy or make and connect the functions that are key for users but do not require any specific reactivity from the industrial system.

FIGURE 5.7 Make or buy matrix

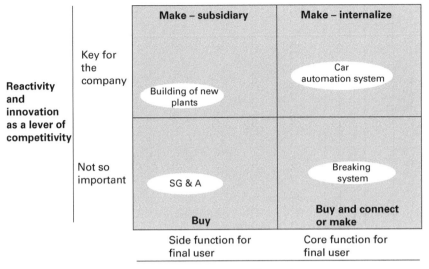

Adopt a clear platformization strategy

In Chapter 4 we saw that some of your businesses or markets could be subject to platformization because they can be disrupted. Once you have identified those markets, the key question is how to launch and achieve platformization. Should you create your own platform, use an existing one or create alliances with your clients and competitors to build one? For that purpose we propose another segmentation here, which will help make this decision, depending on your access to the final client and the digital maturity of the market or sector.

If the digital maturity of the market is low and you have a direct access to the final user, you should create your own platform. If the digital maturity of the market is low but your access to the client is indirect, you should try to build an alliance with your clients and co-create a platform. If the digital maturity of the market is high and you have direct access to the client, you should create an alliance with your competitors: one of them has already probably started to build a platform or might try to do it. Eventually, if the digital maturity of the market is high but you have only indirect access to your clients, you should use an existing platform and simply take advantage of it to get more sales. You will not enjoy the data but at least you can leverage the power of the platform to increase business. See Figure 5.8 for an example of an internal–external platformization decision matrix.

FIGURE 5.8 Internal–external platformization decision matrix

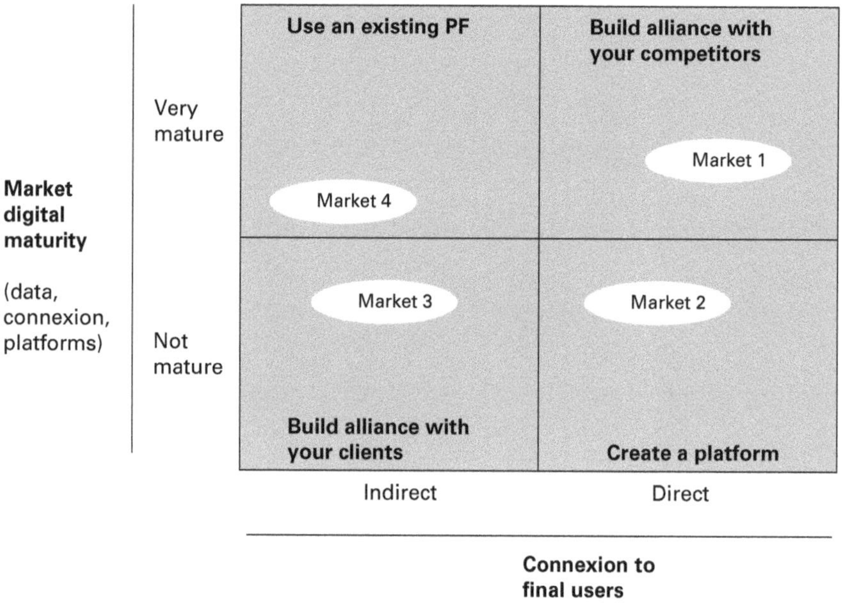

SOURCE OPEO

Once you have decided whether you should create your own platform or not, you need to make the difficult decision about how to do it. There are very important success factors that you should absolutely understand before starting:

- Team: first of all, as we saw in Chapter 4, it is imperative to hire the right team. Most often you will not get one from internal resources because these people will be too defensive regarding the potential risk of cannibalization of the classic business. Airbnb was not invented by AccorHotels for this very reason.

- Methodology: There are five very important ingredients to remember if you wish to create your own platform:

  o Focus on use. You should learn from potential users. User research should be at the heart of your first weeks of seeding your business. Technology at this stage does not matter at all.

  o Kill bad ideas as soon as possible. Learning also requires pivoting and having the courage to leave ideas that do not have any potential.

o Prove the concept before scaling. It is better to spend more time on proving the model and the market, no matter if you lose money, so you can scale without having exponential costs (revenues will be exponentials if you have done a good seed).

o The magic number. Starting a platform is very difficult because you have two sides to convince at the same time: buyers and sellers. Usually one of these sides is more difficult to convince. You should focus on that side and estimate how many users (the magic number) you need to start the platform. For instance, the difficult side for Airbnb was to convince hosts to rent their residence because they were afraid that strangers would damage it.

o Do one thing at a time. Do not try to make an Amazon from the start. Start with one topic and then extend it after you succeed in scaling it up.

Implement an augmented version of your industrial organization

To support the strategic move, you need to set a very robust industrial organization. Before all, this means adapting the ability of your organization to transform itself very rapidly, avoiding waste and taking advantage of the software power to change the operational processes along with the management system.

Guiding principle

The implementation of hypermanufacturing, software hybridization and start-up leadership requires a very subtle balance between test-and-learn, bottom-up approaches and a more integrated, urbanized top-down approach to make sure that technology will lead to concrete improvements in competitiveness that are in line with company objectives and the mission. In any case, one of the keys to success is to lead such developments in a systemic way, identifying the right technologies to implement in order to minimize waste and at the same time adapting the organization and flows, building skills, and managing change to make sure that adequate behaviours grow.

Methodology

Once you have identified the main sources of waste in your organization, an important exercise will be to identify the right technological solutions and compare the potential for improvement versus the difficulty of implementation. But in the 4th Industrial Age the key is not to wait too long: you should leverage your team energy and start very quickly implementing POC with a test-and-learn approach. Failing is an option here. The important point is to learn. A POC will follow a relative generic sequence: identify waste, pre-identify a technology, spend time with users to understand deeply their needs and constraints, test a customized solution without technology, improve the solution on paper, then plug an agile solution with a scrum mindset (fast implementation, fast improvement, short loops).

Example of waste, solution and impact

Bureaucracy is a classical waste in manufacturing. The main consequence is paperwork, which leads to a risk of mistakes, frustration for the teams, a bad carbon print for the planet and a significant amount of time spent on administrative tasks for managers and support functions.

To reduce bureaucracy, a good lever is to simply digitalize the main processes of production planification, quality tracking and preventive maintenance activities. The POC should start with a very concrete shadowing of the planification, quality control and maintenance teams, and then analyse their main paper documents to understand why every piece was created, who acts as a contributor and how it could be replaced by a digital solution. A test then can be performed with simple internet of things solution or bar scans to track the files or production parts and a very basic tablet as a user interface. After a few days of improvements with a test-and-learn approach, the solution can be tried with different users specifically trained for it. An agile solution can be implemented within a few weeks parallel to the existing paper process. When the solution is mature, the paper can then be deleted. The improvement can be major in terms of people efficiency (up to 10 per cent of working time) and quality (reduction of mistakes or versions).

Start small, scale fast but consistently

Of course hypermanufacturing should not have hundreds of competing solutions in every part of the company. The solutions that are reviewed with a test-and-learn approach in the field should be connected to the existing IT architecture (urbanization of the system), and all similar processes should benefit from POCs that have been conducted in other areas of the company. That is where integration is critical: a dedicated resource – an IT-ops architect – should make sure that the best solutions are qualified and rolled out throughout the company. This resource should also prioritize the solutions regarding the company vision and strategy, propose a systemic approach to interfacing the new solution with the existing production system and manage a hybrid IT-ops team to implement the solution in every management perimeter of the organization. Coming back to the zero-paper solution, the qualified technological solutions should be referenced in the production system as a lever to augment the master scheduling process, the quality-control process and the maintenance preventive process. Once the production system is implemented in a new area, this solution will be totally integrated into the local standard operating procedures, and all the teams will work without paper.

Implement a new way of working and learning

Learning is, before all, a mindset – having the courage to take risks; the humility to be challenged; to remain convinced that any difficulty can be overcome with goodwill and obstinacy. How can you create a great place to learn and work differently? Most people think it is simply impossible to achieve in an industrial environment, though we have seen that Tesla and most of the benchmarks of the industry 4.0 companies have transformed their industrial organization and at the same time have created an unrivalled environment to attract and develop people. In reality it could even be the opposite: because these innovative companies have put in so much effort to attract and retain talents, they have managed to leverage the power of these new technologies. We saw in Chapter 4 how to diagnose the skills of the future and the systems to develop those skills continuously.

Start working with the outside world

As we said, one of the keys to creating a massive change inside the company culture can be to hire a significant number of employees who come from the digital sphere. But of course if you lead an SME this is not possible. You then need to be agile in the way the company works with the outside.

Start leading projects with external tech experts, for instance, launching a POC with a collaborative robot or a simple digital manufacturing application. The purpose here is to test and also learn how to work differently and start transferring the skills needed to implement technology.

Build a genuine great place to learn

One of the ways to create a visible change is to invest in a lab. Labs can create team interest in new technologies, especially if the labs are open and easy to access. But do not over-estimate the advantage of this type of initiative. My experience has shown that successful programmes are above all the ones that focus on transforming the actual concrete workstation of daily life. So if you build a lab, make it as close as possible to the production unit and involve teams in concrete projects that will improve working conditions, efficiency or more general performance. Technology is not a hobby, and very few people will come to the lab on Sunday to test 3D printing. The other, and maybe even more important, aspect of building a great learning space to create a learning mindset is the place of work itself: over-invest in your team's cloakroom, sanitary areas, canteen, colour of the walls, light… and in all the areas that are not dedicated to work. Before pretending to install the best technological solutions, you should prove to your team that you can create an environment where they feel good.

Do not be afraid of machine learning and artificial intelligence

Usually, the journey to Teslism starts with the implementation of a few POCs with advanced robotics or digital solutions. Most industrial teams do not feel comfortable with the concept of machine learning and artificial intelligence. There are factual reasons for that – if you are not robust at collecting and storing your data, using advanced analytics to create new business models or improving the competitiveness of the industrial organization. Nevertheless our experience proves that working with new technologies is like a sport: the more you practice the better you get every day. The sooner you start implementing basic tests with machine learning the better it is for your future capability building. Of course artificial intelligence (AI) skills are very seldom needed, especially in the industrial sphere. The shorter way to success is to leverage the expertise of an outside company. In process industries, there are usually lots of opportunities to use better parameters to predict a risk, quality level or performance result. Just pick one and try measuring, storing and then analysing data to improve yield. The investment is low but the result can be huge. For example, a major actor in the food industry saved 1.5 hour per day by avoiding cleaning a tank – because machine learning made it possible to predict the risk of bacteriological contamination. Imagine the impact at that level (100+ factories).

Leverage the power of scrum and agile methods to instil test-and-learn approaches into the DNA of your company

Eventually, train all team functions to work in a test-and-learn mode. To do so you should leverage the younger teammates of your organization: digital natives have a natural inclination to think differently and improve things in an iterative way by testing opportunities with very short loops. This applies not only to continuous improvement in digital production but also in engineering and even in R&D and more generally in all project management processes, as long as the methodology is shared among all project stakeholders. Test and learn is also a very good way to reconcile the two ends of your age pyramid: use the millennials' agility and combine it with the expertise of your older employees. Start with a pilot project, over-communicate it and then roll out the method across your organization. To be successful, do not forget to mix teams with both operations and IT basic skills. Developing agile solutions requires agility, and so you must be able to code very quickly and improve the solution every day, based on user experience.

WHAT DOES THE TESLA WAY MEAN FOR STUDENTS?

Manufacturing has long been a boring place in the collective imagination, especially for the fresh, young and dynamic student brain. But with the recent hybridization of digitalization and manufacturing, new models of organization and work culture have infiltrated the plants. The Tesla Way is a very good example of this major change. Nevertheless, it is far from being the only model. There has been a multitude of organizational innovations recently in companies such as Harley Davidson, which officially claimed to 'liberate' their workers with a very solid level of trust and empowerment. But outside this highly important question of why a student should be interested in working in a factory, we would like to emphasize here the new fundamentals that seem unavoidable to learn for any student who would like to specialize in the manufacturing sector. In addition to the soft skills that will be required in the future (empathy, creativity, social connection), there is increasing need in factories for data science, AI and machine learning; then digital solutions design, industrial computer science, internet of things; finally, robotics. The investments in the hard technologies, such as robotics and 3D printing, follow an exponential trend, and the need for digital analytical skills is growing even faster because it is increasingly important to link the processes with each other and to understand the influence of multiple, end-to-end parameters of products, processes and sales. With the growing importance of learning, AI also will become key because the human brain will not be able to follow the need for memory and calculation.

Eventually, Teslism will reconcile students with manufacturing because factories might be the last place where working can be concrete and conceptual at the same time, where you will meet people who never completed higher education working in the same room with highly educated brilliant brains, where digital meets physical laws every day and where innovation and improvement have always been at the heart of the system. To summarize, manufacturing is a natural and very great place to learn. As we have said, learning is at the heart of human development.

Conclusion

Does the 4th Industrial Revolution constitute progress?

The 4th Industrial Revolution is under way although some may wonder whether that is a good thing. As always, it is normal to want to scrutinize the factors driving technological progress in order to determine whether they truly benefit us. The paradigm shifts accompanying each industrial revolution have been so substantial that they created disruptive opportunities but also serious risks to economic development and human happiness. Above and beyond simple natural resistance to change that everyone carries, to some extent, within themselves, it is healthy to note that reactions to this phenomenon are not uniform given the great complexity of the transformations associated with it. The same applies to the 4th Industrial Revolution.

First, a use-based economy is a formidable opportunity to improve mankind's planetary footprint. Greater sharing of consumer goods, by definition, helps to reduce consumption – hence save resources. At the same time, this new behaviour creates major risks for entire swathes of economic activity, with very negative consequences for employment, and without even talking about the legislative challenge of earning sufficient tax revenues from new activities that may well be decorrelated from the traditional economy. One previously mentioned example is Airbnb. This has been a great thing for householders and guests since it creates a new market that does a better job at balancing supply and demand, while also optimizing the existing housing stock and reducing over time the total number of housing units that the world needs. On top of this, Airbnb facilitates human encounters and helps people to travel differently. At the same time, it employs 25 times fewer people than the AccorHotels group. Moreover, tax revenue calculations for an activity based on direct interactions between housing consumers and providers are by their very nature much more complex, hence harder to control. This creates new problems, like how to design an innovative system to regulate these platforms.

Second, hyper-connectivity between humans, machines and products is a great opportunity to improve people's quality of life. Being able to purchase products through 'one-click' online, work away from the office while caring for one's children, avoid superfluous travel thanks to video conferencing, etc – these are all wonderful things. In addition, the connectivity that they embody creates abundant data. This helps industrialists to constantly innovate and optimize their responses to the demands of customers whose uses they are more familiar with nowadays. Data also helps companies to optimize their internal production processes and manufacture products more cheaply. Of course, the shift has also come with a number of major risks: the misuse of individual data; blurred borders between the private and professional spheres; and cyber-security issues. The optimal balance between individual freedoms and the opportunities that new technologies create has yet to be determined.

Third, exponential progress has enabled the development of tools that did not exist before, thanks to a combination of new technologies and the maturation of concepts that had yet to be fully formed during the 3rd Age of Industry. Robotics will ultimately make people's daily lives much more comfortable by automating many arduous household tasks; and 3D printing is highly likely to simplify complex processes while reducing the industrial sector's ecological footprint, healing the planet by creating greater proximity between the places where things are produced and where they are consumed. Lastly, progress can represent a great source of fulfilment for new generations who will benefit from lifelong learning in technologies that are themselves always changing. But once again, the same phenomena might also have the opposite effect, possibly leading to massive job destruction before the new creation dynamic takes off. Analyses at this level are contradictory. On one hand, those countries that have the highest degree of robotization (International Federation of Robotics, 2017) – such as Germany (250 robots/10,000 employees), South Korea (450 robots/10,000 employees) or Japan (350 robots/10,000 employees) – also have very low unemployment rates, which is encouraging. On the other hand, historically the industrial sector's job creation rates have been lower than its GDP growth rates, explained by the fact that industry has always generated higher productivity gains than other sectors. All in all, technological progress does not necessarily create employment, or at least not directly.

Lastly, hyper-concentration is by its very nature a divisive phenomenon. For people already 'in the system', meaning those who are working in one of the world's 10 leading clusters or in a megalopolis, who have a university degree and maybe speak several languages, this is clearly a wonderful opportunity since it leads to talent being concentrated in just a few places worldwide, hence creating great economic and personal opportunities in these locales. For everyone else, however, the phenomenon needs to be counterbalanced by public policy or industrialists' willingness not to aggravate the imbalance between hyper-centres and their peripheries, with the latter having been industry's natural development zones for decades.

The starting point for ensuring that the pendulum swings in the right direction is to remember, as aforementioned, that industrial revolutions are characterized by economic, technological and organizational movements. The organizational model is a natural regulator of the potential imbalances that can stem from economic and technological change. It helps to define a framework for human development, one where people can fulfil themselves through work, individually and collectively, even as they generate collaborative value for the whole of society. In short, the organizational model transcends the economic framework and becomes a key factor of success by preserving a balance between the different forces constituting the 4th Industrial Revolution. There are, however, a great many different operational models intimately associated with each company's sector, culture and trajectory. The question then becomes whether Teslism constitutes a suitably adapted model.

Is Teslism the right organizational model for the 4th Industrial Revolution?

As discussed throughout this book, the Tesla model is deeply disruptive yet generally coherent, hence robust. It offers a business model that is responsible, efficient and geared towards an intelligent use of mobility and energy, all of which is perfectly congruent with the four major challenges characterizing the 4th Age of Industry.

But let's be clear, this model is not applicable everywhere and has three main limitations. First, the qualities of the man who embodies it today – Elon Musk. Second, access to cash. If it is rather easy for Elon Musk to release money for his projects, that is not necessary the case for an SME owner. Finally, a start-up leadership that is applied directly between Elon Musk and his teams, which may give middle management a feeling of uselessness.

The model is far from perfect, as witnessed first and foremost by Tesla's financial situation. As of year-end 2017, Tesla Inc's total debt was five times greater than its shareholder equity, after recording an annual operating loss of US $1.9 billion (despite revenues being up by 55 per cent). Many analysts predicting a future speculative bubble are concerned about the company being valued higher than Ford or Renault, despite only selling 76,000 vehicles in 2016 and 100,000 in 2017, compared to 10 million for each of its big rivals.

In 2018, Tesla's operational situation was at a critical stage with the ramping up of its Model 3 being much slower than predicted, mainly due (apparently) to initial automation difficulties on the transmissions group line. This could be explained by Elon Musk doing the opposite of other carmakers, having started with full-blown automation before reverting – when that did not work – to more manual input. At first, this caused the market to lose confidence, a problematic outcome since succeeding in this first mass-market adventure is a key factor in the trust that Tesla must benefit from in the future, when it planned on moving from top-of-the-range models to ones targeting the wider public. As Musk himself has explained, the goal had been to do 5–10 times better than the competition by having a line capable of turning out a vehicle every five seconds. Success at this level would stave off any doubts and have a radically disruptive effect on the automotive world, where the best production lines tend to produce one vehicle every 30 seconds, more or less. Of course, back then, it was difficult to see how this would play out until things started working.

By late 2018, Elon Musk was already talking in the press quite openly about the situation at Tesla. Just a few months after this difficult period, weekly output rates were already up for the Model 3, reaching 5,000 units by year-end 2018 and 8,000 units in 1Q2019.

Elon Musk achieved this by remaining faithful to the management methods that he had pursued since the beginning of the Tesla adventure. This mainly involved getting teams to adopt a 'problem-solving' mode where they got their hands dirty fulfilling very specific objectives. Tesla fans would have heard Musk saying how exhausted he was in late August (something he referred to again in the HBO interview), explaining that he had been working 120 hours a week and had slept weeks on end in the Fremont factory, because he wanted to supervise Model 3 production and make sure it hit all targets. Of course, the atmosphere that Musk created in this way had an enormous effect on his teams.

Early 2019 has seen Tesla's adventure continue its merry way. Things are looking up, starting with the announcement of three new models: the Model Y (due to come out in 2020); the electro punk pick-up (timeline yet unknown); and the Tesla truck (which the company has already started operating in-house). Tesla is also advancing in its bid to build a new Gigafactory in China: US $2 billion has already been invested on a project that Musk hopes, quite amazingly, will already be up and running in July 2019. Note similar plans for a new Gigafactory in Germany or the Netherlands – alongside which, Tesla has also announced a densification of its network of superchargers.

In commercial terms, Tesla has 10 per cent of the global electric vehicle (EV) market and its Model 3 is the world's most widely sold EV, despite marketing having only just begun in Europe and China. EV sales are skyrocketing at a rate of around 50 per cent per annum, notably in China (where they account for 3 per cent of all cars, versus a global average of 1 per cent).

On the manufacturing side, Model 3 output rates have increased, reaching 8,000 units weekly thanks to Tesla Grohmann, which is constantly working on production-line improvements. Lastly, Elon Musk recently signed a new 10-year contract tying his own remuneration to the company's stock-market performance. The goal is to reach market capitalization of $650 billion (versus $55 billion today). It would be exponential growth, seeing company size increase by a factor of 10 within 10 years.

Teslism as a model that transcends Tesla

It would be wrong, however, to assimilate Teslism with nothing more than the Tesla brand model. As this book has demonstrated, many other 4th Age of Industry lighthouses stand out precisely because of their trailblazing characteristics in one or several of the seven dimensions constituting Teslism. As Elon Musk says, even if the project were to fail, it would still be a success because its knock-on effects outweigh everything else.

In the 40 years that have elapsed since the 3rd Industrial Revolution, many industrial companies have drawn inspiration from the Toyota model by adopting its key principles while adapting its operational and managerial system to fit their company's culture and sector.

Teslism's vocation is to become the Toyotism of the 4th Age of Industry. It is therefore high time to think about the best way of leveraging this radically disruptive model and take full advantage of its strengths, even if this means adapting the system as thousands of industrialists did during the 3rd Age of Industry. In this New Age, which carries within itself the DNA of exponential progress, every day counts. Even if it means making mistakes, it is better to act than to wait. Teslism is not the be all and end all – but it is a great source of inspiration for getting a foothold in the 4th Age of Industry.

APPENDIX

A brief history of Tesla Motors

July 2003 – Tesla is born

Two American engineers (Martin Eberhard and Marc Tarpenning) launch Tesla Motors, an electric car manufacturing company, named after Swedish inventor Nikola Tesla, in Palo Alto (California).

February 2004 – Elon Musk joins Tesla Motors Board of Directors

Elon Musk funds a large part of Tesla Motors' Series A investment with a capital injection of $7.5 million. He joins the Board of Directors and is appointed chair.

August 2006 – Tesla announces a corporate 'master plan' road map

Tesla, via Elon Musk, announces a 'master plan' serving as a road map for its carmaking activities. The goal is to manufacture and sell sports cars, with initial profits being used to develop a more affordable car, enabling the future production of an even more affordable model that produces less pollution while achieving higher performance.

February 2008 – first model (the Tesla Roadster) goes on the market

First sales of the Roadster, Tesla's first car model; 2,450 units will be produced all in all, retailing for prices starting at $109,000. The model is based on an existing car – the Lotus Elise – and equipped with a revolutionary battery enabling a level of autonomy that is unprecedented for electric vehicles.

October 2008 – Elon Musk becomes Tesla Motors CEO

After Martin Eberhard is forced to resign in 2007, Elon Musk takes over the company (having made a name for himself following his active involvement and role in designing the Tesla Roadster). Facing a critical financial situation, Musk decides to reduce the workforce by 25 per cent and raises $40 million to avoid bankruptcy.

October 2010 – Tesla's first factory opens

Tesla inaugurates its first plant, the Tesla Factory, at Fremont in California. This is an old car-manufacturing unit that General Motors and Toyota had owned since the 1980s and called the New United Motor Manufacturing, Inc (NUMMI).

June 2012 – launch of Model S

Tesla's first car produced in series, the Model S, is launched officially on 22 June 2012, with the delivery of the first 10 vehicles manufactured by the Fremont factory.

June 2014 – Elon Musk makes Tesla patents accessible to all

In an official Tesla press release dated 12 June 2014, Elon Musk declared that, 'Technology leadership is not defined by patents, which history has repeatedly shown to be small protection indeed against a determined competitor, but rather by the ability of a company to attract and motivate the world's most talented engineers.' The words reflect his desire to democratize the manufacturing and use of electric vehicles for everyone's benefit.

March 2016 – the Model 3 arrives

Tesla unveils the Model 3, its new affordable electric vehicle model, which in 2018 becomes the US's most widely sold plug-in EV, with a record of around 140,000 units being delivered.

July 2016 – opening of first Gigafactory

Tesla inaugurates the first Gigafactory, a Nevada (United States) plant enabling the company to produce its own lithium-ion batteries. With a workforce of more than 3,000, Gigafactory's annualized production of batteries is the equivalent today of around 20 GWh, making it the world's largest battery manufacturing plant. A second Gigafactory opened in Buffalo (New York) in 2017, with a third in the process of being built in Shanghai (China).

October 2018 – Tesla finally in the black

Tesla announces a key breakthrough as it finally moves into the black, with 3Q 2018 earnings of $312 million versus losses of $717 million the previous quarter. Turnover reaches $6.8 billion and the company's cash position is finally positive ($881 million).

REFERENCES

BCG (2015) *The Robotics Revolution*

Fabernovel (2018) *Tesla: Uploading the future*

Gartner (2017) *IoT Technology Disruptions*

Guilluy, C (2014) *La France périphérique*, Flammarion, Paris

International Federation of Robotics (2017) *World Robotics* 2017 Edition

La Fabrique de l'industrie (2016), L'industrie du future à travers le monde, *Les Synthèses de La Fabrique*, **4**

La Fabrique de l'industrie (2017), Industrie du futur: regards franco-allemands, *Les Synthèses de La Fabrique*, **15**

Liker, J (2018) Tesla vs. TPS: seeking the soul in the new machine, *The Lean Post*

McKinsey Global Institute (November 2012) *Manufacturing the Future: The next era of global growth and innovation*

New York Times (2018) Tesla achieves a key weekly goal for producing its Model 3 (2 July)

Parker, G G, Van Alstyne, M W, Choudary, S P (2016) *Platform Revolution*, W W Norton and Company, New York

PwC (2016) *Global Industry 4.0 Survey*

PwC (2018) *21st CEO Survey*

Valentin, M (2017) *The Smart Way: Excellence opérationnelle, profiter de l'industrie du futur pour transformer nos usines en pépites*, Lignes de Repères, Paris

Vance, A (2015) *Elon Musk: Tesla, SpaceX, and the quest for a fantastic future*, Harper Collins, New York

Veltz, P (2017) *La Société hyperindustrielle*, La République des idées, Seuil, Paris

Womack, J P, Jones, D T, Roos, D (1990) *The Machine That Changed the World*, Free Press, New York

World Economic Forum (2018) *The Future of Jobs*

YouTube (2016) Elon Musk: Gigafactory opening speech, 30 July

YouTube (2018) How Tesla Nearly Died: Elon Musks's long nights, 25 November

INDEX

Page numbers in *italic* indicate figures or tables.

Hooked: How to build habit-forming products 157 *see also* Eyal, N
how you can implement the Tesla way in your organization *see* implementing the Tesla way in your organization
human and machine learning (and) 124–39
  Bosch interview 132–35 *see also subject entry*
  a great place to learn 127–28
  introduction to 124–25, *125 see also* studies
  lessons from Tesla 130–31 *see also* Musk, E
  lifelong learning 126–27
  link between humans and work changes with each industrial revolution 125–26
  machine learning: hybridizing with machines 128–29
  questions for leaders 132
  Schmidt Group interview 135–39 *see also subject entry*
  testing and learning: mindset for learning and benefiting collectively 129–30
hypermanufacturing: Principle 1 of Teslism (and) 39–55
  agility 45–46
  collaborative value 46–52, *47*
    inhibitors blocking creation of 47–49, *47*
    lessons from Tesla 49–52 *see also* Musk, E
  frugality 44–45
  introduction to 40–41, *40, 41*
  Kimberly Clark: breaking down silos to implement hypermanufacturing 53–55
  lean, just-in-time and value added 41–44, *42, 43*
  new codes for the 4th age of industry 44
  questions for leaders 52–53

implementing the Tesla way in your organization 151–84
  design a customized story-making strategy 166–69, *167*
    1: understand foundations of the company
    2. list key challenges of company in specific sector and context 167
    3. determine the evolution dynamic 167–68
    4. assess governance mode 168

  and adapt personal leadership style to foster organizational consistency through external review, communication and field behaviour 168–69
  diagnose cross-integration with augmented version of Porter Forces 158–62, *158, 161*
  assess new opportunities of partnership with your ecosystem 160–61
  improve value proposition for clients/disrupt value chain if needed 158–59
  reinforce any barriers to entry in terms of platform threats 159
  review connection level with supplier network and disrupt some upstream activities 159–60
  revisit core value proposition: focus on important business lines *and* speed up collaboration level among key internal functions 161–62, *161*
  diagnose hypermanufacturing with a 4.0 VSM (and) 151–57
    virtual waste 154–57 *see also* user friendliness
    visual waste 152–54
  diagnose people and machine learning with skill-centric assessment (and) 171–84
    capability-building system: three aspects to diagnose 183–84, *184*
    manufacturing skill set of the future: technological and soft 171–72
    transformation skill set and organization 172–73
  diagnose software hybridization with a smart matrix 162–63
    methodology 163
    software and new technology classification 162
  diagnose start-up leadership systems and behaviours (and) 169–71
    adapted behaviours 171
    a robust management system – three bricks for 170–71
  diagnose tentacular traction with business segmentation 163, 165–66
    bottom-line opportunities 166
    centricity-dynamic segmentation 163, *164, 165*

Milton Keynes UK
Ingram Content Group UK Ltd.
UKHW051308300723
426028UK00009B/33